PRAISE FOR *MEMPHIS 68: THE TRAGEDY OF SOUTHERN SOUL*

Winner of the Penderyn Music Book Prize, 2018
Mojo – Books of the Year #4, 2017
Shindig – Book of the Year, 2017

'Offers us a map of Memphis in that most revolutionary of years, 1968. Music writing as both crime reporting and political commentary.'
The Herald

'Stuart Cosgrove's whole life has been shaped by soul – first as a music journalist and now as a chronicler of black American music's social context.'
Peter Ross, *Sunday Herald*

Printed and bound in Great Britain by Clays Ltd, Elcograf S.p.A.

'A trilogy of books by Stuart Cosgrove will become a vast tale of three cities, melding two of his great passions, soul music and American history. In *Memphis 68* he continues his compelling account of the last tumultuous years of the 1960s as the decade of love shuddered to a halt in cities ablaze with civil unrest, race riots and political assassination.'
Sunday Post

'It's perfectly feasible that Stuart Cosgrove's exhaustive, but briskly readable trilogy of social, political and musical histories of Black America in the late 1960s will go on to become deserved future classics . . . Cosgrove's selection of his subjects is unerring, and clearly rooted in personal passion . . . The substance of the book is forensic and journalistic, but Cosgrove masks his wealth of detail beneath an authorial voice which is as easily, blissfully evocative as a classic soul seven-inch.'
David Pollock, *The List*

'This is a book that grabs you from the off . . . If *Detroit 67* was the first part of a three-act play, then *Memphis 68* fulfils the role of the second act, where things get worse before they can get better, setting the scene perfectly for the denouement . . . There are few writers who so clearly and powerfully evince the relationship between popular culture and politics as he is doing with these books. *Harlem 69* can't come quickly enough.'
Alistair Braidwood

'Highly recommended! Astounding body of learning. Future classic. Go!'
SoulSource.co.uk

'As ever, Cosgrove's lucid, entertaining prose is laden with detail, but never at the expense of the wider narrative. Hinging on that Memphis destination, he traces the savage dichotomy at the city's heart: it was the site of multi-racial soul imprint Stax, but also the place where Martin Luther King was killed. A heartbreaking but essential read, and one that feels remarkably timely.'
Clash Magazine, Best Books of 2017

PRAISE FOR *DETROIT 67: THE YEAR THAT CHANGED SOUL*

'Cosgrove weaves a compelling web of circumstance that maps a city struggling with the loss of its youth to the Vietnam War, the hard edge of the civil rights movement and ferocious inner-city rioting. His prose is dense, not the kind that readers looking for a quick tale about singers they know and love might take to, but a proper music journalist's tome redolent of the field research that he carried out in Detroit's public and academic libraries. It is rich in titbits gathered from news reports. It is to be consumed rather than to be dipped into, a whole-hearted evocation of people and places filled with the confidence that it is telling a tale set at a fulcrum of American social and cultural history.'
The Independent

'Broadcaster Stuart Cosgrove lifts the lid on the time when the fight for civil rights and clash of cultures and generations came together in an incendiary mix.'
Daily Record

'The set-up sparks like the finest pulp thriller. A harsh winter has brought the city to its knees. The car factories are closed and Motown major domo Berry Gordy is fighting to keep his empire afloat. Stuart Cosgrove's immaculately researched account of a year in the life of the Motor City manages a delicate balancing act. While his love for the era – particularly the music, best exemplified by the dominance of Motown, whose turbulent twelve months are examined in depth – is clear, he maintains a dispassionate, journalistic distance that gives his epic narrative authority and depth. *****'
The Skinny

'A gritty portrait of the year Motown unravelled . . . *Detroit 67* is a wonderful book and a welcome contribution to both the history of soul music and the history of Detroit.'
Spiked

'A thoroughly researched and fascinating insight into the music and the times of a city which came to epitomise the turmoil of a nation divided by race and class, while at the same time offering it an unforgettable, and increasingly poignant, soundtrack . . . By using his love of the music as a starting point he has found the perfect way to explore further themes and ideas.'
Alistair Braidwood

'The subhead for Stuart Cosgrove's *Detroit 67* is "the year that changed soul". But this thing contains multitudes, and digs in deep, well beyond just the city's music industry in that fateful year . . . All of this is written about with precision, empathy, and a great, deep love for the city of Detroit.'
Detroit Metro Times

'The story is unbelievably rich. Motown, the radical hippie underground, a trigger-happy police force, Vietnam, a disaffected young black community, inclement weather, The Supremes, the army, strikes, fiscal austerity, murders – all these elements coalesced, as Cosgrove noted, to create a remarkable year. In fact, as the book gathers pace, one can't help think how the hell did this city survive it all? In fact such is the depth and breadth of his research, and the skill of his pen, at times you actually feel like you are in Berry Gordy's office watching events unfurl like an unstoppable James Jamerson bass line. I was going to call this a great music book. Certainly, it contains some of the best ever writing and insight about Motown. Ever. But its huge canvas and backdrop, its rich social detail, negate against such a description. *Detroit 67* is a great and a unique book, full stop.'
Paolo Hewitt, *Caught by the River*

'Big daddy of soul books . . . Over twelve month-by-month chapters, the author – a TV executive and northern soul fanatic – weaves a thoroughly researched, epic tale of musical intrigues and escalating social violence.'
TeamRock

'As the title suggests, this is a story of twelve months in the life of a city . . . Leading black music label Motown is at the heart of the story, and 1967 is one of Motown's more turbulent years, but it's set against the backdrop of growing opposition to the war in Vietnam, police brutality, a disaffected black population, rioting, strikes in the Big Three car plants and what seemed like the imminent breakdown of society . . . *Detroit 67* is full of detailed information about music, politics and society that engages you from beginning to end. You finish the book with a real sense of a city in crisis and of how some artists reflected events.'
Socialist Review

'A fine telling of a pivotal year in soul music'
Words and Guitars

Two young kids stand in the doorway of 2026 Seventh Avenue in Harlem at the offices of the Black Panther Party, where breakfast programmes fed local children. The doorway is now that of Jenny's Food Corporation, which sells chicken wings and French fries, and the address is 2026 Adam Clayton Jr Boulevard.

HARLEM 69

The Future of Soul

STUART COSGROVE

Polygon

First published in Great Britain in 2018 by Polygon,
an imprint of Birlinn Ltd.

Birlinn Ltd
West Newington House
10 Newington Road
Edinburgh
EH9 1QS

www.polygonbooks.co.uk

1

ISBN 978 1 84697 420 5
eBook ISBN 978 1 78885 025 4

British Library Cataloguing-in-Publication Data
A catalogue record for this book is available on request
from the British Library.

Typeset by 3btype.com

Printed and bound in Great Britain by Clays Ltd, Elcograf S.p.A.

For Michael Tabor and Donny Hathaway

'For the first time in years, he felt the deep sadness of exile, knowing that he was alone here, an outsider, and too alert to the ironies, the niceties, the manners, and indeed, the morals to be able to participate.'

—Colm Toíbín

CONTENTS

FOREWORD

Harlem 69 is the final book in a trilogy of books on soul music and social change in the sixties. The two previous books – *Detroit 67: The Year That Changed Soul* and *Memphis 68: The Tragedy of Southern Soul* – focused on a specific place in an eventful year. Each of the books is self-contained and can be read independently, but read in sequence they tell a much bigger story of black music's place in the many epoch-defining issues of the times: the evolution of ghetto sociology and culture in America; the civil rights movement; the emergence of Black Power; the assassination of the leaders of political change such as Malcolm X and Dr Martin Luther King; the war in Vietnam, both in South East Asia and on the home front; the impact of drugs and criminality on inner-city America; and how underground music became mainstream. This book is dedicated to two of its principal characters, the Harlem Black Panther Michael Tabor, a street kid who overcame heroin addiction to become one of the most influential street radicals of the sixties, and the great Donny Hathaway, one of black music's towering geniuses, whose 1969 single 'The Ghetto' changed the direction of soul music.

What separates *Harlem 69* from the two preceding books is its look to the future of soul. Rather than ending the trilogy on the final days of 1969, which would follow the logic of the decade, this book argues that Harlem in 1969 was the place where many of the seeds of soul music's rich future were planted and nourished. The metaphor of creative growth in the ghetto was first imagined on the picture cover of Ben E. King's song 'Spanish Harlem', in which a blooming red rose emerges from the cracks in a dilapidated Harlem sidewalk. It is self-evidently the rose of youth, of hope, of love, and, most importantly, of a new future. So, throughout the book you will meet soul in all its many emerging manifestations: jazz-funk, message music, psychedelic soul, disco and boogie, rare groove, house and hip-hop.

Inevitably, the trilogy focuses on the major labels of the era – Motown in Detroit, Stax in Memphis and Atlantic in New York – but all three books dig below the surface of commercial success and shine a light on independent labels and the artists who in many cases have been airbrushed from conventional histories of soul.

Writing the trilogy has been borne out of a lifetime passion which I hope comes across to readers. There are many people to whom I'm grateful. I'd like to thank the staff of Harlem's Schomburg Center for Research in Black Culture, a research library of the New York Public Library and an archive repository for information on people of African descent worldwide; the Performing Arts Division of the New York Public Library and the archival staff of *The New York Times*. I'd like to thank the staff at my publishers Polygon, especially my editor Alison Rae and cover designer Chris Hannah, and I'm grateful to Michael Randolph for the use of his father PoPsie's photograph of Wilson Pickett and Jimi Hendrix. Personal thanks to my dearest friends and family both living and dead. Finally, I'd like to thank my many friends on the rare and northern soul scene – the ultimate academy – whose collective knowledge and belligerent wisdom has informed the trilogy throughout. I owe a debt of gratitude to 'the scene' and all its eccentric characters. For those many people who have bought the two previous books, I hope this one lives up to your expectations.

Stuart Cosgrove
Glasgow
September 2018

Bearing gifts: Fat Jack Taylor dressed as Santa Claus at a Harlem children's party in the early sixties. Taylor was one of Harlem's most flamboyant characters; a heroin dealer, he was also the local boss of infamous indie label Rojac Records.

JANUARY

Fat Jack Taylor's Curious Empire

Christmas was a fading memory for Fat Jack Taylor. He folded his Santa costume carefully and stored it away in his wardrobe for another year. The red coat reeked of alcohol and the tatty furry hat was discoloured with tobacco. Fat Jack briefly thought of taking it to the laundromat on 116th and Lenox, but it would be another year before the costume was needed so he doused it with cologne and closed the wardrobe door. When Fat Jack looked in his mirror it was always with a sense of disappointment. He had access to the latest gear – sharkskin shoes, cascading purple shirts and canary-coloured jackets tailored with the finest velvet edgings – but his face remained stubbornly round. Bulging rolls of fat crept up from his neckline, straining his top button and ruining whatever ensemble he tried on. He wore stylish Homburg hats and caused a commotion wherever he went but his greatest battle was neither with his rival heroin dealers nor the young soul singers who crowded hopefully around him: it was a fundamental anxiety he had fought since childhood – how to be both fat and fashionable.

Fat Jack was one of Harlem's restless pioneers, an enigmatic figure who kept his private life close to his chest. He was a drug dealer and a tireless musical entrepreneur, boisterous with those who hung around him and confident that the next rising star would gravitate to him. He was in many respects a shepherd in wolf's clothing, protective and threatening in equal measure. One of his most persistent routines was to clatter into his office on 116th Street and spend an hour among his young acolytes at Rojac Records, playing his way through piles of acetate discs or listening to promo records that had yet to hit the streets. It was a habit that had brought Fat Jack talent before anyone knew their names or, on several occasions, alerted him to fading stars of yesteryear, singers still clinging on to the life raft. He had worked out that those who were most in need of his services were either young and naïve or old and wasted.

In the early weeks of 1969 one particular record nagged at his mind, a standard lovers' duet recorded in Chicago called 'I Thank You Baby' by June and Donnie. The song opened with a curiously poetic lyric, 'Mama said thank you for the rain.' It was a sound that appealed to Fat Jack and could have been recorded at any time in the sixties. He called the Chicago-based producer Curtis Mayfield to enquire about a national distribution deal but was rebuffed. He was told that the song had only materialised when Sam Cooke's brother, L.C. Cooke, failed to show up for a recording session and, under pressure of time, Mayfield drafted in his colleague Donny Hathaway to partner local singer June Conquest. The record had already stalled, and having fallen out with Mayfield, Hathaway had moved to New York where he was staying on the fringes of Harlem not far from Fat Jack's luxury apartment. He was now within touching distance, but within a year would be out of reach and one of the most talked-about musicians in black America. Hathaway's era-defining single 'The Ghetto' would be stellar and his career would propel at a pace that was neither healthy nor sustainable. Hathaway was in need of medication, but way beyond the coke and dope that Fat Jack prescribed.

For much of the sixties, soul music had been dominated by Berry Gordy's Motown empire in Detroit and the earthier Stax sound from Memphis; by contrast Fat Jack Taylor's label never exerted the same influence but he was by some distance the most successful independent producer in 'the capital city of black America' – Harlem. As pop music diversified and took inspiration from the Summer of Love and psychedelia, Fat Jack's label Rojac Records stayed hardwired to the streets, taking its influence not from world trends or international artists but from Harlem itself. Fat Jack had an unshakable belief that if anything was to change in music he would know about it first, because it would erupt in the streets he now called home: from the festering alleyways around Lenox, the impenetrable housing projects that lurked behind the Apollo Theater, or the impoverished teenage bedrooms of Harlem and the Bronx. He had seen it all before; the rest of the world might run out of energy but Harlem never would.

For much of the post-war period, Harlem was a magnet for musicians, offering opportunities in bars and nightclubs or as session musicians working on call for the Midtown studios. Although his origins are unknown, the most likely scenario is that Fat Jack was part of the great migration from the Deep South. Six million African-Americans had moved north from the largely rural communities of the South, first to escape slavery and segregation, but more often to seek out work in the industrial North, in Detroit's bustling car plants and the processed-food plants of Chicago. Thousands flocked to New York and its myriad opportunities, joining the queue of hopefuls who saw the Apollo's weekly talent competitions as a route to success. The Apollo was not only a magnet for the young and hopeful, it occupied a crucial place in the so-called Chitlin' Circuit, the itinerary of mainly black venues that stretched across America. Most tours began or ended at the Apollo. It was a place of unrivalled opportunity but what few fully understood was the sheer scale of the competition. Harlem had become a graveyard for music's might-have-beens: those walking corpses who found refuge in heroin, those who had given up and taken a low-paid job in public service, and those who simply hung around in the bars hoping to be remembered. Fat Jack knew them all and where they hung out. He could recite the dive bars and jazz joints as if they were old schoolmates: there was the Hi-Hat, the Baby Grand and the Palm Café; there was Mr B's, Willie Abraham's Gold Lounge and the Shalimar. He was guaranteed a seat wherever he went and he knew what secrets the barman hid beneath the counter.

Among the many musicians who had been abandoned in Harlem were two of Fat Jack's associates, Bobby Lewis and Ritchie Adams, a couple of singers who had appeared at the Apollo with Jackie Wilson and the Fireflies. Having paid for their own travel from Detroit to New York, they were left penniless when Wilson's entourage moved on, and so tried to earn a living by hawking their songs along Broadway. One of their most fruitful meetings was with Beltone Records, a start-up owned by producer Les Cahan and his studio director Joe René. Beltone had already secured a contract with the in-demand Harlem singer Chuck Jackson when, in an act of brinkmanship, Jackson insisted the contract was ripped up to allow him to join a better-resourced New York indie, Wand Records. In the hiatus Bobby Lewis and Ritchie Adams filled a vacuum with a string of solo R&B singles, as well as working in tandem with the doo-wop group the Jive Five. At almost exactly the same time, Fat Jack had found his way to the Beltone offices, where he sold them a song called 'Peepin' Tom' (1960), which he recorded with a singer called Chuck Flamingo. The identity of Chuck Flamingo has never been established, and it's possible, given Fat Jack's capacity for deception and manoeuvring, that he may have successfully talked Chuck Jackson into breaching his newly signed Wand contract and moonlighting under the pseudonym. As Jackson's career at Wand exploded, Flamingo's records began to appear on the discount counters of the Acme supermarket chain, which at the time bundled discounted records into a bag known as 'The Bag o' 45s'. Humiliated that his debut single was being hawked in discount stores, Fat Jack bought up all the cheapskate bags and gave the records away as promotional gifts.

Between 1963 and 1970 Fat Jack's drugs enterprise flourished. He was an O.G. – 'original gangsta' – one of the small army of high-ranking black drug dealers whose flamboyant names became etched in Harlem nightlife. Mookie Jackson, William 'Goldfinger' Terrell, Sylvester 'Radar Man' Hoffler, 'Red' Dillard Morrison and the notorious kingpin Bumpy Johnson were all part of a Harlem underworld engaged in a pathological business that was on the verge of spiralling out of control and bringing Harlem into national disrepute.

Unlike most of his flashy and heartless contemporaries, whose conspicuous consumption led them to jail, Fat Jack diverted much of his drugs profit into music; he released over fifty singles, many on labels that were misspelt and garishly designed. It may well have been his loss-making music ventures that kept the IRS at bay and allowed him to evade serious detection for years. Surreptitiously, Fat Jack bought up properties across Manhattan, eventually owning several luxury apartments in Riverside Drive, which variously became the gifted or sub-let homes of Big Maybelle, Etta James and, for a spell, the itinerant master guitarist Jimi Hendrix. Although his precious vinyl frequently stiffed, failure never dented Fat Jack's boundless enthusiasm and, regardless of their obscurity, he paraded his artists around the ghetto as if they were superstars. He instinctively understood one of the most basic unwritten rules of the music industry and rewarded the talent with attention, gifts and glassine wraps of the very best brown sugar in Harlem. He kept the talent happy.

Unlike Motown and Stax, who dominated the soul charts in the sixties, it was a cause for celebration if one of Fat Jack's singles scraped into the Top 100 – and a few did, most triumphantly Big Maybelle's cover version of the garage band hit '96 Tears', which grazed the *Billboard* pop charts in 1967, helped by an introduction shamelessly stolen from the Four Tops classic, 'I Can't Help Myself'. But the odds were stacked against Rojac Records; the label struggled for national attention in an industry still inured against independent soul and both corrupt and biased towards the majors. Nonetheless, being hardwired to the local community had distinct advantages. Rojac released records that screamed of the street and captured the extraordinary urban zeitgeist of Harlem.

Fat Jack was no conventional heroin dealer; his moral code is hard to define and he came shrouded in ambiguity. A man who profited from drugs, he poured resources back into local charities, block association events and initiatives that fed the homeless. For two decades he funded the annual Thanksgiving Dinner for the poor and homeless, using his fast food restaurant Soul Expression as the nerve centre of a charitable effort that spread throughout Harlem and into the Bronx. He was regularly cast as a black Santa Claus at children's Christmas parties, and when big-ticket boxing bouts were fought at Madison Square Garden and Las Vegas, he would fund nights out for soul singers, favoured staff and other Harlem fly guys.

Fat Jack was ashamed of his weight but referred to it constantly, introducing himself as 'Fat Jack' or 'the Fat Man'; he was acquisitive about credits, claiming he had written songs that were the work of others, but then he was fulsome in his praise of his artists; he was loud and gregarious when he entered a room, high-fiving and back-slapping, then would fade quietly into a corner with one or two close friends; he was a wealthy man who always carried greenbacks in his fleshy fists but he liked to give it away as much as to gain it, and frequently handed out gifts, loans and extravagant tips to people he barely knew. Most curious of all, he seems to have been asexual, happiest in the company of older R&B singers. He doted on Big Maybelle and at times was mistaken for her husband.

Of course he was a drug peddler in the most notorious areas of inner-city America and it would be easy with hindsight to cast him in a dark light, as sinister, exploitative and amoral, but the opposite seems to have been the case. The New York street paper *Village Voice* described Fat Jack as 'a gentle behemoth', a strange but accurate description of a man who was a lynchpin in the Harlem heroin trade but much liked, and who passed the time with those less well-off than himself.

Rojac Records and its sister label Tay-Ster (a name that was a conglomeration of Taylor's surname and that of his sometime partner Claude Sterrett) were notable for the phenomenal range of their output, which reflected over twenty years of Harlem music. There was 'Christmas In Vietnam' (1966) by Private Charles Bowens & the Gentlemen from Tigerland, a brutally honest dispatch from the battlefield recorded by a group from Bowens' regimental base in Fort Polk, Louisiana. Fat Jack loyally released the record on successive Christmases until patriotism stalled and the unpopularity of the war risked harming sales. Rojac released a party marijuana song called 'Give Me Another Joint' (1968) by Damn Sam the Miracle Man & the Soul Congregation; the pounding 'I Love My Baby' (1966) by the International 'G.T.O.s'; Big Maybelle's up-tempo 'Quittin' Time' (1968); and Lillie Bryant's uplifting 'Meet Me Halfway' (1966), a song that could have been hijacked from the Motown vaults and packed into jukeboxes along Lenox Avenue. With each new release, Fat Jack lavished money on launch parties, some so expertly conceived that he boasted with some merit that he threw *the* most famous parties in New York. They even had their own name – Fat Jack's sets – a term which signalled their theatricality and the covert way they moved through Harlem, from storefronts to office lofts and community halls. For a man deeply implicated in the heroin trade, Fat Jack had a strange fascination with acting, the theatre and, most intriguing of all, opera, which is why his most successful record label – Rojac – carried the twin masks of tragedy and comedy as its logo. 'There was a whole clique around Harlem,' Lithofayne 'Faye' Pridgon told the *Guardian* newspaper in 2015. At the time she was one of Jimi Hendrix's Harlem girlfriends and one of Fat Jack's inner circle. 'He was the dope kingpin of Harlem – he had everybody in his pocket . . . He was rumoured to be the dope dealer to all the stars . . . We would frequent the same kind of places and run into each other here and there, now and then. And there were always cute guys, cute girls, on the scene. Everybody was young and energetic. And so if you saw somebody you liked you kinda just . . . hooked up with them, took them with you.' These spontaneous hook-ups usually took place at a hotel suite or at an apartment rented by Taylor. 'You'd take the young tenders in and just party to your heart's content. Sometimes a set lasted two or three days.' And Fat Jack was the one who 'always provided the finances, the drugs or whatever was necessary'.

In the spring of 1969 Fat Jack was planning a loft party to promote a slate of new Rojac releases, among them a reissue of a sadomasochistic funk song by Chuck-a-Luck & the Lovemen Ltd, snappily titled 'Whip You'. The record had been out before, but Fat Jack had huge faith in it and was determined to make it a hit. Chuck-a-Luck had taken his name from an old Harlem dice game still played on ghetto street corners, but his real name was Little Charles Whitworth and he hailed from the Triad area of North Carolina. Whitworth had moved to Harlem after he toured Europe as Sam and Dave's bassist, on the historic Stax tour of Europe two years earlier.

There was already a buzz about the night. Fat Jack had sent embossed invitations to the Apollo and they were laid out in the dressing rooms of that month's roster of artists. Most of them were in town from Chicago – Gene Chandler, Tyrone Davis, Barbara Acklin, and the Chi-Lites featuring vocalist Eugene Record. He had tracked down Donny Hathaway's home and left an invite there but it lay unopened.

Fat Jack's big idea was not his best but it had audacity. He had told his inner circle to scour Manhattan for leather whips, which he planned to distribute to party guests on their arrival. Fat Jack had an eye for drama and he had put the word out that Harlem's painted ladies should dress to impress, and that the 'sophisticated cissies' who hung out in the bars on Lenox were more than welcome. He liked gay men and had predicted the impact of gay disco before the term was in common use downtown. He had a passion for the great soaring gospel voices of the past allied to party music. In 1968 he signed the Cleveland vocalist Kim Tolliver and then Joshie Jo Armstead, a Mississippi singer who had relocated to Harlem after struggling to make an impact in the fiercely competitive downtown New York music industry.

In a gesture of largesse, Fat Jack had hired a private jet to bring in his Detroit business partners, mostly drug dealers, soul music contacts and rival label owners. Prominent among them was the Motor City producer Dave Hamilton, a one-time member of the legendary Funk Brothers and a talented guitarist who released records on the Motown subsidiary Workshop Jazz. Hamilton became Fat Jack's most gifted collaborator and co-producer. It was through Hamilton that he became involved with a generation of talented singers who had slipped through Motown's net, among them Little Ann, Tobi Lark and a gospel singer who would eventually relocate to Harlem to become Fat Jack's trusted lieutenant and bodyguard, O.C. Tolbert. With Tolbert's pure soul voice and

Taylor's instinctive feel for the street, they went on to produce an album that was destined to become the ultimate underground classic, *Damn Sam The Miracle Man And The Soul Congregation*, a rousing compilation of meandering jazz, madcap lyrics and hardcore funk that became a template for the music of Parliament, Funkadelic, Bootsy Collins and other insane street warriors yet to come. For much of 1968 he lived in rented property in Detroit where his Harlem-born runner Li'l Buster Robinson and a former Harlem Globetrotters star, Ernie Wagner, had set up his Detroit-based heroin operation.

Fat Jack was keenly aware that his party sets helped to promote records and sell drugs but most of all they brought him status. Harlem had a long and fascinating history of illegal or unlicensed parties, which ran through the night and into the next day, often emptying with the church bells. It was through parties, as much as the famous uptown clubs, that music made its atonal journey from ragtime to jazz to R&B and on to street funk. Sets were one of the links that connected back to the twenties, a period of intense creativity. The famous Harlem Renaissance – or as it was more commonly known then, the New Negro Movement – unlocked a spirit of freedom as the jazz age adjusted to the restrictions of Prohibition. Clubs became more secretive, more subterranean and more word-of-mouth, lending them a special allure for music lovers and white visitors from downtown. A network of parties began to flourish in tenement basements, in upstairs lofts, in storefronts, and even in the function rooms of Harlem's once spectacular hotels. It was the area of 'rent parties' – illegal all-night drinking dens – where a small entrance fee of twenty-five cents helped the home-owners pay for their rent during a period of escalating costs and discriminatory land practices. Underground house parties were so common in the thirties that the superstar of the Harlem Renaissance Langston Hughes collected the 'calling cards' that were issued to promote the parties. On the surface they were polite and deceptively twee: 'Satisfy Your Souls and Let the Good Times Roll at Joe Baker's Social Whist, Apartment 3-11, 305 West 150th Street. Refreshments served'; 'The lights are low, the music is fine, come on up and cop a tough grind with Elvira, Shirley and Barbara at Apt. 8. 2375 8th Avenue. Ring one long bell'; 'Why stay at home and look at the wall, come out and let's have a ball, at a party given by the 7 Brothers Social Club. Good music and refreshments. 2254 5th. Ave between 137th and 138th Street'; 'Fall in line, and watch your step, there'll be lots of browns and plenty of pep. A social whist given by Lucille and Minnie, 149 West 117th Street.' But these coded invitations were fully understood by the bohemian Harlem community: 'refreshments' meant liquor, 'grind' referred to the latest sexually explicit jazz and blues tunes, and 'browns' and 'pep' meant heroin and amphetamine. This Harlem subculture of illegal parties preceded New York's underground club scene, the UK's northern soul all-nighters and the techno-rave scene by over forty years. By 1969 Fat Jack was the grandmaster of the secret venue, and his invite-only events had morphed into spectacular loft parties.

Harlem's underground party scene was paralleled by another forerunner of club culture, a network of places not formal enough to be commercial venues like clubs or theatres where music was not simply played, but eulogised. Among them was Niggerati Manor, the brownstone rooming house on 136th Street that became the lawless home to the writers of the Harlem Renaissance and their short-lived magazine, *Fire!!*. One resident, the writer Bruce Nugent, painted giant multicoloured phalluses on the wall and encouraged gay bacchanalia into the small hours. In 1926 the drama critic Theophilus Lewis described it as a place of delirium and debauchery: 'Those were the days when Niggerati Manor was the talk of the town. The story got out that the bathtubs in the house were always packed with sour mash, while gin flowed from all the water taps and the flush boxes were filled with needle beer. It was said that the inmates of the house spent wild nights in tuft hunting and in the diversion of the cities of the plains and delirious days fleeing from pink elephants . . . Needless to say, the rumours were not wholly groundless; where there is smoke there must be fire. In the case of Niggerati Manor, a great deal more smoke came out of the windows than was warranted by the size of the fire in the house.'

Another place that came to inform Harlem folklore was the riotous home of A'Lelia Walker – a black society hostess and patron of the arts whom the writer Langston Hughes called 'the joy goddess of Harlem's 1920s'. Her brick and limestone house at 108–110 West 136th Street near Lenox had a converted floor called the Dark Tower, a cultural salon that became legendary as one of the gathering places of ragtime, jazz and blues musicians. Hughes was a regular and described it as a place where sobriety was an unwelcome stranger. 'A'Lelia Walker had an apartment that held perhaps a hundred people,' he wrote. 'She would usually issue several hundred invitations to each party. Unless you went early there was no possible way of getting in. Her parties were as crowded as the New York subway at the rush hour – entrance, lobby, steps, hallway, and apartment a milling crush of guests, with everybody seeming to enjoy the crowding.' But the parties at the Dark Tower came to an end with the onset of the Great Depression. Antiques and luxury items were auctioned off, and in the early hours of 16 August 1931, after hosting a birthday party for a friend, A'Lelia Walker, Harlem's irrepressible hostess, passed away.

Harlem's list of secret venues was legend. Harry Hansberry's Clam House on 133rd Street was the residence of the transvestite blues singer Gladys Bentley, whose recording career, in part fortified by her dynamic cross-dressing, was backed by the legendary OKeh Records. Bentley was a forerunner of the soul singer Clarence Reid aka Blowfly, who in 1968 had forsaken his Florida base and his own indie label Reid Records and was living in Harlem, recording for Dial and Wand Records, before he joined Fat Jack at Rojac. Separated by decades, both Bentley and Blowfly specialised in doing bawdy and sexually explicit cover versions of the popular hits of the day. Reid had unsuccessfully tried to convince Fat Jack to release his puerile show-stopping version of 'Shitting On The Dock Of The Bay', a gross parody of the late Otis Redding's song. His ability to impersonate the greats of soul music was renowned in Harlem and Miami, but it was a blessing and a curse. He was so good at descanting on the voices of the famous that for years he struggled to promote a style of his own.

Since 1963 Fat Jack's sets had borrowed from the historic Harlem underground. When he held a launch party for Rojac releases in 1967 and 1968 Blowfly performed and set out to shock the house with songs that were outrageous and anatomical, never missing a body part in the pursuit of laughs. Fat Jack prided himself on throwing the most lavish parties: a room drenched in blue neon, elegant crystal glasses, crushed ice, pure white cocaine, and, of course, throbbing street funk. His sets were a source of great personal self-respect, and it niggled away in his mind like an irritating put-down when the soul singer Benny Gordon told him about the writer and bon viveur Truman Capote throwing a party at the Plaza Hotel. Harlem and the high society scene in Midtown Manhattan were closed off to each other by race, class and social snobbery, and Gordon was the only connection between Capote and Fat Jack. Capote certainly knew nothing of the ghetto or soul music; in fact he had hired Gordon because he fronted the house band at a celebrity nightspot, Trude Heller's discotheque on Sixth Avenue in the Village.

Truman Capote's Black and White Ball was held at 10 p.m. on Monday, 28 November 1966 and became a defining moment in the rise of New York celebrity. Sinatra was there; so was Tallulah Bankhead and old Rose Kennedy. The party had been thrown in honour of Katharine Graham, the society hostess and president of *The Washington Post*. The newspapers christened it 'The Party of the Century' but Fat Jack insisted that none of the guests had ever ventured up to Harlem. The hardened soul communities of the ghettos and the privileged elite of Manhattan may as well have been millions of miles apart. Yet Harlem was in touching distance of what the mayor of New York, John Lindsay, had called the 'silk-stockinged districts', swathes of expensive homes on the Upper East Side and Central Park, which had a long tradition of electing well-heeled liberal Republicans, and where the managers of the advertising and music industry mainly lived.

Describing Fat Jack and Truman Capote as a clash of cultures would be to seriously underplay the gulf of difference. Only six people had ever bridged the two worlds and they were Benny Gordon and the Soul Brothers. At the time, Gordon was living in Bedford-Stuyvesant, Brooklyn, running the northern wing of Estill Records, a cash-strapped indie from his hometown of the same name in South Carolina. He had first met Fat Jack when he arrived in Harlem with his cousin Sammy, as part of the southern gospel caravan group called the Harmonizers. Just days after they arrived in Harlem, they played the Apollo, and, desperate for cash and exposure, secured a return booking by changing their name to the Soul Brothers, thus conning the management and reappearing as a new act.

Staying one step ahead of the law, Fat Jack rented or bought business premises across Harlem, shifting his main address almost annually, and used them as fronts for his labels and as temporary business dropboxes. Besides drugs, his biggest source of income was not music, it was fast food. He owned Fat Jack's Chitlin' House, a broiled chicken and southern soul food restaurant, which he frequently talked about franchising but never did. What is difficult to reconcile with Fat Jack's drug empire and gangster lifestyle was his uncanny ability to spot talent on his doorstep. Like the Dickensian character Fagan in *Oliver Twist*, he had a coterie of young boys who buzzed around him like bees; some were orphans from the streets, some were attracted to him in the hope of money or fame, and some simply saw him as a generous father figure. It would be easy with hindsight to characterise Taylor as a predatory figure, preying on the young for his own gain, except that the young people he attracted were smart young men, some of them fearsomely bright, and many talented well above their natural age.

Private Charles Bowens, who sang lead on 'Christmas In Vietnam', was conscripted in the early sixties. He had been a standout pupil in the Harlem public schools system, a successful debating champion and a YMCA charity volunteer. At sixteen, he was nominated for Harlem's outstanding boy of the year. Another Harlem high school standout was Michael Tabor, a basketball star at Rice High School who had taken a job at Rojac delivering flyers and running errands. Fat Jack loved Tabor's booming *basso profundo* voice and they often discussed recording songs in the style of Paul Robeson but for the Black Power generation. Nothing came of it, and as the sixties intensified Tabor drifted further north, to a storefront near 141st Street, the headquarters of the Harlem Branch of the Black Panthers. The year of 1969 marked his life in the most extraordinary way; within a few short weeks he would be under police surveillance and at the centre of one of the most controversial show trials in American legal history.

Tabor was not alone. Although conventional wisdom has portrayed Rojac Records as a label surrounded by gangsters, the vice-president was a hip young civil rights activist called Claude Sterrett, whose heavy spectacles made him appear more like a geek than a gunman. Sterrett had a macabre back story: he was the son of an infamous Harlem undertaker, who in 1953 had shot his wife in a dispute that dated back to a failed business in South Carolina. The family still lived together on 113th Street, making ends meet by embalming bodies. Sterrett had been marching with his friend James Meredith when the famous civil rights leader was shot by a sniper in Mississippi during the voter-registration demonstration 'The March Against Fear' back in June 1966. The march had the high-profile support of Martin Luther King and the comedian Dick Gregory, an Apollo regular, who on a trip to Harlem recommended Sterrett to Fat Jack.

Fat Jack's young recruits became his surrogate family – none more so than Herman Robinson. Although there is no evidence of formal adoption papers, Taylor had taken care of the wayward teenager, who was known on the streets by his nickname 'Li'l Buster'. Robinson was only thirteen and homeless when he met Fat Jack. He was given a job (below the legal age) at Fat Jack's fast food restaurant in premises below his offices on 116th Street, a corner that was the bustling front for drugs connections. Unmarried and possibly yearning for another life, Fat Jack described Robinson variously as his son or his nephew. He was neither. Fat Jack persisted with the deception and became a protective father figure, promoting Robinson within the business and mentoring him until the dying days of 1969 when Robinson was caught up in a botched robbery at a bar and sentenced to ten years. Such were the historic threads of Harlem at the time that Li'l Buster Robinson was sent to Attica State Prison in upstate New York – a place seething with violence, brutality and overcrowding that was about to erupt into the history books. Records show that Robinson was the youngest inmate in Attica when a riot broke out on 9 September 1971.

On the fifth day of the uprising, Governor Nelson Rockefeller ordered state troopers to take back control. More than 2,000 rounds of ammunition were fired over six minutes, and when the smoke cleared, twenty-nine inmates and ten prison officers lay dead, most of them shot during the raid. Robinson survived. He was in the prison hospital at the time recuperating from a burst appendix and witnessed the mayhem through a window; years later he acted as a witness for the families who subsequently sued the New York State authorities.

By far the most famous members of Fat Jack's street family were his close lieutenants and sometime business partners, the identical twins Arthur and Albert Allen. In their vivid description of Fat Jack, they described him as looking 'like the Ugandan dictator Idi Amin' and, like Amin, a man who was prickly and self-conscious about his weight. In the rough and tumble of Harlem nightlife, he had learned to laugh off insults but kept a surreptitious ledger of those who pushed it too far. The Allen twins had been born prematurely on Valentine's Day in 1946 and grew up in a brownstone block on 141st between Seventh and Eighth Avenue. As children they hung out at the Woodside Hotel where their father often drank in the hotel's down-at-heel Victoria Bar. They ran errands for the high rollers, earning cheap change from jazz musicians too blissed out to walk to the convenience store for a box of matches. The Woodside was a decaying place which had long lost its grandeur but it was where Count Basie had performed 'Jumping At The Woodside'. Even in 1969 it remained a favourite watering hole for old jazz cats. The Allens' mother was a music teacher and skilled pianist but it was their father who exerted the greatest influence. He worked on the railways for the Pullman Car Company and was a member of the Brotherhood of Sleeping Car Porters, a pioneering labour union that fought the thinly disguised master–slave conditions that black workers faced in Pullman cars in the Depression years. Dependent on tips to supplement a low basic wage, their father became an ardent civil rights supporter and a close friend of the union leader, A. Phillip Randall. His views on desegregation and community politics were common conversation in the Allens' crowded home, and it was through the Harlem branch of the Brotherhood, rather than through the more visible Martin Luther King Jr, that the twins first came to understand the power of collective action. Both were keen bodybuilders and members of the Harlem Gladiators, and provided physical support to Fat Jack, but to call them bodyguards would be a disservice. They were among the most talented and far-sighted young musicians in Harlem and only when they had converted to Islam did they become known by their stage name, the Fantastic Aleems.

By 1964 the Allen family were living in the St Nicholas Projects on 129th Street, in the same block as the Harlem funk star Jimmy Castor, and for the first time the twin brothers were torn apart. Arthur had been shot in the back during the Harlem riots of 1964 – one of over a hundred injuries – and his incapacity ruled him unfit for military service. As the Vietnam War intensified, Albert was swept up in a military conscription drive that targeted inner-city ghettos and was sent to Vietnam aged seventeen. When he asked what to expect in the malarial jungles of Vietnam, Albert was told by a commanding officer, 'Marijuana, partying and freaky young oriental women.' He had witnessed them all two blocks from home at one of Fat Jack's sets and was unimpressed. While one brother went to Vietnam, the other stayed behind and grew closer to Taylor, joining a great Harlem soul group called the International 'G.T.O.s', who recorded for Rojac. Like many harmony groups before – the Cadillacs, the Chevrons, Maurice Williams and the Zodiacs, and Dennis Edwards and the Firebirds – the International 'G.T.O.s' were named after one of the *de rigueur* automobiles of the era: the Pontiac GTO. The 'G.T.O.s' were in every respect the classic mid sixties soul group, not unlike the Four Tops. Lead singer Tommy Lockhart was upfront with a powerful falsetto voice that preceded the great lead singer of the Stylistics, Russell Thompkins Jr, by years. Arthur Allen was the group's second tenor. The International 'G.T.O.s' played bars in Harlem but struggled to make an impact nationally, so Arthur tried again. This time they changed the group's name to the Master Four, and Taylor released a ridiculously catchy novelty record, 'Love From The Far East', which employed cod-oriental tropes over a pounding Motown beat. Harlem's innovation seemed limitless.

Within a year Albert was back in Harlem, his military uniform confined to the cupboard, and reunited with his brother. They joined a generation who took their influence from the wave of Muslim teachings sweeping Harlem in the wake of the assassination of Malcolm X and changed their names to Tunde' Ra Aleem and TaharQa Aleem respectively. More than any of Harlem's thousands of restless children, it was the Fantastic Aleems who came to map out the shifting cartography of soul music and make the connection between sixties soul, disco boogie and hip-hop. By the summer of 1969 they had become the local promoters of guitar superstar Jimi Hendrix and were his closest companions in Harlem. Years later, they became the creative force behind Fat Jack's pioneering hip-hop venue Harlem World, which he bought in partnership with the Aleems and his one-time gangster rival Mookie Jackson. The venue was a vacant lot on the corner of 116th and Lenox near Fat Jack's fast food joint, which had once housed a struggling Woolworth store. As you emerged from the bowels of the IRT subway at Lenox, the club's stained white facade met you; scattered near the doorway, multicoloured parasols sat incongruously in the rain, as if a Sandals resort had opened in the ghetto.

Sensitive to the sounds he heard in the bars of 125th Street, Fat Jack was quick to recognise the merits of street funk, and – again without conspicuous success – released some of the best of the genre. Curtis Lee & the KCP's 'Get In My Bag' was one among many tributes to Godfather of Soul James Brown, but one specific release, recorded in the dying days of 1969, screamed of Harlem's creative intensity and the sheer weirdness of Fat Jack's parties. Recorded in Detroit, Chico and Buddy's 'Can You Dig It' opens with blaring police sirens and then the action kicks in. A tireless funk soundtrack carries you up from the crowded sidewalk through a loft window to a full-scale set, heavy with sweet smoke, the floor heaving with dancers and drag artists. Bodies gyrate to percussive cowbells as the room is filled with insane druggy lyrics that shift from southern soul food to space-walk nonsense and surreal half-spoken soliloquies that could have been parsed by George Clinton's Funkadelic. This was new funk at its rawest – urban street music breaking free of the feelgood stranglehold that Motown held over mid sixties soul and pointing forward to decades of more disruptive music yet to come. 'Can You Dig It' was one amongst hundreds of new releases circulating in the stores of Harlem and Bushwick that summer, local indie vinyl that was testing the coherence of traditional soul music in the civil rights era.

Although Fat Jack – and his local contemporaries Paul Winley and Joe Robinson – struggled to take lo-fi independent soul music much beyond Harlem, they had one overwhelming advantage over their contemporaries in Detroit, Chicago and Memphis. The shifting rhythms and quixotic fashion trends of 125th Street were on their doorstep. Robinson described a phalanx of record industry executives sifting through his shelves, checking the action and jotting down titles as he tried to manage a bustling store, the speakers spilling out on to the sidewalk, the sounds competing with screeching traffic. Despite their limited resources, the Harlem indies – and the questionable characters who drove the local music market – became bellwethers of the evolution of soul and how its future was fragmenting and changing. Record industry executives, sometimes apprehensive about their safety, hung out in Harlem record stores, hoping to crack the codes of black music and anticipate the next big shift in the shuddering journey of R&B.

Fat Jack and his retinue were a familiar sight cruising 125th Street in his classic-style Buick Electra 225. (Although his records were at the cutting edge of new funk and street boogie, his personal tastes were more retrospective.) Harlem's indies such as Rojac, Tay-Ster, Sprout and Winley Records were typically under-capitalised and lived from one release to the next, often funding records from the proceeds of other local businesses. Compared with New York's most established Midtown labels, like Florence Greenberg's Scepter/Wand group and the towering Atlantic Records, these were makeshift organisations, often existing in a twilight world closer to street crime than global distribution deals. Atlantic, the self-styled 'West Point of Rhythm and Blues', could boast the towering talent of Aretha Franklin and the recording catalogue of the late Otis Redding. Their roster of artists included Patti LaBelle, Wilson Pickett, Sam and Dave, King Curtis, Don Covay and both Roberta Flack and Donny Hathaway. Set against the established R&B labels which were already diversifying into the next generation of progressive rock, Fat Jack was reliant on cash derived from multiple questionable sources including illegal street gambling, the drug trade and vinyl bootlegging.

His relationship with the soul vocalist Big Maybelle was a bundle of intrigue. He was her manager, her producer and almost certainly her 'doctor', the intimate word that the declining and distressed R&B singers of Harlem used to describe their most trusted and reliable heroin dealer. But to describe their relationship as simply one of addict and dealer would be to diminish a bond that held fast for many years and was one of both love, artistic support and dependency. Fat Jack poured money into making her a star again, taking out adverts in *Billboard* to back her 1966 album *Got A Brand New Bag* and building a distribution team focused almost entirely on reviving her fortunes in stores across the US. It never quite came to anything, but their relationship lasted until Big Maybelle was too ill to continue working and was finally forced to leave Harlem. She returned to her mother's home in Cleveland where she succumbed to diabetes, never able to shed weight or her drug dependency.

Fat Jack's contradictory personality lurched from an intimidating hard exterior to an emotional soft core. He was considerably more sensitive to the shifting fortunes of his roster of artists than more established record producers and his advice to those around him was a coarse interpretation of Black Power – 'Don't let them intimidate you, intimidate them.' He was admirably blind to age and to reputation, courting new artists with nothing more than an idea, and then the next day revivifying those whose careers were spiralling towards ignominy. He was a close confidant of Etta James and was with her when she recorded 'Miss Pitiful', her self-reflective cover version of the Otis Redding standard, 'Mr Pitiful'. At the time of the recording in June 1969, James's life was already seriously compromised by drug and alcohol problems. Rather than blame her supplier, the singer described Fat Jack as a saviour, a man who had protected her from the darkest forces of the recording industry.

He had also held out a hand of hope to a third great female singer, Joshie Jo Armstead, whose career had brought her to

Harlem from a period as a recording artist at Giant Records in Chicago. Armstead befriended Nicholas Ashford and Valerie Simpson, then two budding songwriters from Harlem's White Rock Baptist Church, and held their hands as she led them around the publishing companies of Midtown, until they were spotted by Motown and relocated to Detroit to become the chosen writers for Marvin Gaye and Tammi Terrell. Working as a threesome throughout the mid sixties, Ashford Simpson and their mentor Armstead wrote several great soul songs, not least Ray Charles's 'Let's Go Get Stoned' (1966) and another partially disguised drug-addiction song, 'I Don't Need No Doctor' (1966). By then Charles's career had stalled and he could often be found in the Woodside Hotel talking race relations with the Allen twins' father William. He had been arrested for possession of heroin for a third time and was one among many major singers of the era facing rehab.

Heroin was not only gripping Harlem, it had travelled like a hurricane through R&B. In January 1969 Esther Phillips's contract with Atlantic had expired. Frustrated by her unreliability, Atlantic let her go, and she signed to another New York indie, the notoriously uncaring Roulette Records. It was one of the many low points in her career. Ravaged by heroin addiction, she took the brave but risky decision to check herself in to the controversial Synanon clinic in Los Angeles, where she met the singer Sam Fletcher. Together they worked on a live album at the local Pied Piper Club. Phillips' therapy was brutal in the extreme. Under the tough regime of the untrained Charles E. Dederich, she suffered for weeks in a former hotel in Santa Monica. Dederich, a reformed alcoholic, was one of the West Coast's irrepressible fantasists who wanted to create an experimental cult that would transform the world. 'Crime is stupid, delinquency is stupid and the use of narcotics is stupid,' opined Dederich. 'What Synanon is dealing with is addiction to stupidity.' His programme rejected any form of pharmaceutical treatment, and Phillips, along with most of her fellow patients, suffered an unforgiving 'cold turkey'. Those who visited the facility at the time described seeing junkies left on couches to writhe and vomit for days while they suffered withdrawal. Then they were confronted with 'The Game', a group therapy set-up where people sat in a circle barking their frustrations at each other. It was a ragbag of bogus science, half-digested psychology and punishing behaviourism. But by sheer fluke, rather than any underlying therapy, it worked for Phillips and she returned to her spiritual home at Atlantic. In 1972, on her painfully honest album *From A Whisper To A Scream*, Phillips recorded one of the era's greatest self-critical heroin songs, Gil Scott-Heron's 'Home Is Where The Hatred Is'. A song of dramatic complexity, it recounts the personal experiences of a junkie walking through the ghetto twilight and trying to avoid returning to a broken home. As the song unfolds, memories of home and of domestic abuse intertwine with the rash of needle marks.

As Phillips headed optimistically to rehab in California, back in Harlem Fat Jack was also looking to the future. A new generation of musicians who did not share the great R&B and jazz lineage of Big Maybelle, Etta James, Esther Phillips and Ray Charles were hustling for attention. They were mostly young, untried and from the ghetto tenements of Harlem, earning cash working for Fat Jack's string of businesses or dealing on his behalf on street corners.

By 1969 Fat Jack's greatest hope – one among many – was yet another southern soul singer, O.C. Tolbert, who had come to Harlem from Detroit seduced by Fat Jack's promises. Tolbert was born in Selma, Alabama, a stone's throw from the Edmund Pettus Bridge on the so-called 'Freedom Highway', a historic flashpoint at the height of the civil rights era. Tolbert had witnessed the tensions in the area, but by the time the civil rights marchers had been clubbed to the ground as they attempted to cross the bridge in March of 1965, he had moved north to Detroit to join the great migration of southern soul talent who saw the Motor City as an oasis of opportunity. By 1968 he had moved again, this time to Harlem where his unfulfilled career took a significant turn: he led a funk coalition known as Aleke Kanonu Meets Tolbert the Miracle Man. Only one record was released, again funded by Fat Jack. The pulsating 'Nwanne, Nwanne, Nwanne' captured the rising wave of pan-African nationalism that was gusting through the community, but again was ahead of its time and disappeared from view. It did, however, lay the foundations for one of the greatest obscure soul albums of all time, *Damn Sam The Miracle Man And The Soul Congregation*, released by Fat Jack on Tay-Ster in 1970.

For all his generosity, Fat Jack's approach to releasing records was at best scattergun, and his legacy says as much about ego as inspiration. He was prone to taking credit for writing songs he had little to do with, and like his Detroit-based colleague Diamond Jim Riley, or another ghetto producer George Blackwell at Smoke Records in Newark, Fat Jack added his name to nearly every release, claiming to be either writer, producer or both. It was a common conceit in independent soul music – that the tough-talking guy who put up the money took the credit as copyright law cowered in the corner.

In the early months of 1969, as NASA's scientists were making their final calculations for a manned lunar landing, a joke spread through the independent soul scene: what was the quietest place in the galaxy? The answer was the royalties department at Roulette Records. Roulette was led by the Harlem-born gangster Morris Levy, whose tentacles stretched into the darkest areas of music industry crime. From the company's base in office suites at Broadway and 50th Street, it enjoyed the tacit support of the Genovese crime family, and Levy was guarded wherever he went by the muscular Nate McCalla, a personal friend of Fat Jack, an uncompromising hard man and long-time label owner of Calla Records. A minority shareholder in Roulette, Dominic Ciaffonne, a member of the Genovese mafia, took on the role of controlling record stores and rack jobbers, either directly or via compliant mob-controlled labour unions. In 1969 Levy and McCalla, often working in tandem, controlled the careers of Jean Wells, Tony Fox, Charlie Hodges, Ila Vann and Geraldine Hunt – all decent singers in an industry where the odds were stacked heavily against them. More mainstream than Fat Jack's roster of artists, they fell afoul of similar barriers: poor distribution, limited promotional support and aggressive copyright theft. Few, if any, were paid in full. Tommy James, one of the most successful artists in the Roulette stable, exposed the extent of criminality he witnessed in his autobiography *Me, the Mob and the Music*, describing a claustrophobic world of tax evasion, payola and physical violence. For years he claimed IRS investigators were virtually camped out in the company's offices poring over royalty returns and record invoices. But even under the noses of the tax men, Roulette's malpractices continued. Morris Levy was the master of voodoo economics, claiming spurious writing and production credits – mostly by adding his own name to royalty return sheets, and when in doubt inserting the name of his son Adam. Bizarrely, it was the corporate buildings of Manhattan that had provided the inspiration for his greatest hit. While looking up at the illuminated sign of the giant insurance company skyscraper Mutual of New York Building – MONY – he found the hook for the global pop hit 'Mony Mony' (Tommy James and the Shondells, 1968).

Fat Jack was smart enough to know that his image in the industry came with a question mark, and so for two years Claude Sterrett was the 'acceptable face' of Rojac. He was a young man who gave the label's releases the illusion of credibility and he was a prominent member of the Fair Play Committee, the notorious Harlem-based organisation that spooked the mainstream recording industry by using strong-arm tactics to demand better terms and conditions for black artists and their labels. Their cause was noble, their tactics horrific. The Fair Play Committee had enraged the established industry when they bulldozed into a NATRA convention in Miami, in the late summer of 1968, bearing arms and threatening executives. Atlantic's Jerry Wexler, who was threatened with his life, described them as Harlem 'shakedown artists', although he himself had secured numerous dubious co-writing credits on songs at Atlantic. Among the ranks of the Fair Play Committee were Fat Jack's collaborator Clarence 'Mookie' Jackson and two other notorious hustlers with a background in the uptown soul scene: Johnny Baylor, the owner of KoKo Records, and his sidekick Dino 'Boom Boom' Woodard, who by 1969 were acting as armed executives for the Memphis-based Stax Records. Despite having right on its side, the Fair Play Committee divided opinion, in part because it was driven by Fat Jack and 'Mookie', two men with questionable business backgrounds who were easily dismissed as criminals rather than some sort of civil rights pressure group. One remarkable sidebar to the story of the Fair Play

Committee was a lengthy copyright dispute that involved Fat Jack, 'Mookie', James Brown and a glamorous Harlem nightclub dancer, Betty Jean Newsome, who befriended Brown during one of his famous residencies at the Apollo back in 1962.

The couple became intimate sexual partners, and on a limousine trip from Harlem down south, she sang Brown the chorus of a song she had improvised in her mind. It was the kernel of what became one of Brown's signature songs, 'It's A Man's World'. According to *Village Voice* journalist Michael Clancy, 'like two parents in an ugly custody battle, Brown and Newsome – or at least their proxies – have tussled over ownership of the song for decades. First recorded as "It's A Man's World" in June of 1964 in Chicago, it was Brown's second version of the song, retitled a few years later to slyly echo the Oscar-winning "It's A Mad, Mad, Mad, Mad World" that would became an international sensation, ascending to the top spot on the R&B chart and number eight on the pop charts, evolving onstage into one of Brown's signature showstoppers and personal favourites.' As the dispute over the song's provenance grew, Newsome stood her ground. Back in Harlem she had fallen in love with 'Mookie' Jackson of the Fair Play Committee. Although the committee's original targets were the rich white recording executives who had profited on the back of soul music, Jackson encouraged his girlfriend to pursue James Brown. In an event now mythologised in the story of black music, Jackson travelled to a James Brown concert in Brooklyn with a box of mice and let them loose in the auditorium. Faced with the chaotic scenes in front of him, Brown was forced to abandon the show and face up to the realisation that neither Jackson nor Newsome were going away. Newsome received a partial settlement of $250,000 in 1967, but even today her lawyers are pursuing full settlement and back royalties estimated to run into millions, in what her lawyer Carl Kaminsky claims is one of the 'biggest frauds in modern musical history'. One final twist in the story brought it back to Harlem and Jackson's friendship with Fat Jack. The dispute had encouraged Fat Jack to produce a version of the song featuring Big Maybelle, whose deep soul interpretation not only gives it a feminist force but, by manipulating her pronunciation of the key word 'man', hints heavily at its being a song about drug dependency. The song was released by Rojac and licensed to the legendary Chess label in Chicago. Although Fat Jack is credited as the producer, the law at the time required James Brown to be identified as the composer.

As the independents of Harlem demanded fairness and greater transparency in the industry, sometimes paradoxically at gunpoint, two of the musical forms of the future – funk and disco – were becoming increasingly visible. Among its many adventures into soul's splintering styles, Rojac was a forerunner of street funk, and a rival New York label Samar Records, an indie based upstate in Rochester whose arteries spread down to Harlem, was laying down the blueprint for what became disco. Unable to secure much in the way of national distribution deals, Samar was all but dependent on the crowded record stores in Harlem and Brooklyn's Bedford-Stuyvesant, selling records via Record Shack or Bobby Robinson's Happy House. Among its many featured artists and producers were a number of well-known Harlem faces: Jimmy Norman, Bert Keyes, Johnny Brantley, the Poindexter Brothers and King Curtis's protégé, the saxophonist Lonnie Youngblood. One of the label's now most cherished releases was the Icemen's haunting '(My Girl) She's A Fox' (1966), which features Jimi Hendrix on lead guitar. Samar was short-lived but screamed with importance. The label was part owned by Bob Schwaid, a Brooklyn native with business connections in Rochester, who all but abandoned the label to become Van Morrison's manager at the time of the recording of Morrison's now classic album *Astral Weeks*. Schwaid had cut his teeth on several obscure independent soul releases, including Madeline Wilson's 'Dial "L" For Lonely' and Gloria Parker's 'The Best Thing For You Baby' – both joyous teenage love songs cast in the dominant Motown style. But hidden within the arrangement was another emergent soul style. Schwaid had hired as his arranger an old schoolfriend from Brooklyn, a jobbing producer-arranger with the grandiloquent name of Norbert de Coteaux. Known as 'Bert', he was a thick-set young man with heavy horn-rimmed spectacles who looked more like a schoolteacher than a record producer. He was steeped in orchestral music and had recently graduated from the prestigious New York conservatoire the

Juilliard School. He had a personal mission to combine the R&B of his ghetto childhood with the lush strings and sophisticated orchestration he had studied at the Juilliard. De Coteaux's curriculum vitae was a masterclass in metropolitan soul: he was the talent behind Lou Courtney's 'I Watched You Slowly Slip Away' (1965), Harlem-born Patti Austin's 'Take Away The Pain Stain' (1966), the Charts' 'Living The Nightlife' (1966) and Christine Cooper's ebullient 'Heartaches Away My Boy' (1966). Within a matter of a few more years, ploughing a furrow for subtly crafted orchestral dance music, he offered a sophisticated alternative to street funk and edgy political soul, and thus became one of the most sought-after producers in the New York dance music underground. When disco eventually dominated the charts, his name became an imprimatur of success and he became known throughout the industry by the nickname Bert 'Super Charts' de Coteaux. He was one of many young producer-arrangers who were emerging from the margins of the New York ghettos and who with time would dominate the musical mainstream. He is often cited as the man who brought lush strings to soul music.

By early 1969 Florence Ballard, the recently deposed member of the Supremes, had also arrived in Harlem. Her relationship with Motown was in disarray and she was in the early stages of a catastrophic series of legal disputes that in time would bankrupt her and force her onto welfare. Suffering from depression, alcoholism and the emotional fallout of a violent teenage rape, she had signed a hurriedly arranged solo deal with ABC Records and moved in to a New York hotel. Restless to escape from Midtown and connect with a time when her musical career was exciting and less pressured, she headed uptown to the bars and clubs of Harlem, an area she knew from the earliest years of her Motown past. As a young teenager, she had stayed in the Hotel Theresa near the Apollo, now at the heart of a dispute with Columbia University's land grab. Decay had set in and the once grand hotel was now being sublet as an office block. Seeking familiarity in a time of troubled emotions and tired of eating in show-business restaurants on the Avenue of Americas near ABC's corporate headquarters,

Ballard hung out in Harlem, looking up old acquaintances and turning up backstage at the Apollo to renew old friendships. Despite the near collapse of her career, she was about to cut a record that played its own small place in the history of underground dance – 'Love Ain't Love', a dynamic proto-disco record arranged by Bert de Coteaux and written by another emerging star of the New York underground, Van McCoy.

McCoy was plotting the baby steps of what was to become a truly historic album, *Soul Improvisations* (1972). Viewed with hindsight, it was an album that bridged uptown soul and metropolitan disco, and although no one called it that at the time McCoy's orchestral arrangements and his virtuoso electric keyboard skills created a sound that was not only original but a blueprint of music yet to come. McCoy's impatience about change in African-American music was shared by his contemporary Gene Redd Jr, the son of a well-known swing-era artist and a man who had worked for Motown's New York office. By 1969 he, too, was striking out in a similar direction and had set up two parallel labels, De-Lite Records and Red Coach Records, that would become progenitors of funk and disco and eventually homes to Kool and the Gang, Crown Heights Affair and Everyday People.

In 1969 Robert 'Kool' Bell, a native of New Jersey, had moved to Harlem where his uncle Tommy was a boxing trainer. Earlier in his distinguished career, Tommy Bell had been a major welterweight talent who fought Jake LaMotta and Harlem icon Sugar Ray Robinson. Now living in his uncle's apartment near 125th Street, Robert 'Kool' Bell and his Gang released their eponymous debut single, initially hitting the stores of Harlem on the barely distributed local indie Red Coach. Nothing about its first pressing could have anticipated the stellar success the group would enjoy when disco and jazz-funk came to dominate the club charts. Fat Jack fought for their signature but lost out to Red Coach's sister label, De-Lite Records, and before 1969 was over Kool and the Gang had released 'Let The Music Take Your Mind' and their eponymous single 'Kool And The Gang' on the fledgling New York indie. The journey to their classic mid seventies pop-funk records 'Jungle Boogie' and 'Hollywood Swinging' had begun in earnest.

And so, within a few blocks of central Harlem, the foundations of disco were being laid. Hollywood was typically late to the party. It wasn't until 1977, when the blue-collar Brooklyn film *Saturday Night Fever* became a global hit, that disco – or rather 'the uptown sound' – went mainstream. By then Van McCoy's *Soul Improvisations* was five years old and his ubiquitous album track 'The Hustle' already two years old. The roll-call of early pioneers who either lived or worked in central Harlem is, in retrospect, a staggering checklist of disco talent: Bert 'Super Charts' de Coteaux, Van McCoy, Gene Redd Jr, Kool and the Gang, the Fantastic Aleems, Patrick Adams, Luther Vandross, and a young, then unknown, singer who would rise to become one of the cult superstars of underground club music, Leroy Burgess. For over ten years Fat Jack's micro-indies – Tay-Ster and Rojac – had blazed a trail for independence and for uptown soul, but by the early seventies they had been surpassed by a generation of new independent labels that would take soul music forward to the next chapter in the evolution of the New York indie scene: among them De-Lite, Red Coach, Perception, Today and Salsoul, and in time NIA Records, a home for Fat Jack's prodigies, the Aleem brothers and Leroy Burgess.

It was the summer of 1968 when Leroy Burgess first made his break, and although he was only ever on the periphery of Fat Jack's curious empire he knew the Aleem twins as neighbours. Burgess had taken a summer job opposite the beautiful Gothic-style church nicknamed the 'Cathedral of Harlem' (St Charles Borromeo and the Chapel of the Resurrection) on 141st Street. His story is not the well-worn narrative of a boy graduating from the gospel choir. Burgess had taken on work as a social work assistant, managing unruly kids when school was out. The job took him to the grounds of the church which had witnessed demographic change on a massive scale. It had been established by Irish Catholics, who were the dominant immigrant group in Harlem in the late nineteenth century. By the sixties its congregation was drawing on the local black community, many of whom came from the Deep South or the Caribbean. Burgess was neither a Catholic nor particularly religious and had taken the job because he needed cash. In the heat of a summer's day he had taken a lunch break and was playing basketball at a court next door to the church. In his team was another local kid, Larry Newkirk, the lead singer of an unsigned Harlem soul group called the Mellow Souls. Legend has it that during a break in the game, Burgess sang along to a transistor radio playing Smokey Robinson's harmony-soul song 'Here I Go Again'. It was a virtuoso performance, a pitch-perfect audition, and Newkirk immediately invited Burgess to join his group. In 1969 they changed their name to Black Ivory and would go on to become one of Harlem's truly exceptional soul groups. After turning down an offer from Fat Jack, they gravitated towards a then unknown Harlem producer, Patrick Adams. Within a few years, Burgess and Adams would become hugely significant figures in New York's underground disco scene and pillars of a hedonistic society that remains a religion of its own even today.

A momentum was gathering that led inexorably to disco. Downtown on East 45th Street, at the celebrity hotspot Arthur's which had been opened in 1965 by Sybil Christopher, the Welsh socialite and first wife of actor Richard Burton, two turntables had been installed, one as a back-up in case the other failed. Christopher's in-house DJ Terry Noel put them to a different use and is often regarded as the pioneer who worked the first set of double-decks, allowing him to mix records in what was then a primitive club music fashion. Back up in Harlem, at Fat Jack's infamous sets, the Aleem brothers relied on a single deck and a versatile hand-over-and-play partnership, aided with a live conga drummer, to make it seem as if there was no gap between sounds. Dominating the Harlem nights were the big party sounds of 1968 such as Archie Bell & the Drells' 'Tighten Up', Vicki Anderson and James Brown's 'You've Got The Power' and Charles Wright & the Watts 103rd Street Rhythm Band's 'Do Your Thing'. Then they would drop big shots from the Rojac catalogue – Wesley Paige's 'I've Got To Find Out For Myself' and Curtis Lee & the KCP's 'Get In The Bag'. A familiar blast of big phat Rojac releases kept Fat Jack happy – and the room going – with a threatening clamour of funk and soul, many years ahead of its time.

As the decade neared its close the influence of Fat Jack's sets and Harlem rent parties began to filter downtown, first to the

Upper West Side and then to Greenwich Village where the gay roots of underground New York disco were sown. The most celebrated unofficial venues were the house parties hosted by audiophile David Mancuso, so different from Fat Jack's sets and yet in some ways very similar. In his obituary, *The New York Times* described his loft parties as 'a '60s dream of peace, love and diversity: multiracial, gay and straight, young and old, well-to-do and down-at-heel, singles and couples, all mingling ecstatically in an egalitarian, commerce-free space'. Unable to afford his rent, Mancuso sold tickets for what was the downtown equivalent of a Harlem rent party, hosting his first event on Valentine's Day, 1970, a party which bore the title 'Love Saves the Day' and whose initials were code for LSD. Tim Lawrence, the author of *Love Saves the Day: A History of American Dance Music Culture, 1970–1979*, saw Mancuso's loft parties as the big bang that ultimately gave life to underground disco. 'D.J.'s started to gravitate to the Loft, when they were finished with their own parties for the night,' he wrote, 'and it was there that some of the most influential D.J.'s of the future – Larry Levan, Frankie Knuckles, Tony Humphries, François Kevorkian, David Morales and many more – would learn about the sonic and social potential of the party.'

A direct lineage can be traced back from Fat Jack's sets to the rent parties of the Harlem Renaissance and forward to the unconventional loft parties downtown. There is a further link that is borne out in Fat Jack's own contradictory life. He was a drug dealer given to flashy arrogance and street-level criminality but he surrounded himself with older Christian singers, especially those women gifted with sanctified voices who were falling on hard times. Of all the forms of post-sixties music that have claimed to have been born out of a culture clash, it was underground disco that pulled off the greatest clash of all. Disco and its underground derivatives, boogie and house, had taken over fifty years to mutate, but when it came, it arrived with such blistering force that the thing they once called soul music would never be quite the same again. The uptown rent parties and the independent soul music of Harlem had invented the future: up-tempo, soul-infused club music that literally shook the house. As with Fat Jack's fascinating life, contradictory elements bound themselves together in an unholy alliance. The spiritual voices of the gospel tradition, embodied in women like Big Maybelle, Lillie Bryant, Joshie Jo Armstead, Linda Jones, Loleatta Holloway and Jocelyn Brown, floated like celestial beings above the hedonistic beat of dance music. Disco and club music fed off the same moral paradox that had shaped Harlem nightlife – a society infused with religion and yet consumed by drugs. In his later years, Fat Jack was stricken by ailing health and eventually died of a heart attack, in part induced by heavy abuse of crack cocaine. There is no evidence of where or when he died, and no death certificate to throw light on his passing. Fat Jack Taylor's curious empire left precious few hits behind, but the range and quality of the music – simultaneously respectful of the past and hardwired to the future – pointed to an important fact: Harlem, the crucible of change and soul music, was about to fragment into new and unforeseen shapes.

Alice Faye Williams (aka Afeni Shakur) and her boyfriend Lumumba Shakur of the Harlem Branch of the Black Panthers are arrested at an apartment at 112 West 117th Street in a series of dawn raids in 1969. The arresting officers are members of New York Police Department's undercover unit BOSS – the Bureau of Special Services.

FEBRUARY

The Black Panther Conspiracy

In February 1969, as New York City battled with a crippling snowstorm Eugene Roberts stayed indoors in his apartment in the Bronx and compiled a meticulous ledger of names and addresses. A young navy veteran, Roberts had been keeping a log of the activities of political radicals in Harlem since he graduated from the New York Police Department Academy in the winter of 1963. From a distance or in a crowd his unruly curls looked vaguely like an afro, and that fact alone encouraged senior officers to promote him to detective and train him as an undercover agent. By 1964, working for the NYPD's Bureau of Specialist Services (BOSS), Roberts had successfully infiltrated Malcolm X's nascent political party, the Organization of Afro-American Unity. He had arrived at a volatile time in Harlem street politics; it was in the early days of Malcolm X's dispute with the Nation of Islam, when suspicions were high and murderous plots were afoot. With time Roberts became a trusted member of the organisation – he was referred to as 'Brother Gene' – and was promoted to an inner-circle role as Malcolm X's personal bodyguard. To strengthen his cover, he assumed the name 'Gene X', a nod to Islam, and pursued a course of study that he hinted might lead to full religious conversion. Roberts' handlers had given him the fake identity of a warehouseman, a happily married grafter who lived with his wife and child in the Bronx. Roberts was in fact one of the NYPD's most valued 'deeps' – the police term for a deep penetration undercover officer – who had been charged with monitoring the numerous radical factions and community groups within Harlem's vigorous political world. Roberts was always around, standing by Malcolm, buying the *Amsterdam News* on the corner of Lenox, or huddled with street militants whenever a protest erupted. In the eyes of his controllers downtown, Roberts had been an outstanding success, and by 1965 was a familiar face among the first generation of recruits to the Harlem Black Panther Party. His closeness to Malcolm X had virtually given him a free pass into the newly emergent movement. Although the official history of the Black Panther Party normally begins on the streets of Oakland on the West Coast, Black Power had been embedded in Harlem's community life for decades. The first real evidence of a group calling themselves the Black Panthers in New York came in the context of school strikes in 1964 when hundreds of thousands of parents, students and civil rights activists took part in a city-wide boycott of the public school system in support of full integration. More than 460,000 students refused to go to school on 3 February. A small group of Harlem teenagers supported the boycott and took on the identity of 'panthers' in their flyers and street banners.

Roberts watched it all unfold. His sparse woolly hair grew out over the years and his quiet demeanour made him seem unspectacular and trustworthy. He had not only been handpicked by the NYPD; his credentials had been cleared in advance by the FBI, who had set up a network of informers and undercover agents in the major ghettos. Despite years of local service in Harlem, Roberts was virtually unknown except to a small elite of senior officers downtown. His recruitment photograph had been hidden in a locked box and he had been advised never to call in at the office or make connections with other serving officers. The police had even trained him to be hostile to uniformed officers and to immerse himself in Harlem street crime so that his cover could not easily be blown. It was a lonely job. He was never fully comfortable with the armed and erratic underworld of internecine Muslim politics and not only feared for his own safety but became concerned about the likely impact on his family. As a precaution, he sent his infant daughter to stay with his mother-in-law in Virginia.

Roberts had been with Malcolm X in February 1965 when he was assassinated at the Audubon Ballroom in Washington Heights. According to Manning Marable, in his authoritative biography *Malcolm X: A Life of Reinvention*, 'an incendiary smoke bomb ignited at the extreme rear of the ballroom, instantly creating panic, screams and confusion. It was only then that Willie Bradley, sitting in the front row, got to his feet and walked briskly toward the rostrum. When he was fifteen feet away, he elevated his sawed-off shot gun from under his coat, took careful aim, and fired. The shotgun pellets ripped squarely into Malcolm's left side, cutting a seven-inch-wide circle around his heart and left chest. This was the kill shot, the blow that executed Malcolm X . . .' Roberts had fought his way to a stage littered with drum kits and amplifiers and clambered up to the bullet-ridden lectern, evading gunfire as he ran, and attempted to give Malcolm X mouth-to-mouth resuscitation. But it was too little too late.

Although the assassination has led to countless conspiracy theories, it is now the settled presumption that the assassins were a gang of conspirators from Newark's Mosque No. 25, working on assignment for Elijah Muhammad, leader of the Nation of Islam. Although there has been claim, counterclaim and outright denials, it is now believed that the unit sent to kill Malcolm X consisted of five men: Benjamin Thomas, Leon Davis, Wilbur McKinley, Talmadge Hayer and William Bradley. The five conspirators all had criminal records and hailed from the East Orange area near Newark, New Jersey, where they were associates of the boxer Rubin 'The Hurricane' Carter (who was wrongfully convicted of a triple murder in 1966 and spent twenty years in prison before being released) and George Blackwell, a producer with the Newark soul label Smoke Records.

Curiously, in the months before the assassination, Malcolm X and Eugene Roberts had developed a friendship of sorts. Roberts frequently travelled with Malcolm X in his Oldsmobile and, according to the retired police officer Edward Conlon, writing in *Esquire* magazine, 'was recognized for his quiet competence and the sincerity of his allegiance, which was unfeigned – (and) he came to admire Malcolm with fervour'. One subject Roberts and Malcolm X often returned to as they travelled together between meetings was the relatively safe topic of music. After surviving a tough childhood – his father died when he was six and his mother was incarcerated in a Michigan mental hospital when he was thirteen – Malcolm Little drifted towards petty criminality, becoming a pimp and street hustler known as 'Detroit Red'. By 1943 he had been moved to Harlem where he was subsequently jailed for larceny. In jail he converted to Islam and re-emerged as Malcolm X, a charismatic and serious young man whose passionate intelligence made him a formidable leader. In his hoodlum days, he was a fan of the early pioneers of R&B such as Johnny Otis and Big Mama Thornton, but as he grew older he preferred jazz to the coarser juke-joint sounds and eventually graduated to his favourite singer, Dinah Washington, the most popular black singer of the fifties. Then, with his conversion to Islam, he told Roberts that he felt morally obliged to support those artists who had also converted, naming Ahmed Abdul-Malik, a bassist with the Thelonious Monk band, the pianist Ahmad Jamal and, most passionately of all, the vocalist Dakota Staton, his all-time favourite singer. Staton had been discovered at the Baby Grand in Harlem and signed to Columbia Records before changing her name to Aliyah Rabia after religious conversion. She married one of Malcolm X's closest musical friends, the trumpeter Talib Ahmad Dawood, and for a time the couple operated one of Harlem's busiest record stores, which not only serviced the local jazz and independent soul scene but was a meeting place for members of the Organization of Afro-American Unity. Significantly, it became the first record store in Harlem to import records from Africa and thus became a centre for the supporters of pan-African politics. Malcolm X had many other reasons to list Dakota Staton as his favourite singer. Not only was she a high-profile supporter of his movement, her husband was a noisy critic of the Nation of Islam and despised Malcolm X's nemesis, Elijah Muhammad. Some suspected that Dawood's scathing opinion pieces about the Nation of Islam, which appeared in the *New Crusader*, a daily newspaper widely distributed in the black community, were inspired, if not actually written, by Malcolm X. In the fifties Malcolm X had given his vocal support to a group put together by Dawood, a seventeen-piece big band composed entirely of Muslim musicians called the Messengers. Members included Yusef Lateef, Ahmad Jamal, McCoy Tyner, and latterly Art Blakey, who kept a core of the group together as his Jazz Messengers. Harlem's various nations of Islam were producing popular music long before the term soul was coined.

Music was digging deeper into the very soul of Harlem, driven by jazz, a rising fascination with pan-African rhythms and the more politicised beliefs of a new generation of musicians, many of them opponents of President Nixon and converts to Islam. But by far the biggest influence was the ghetto itself and the deepening social problems that were infecting the dilapidated buildings across 110th Street. A network of poorly funded community centres and welfare programmes had sprung up across Manhattan, often in spite of severe cutbacks in spending. The cost of the war in Vietnam had bitten hard into public expenditure and community groups across Harlem had suffered more than most. One of the few positive developments they could point to was an upsurge in self-awareness and a new kind of soul music that had its roots firmly planted in social deprivation. This was a form of soul imbued with the history of civil rights but it was angrier, more politically demanding and owed more to the crumbling projects of Harlem than to the Christian battle cries of Selma and Birmingham.

Harlem had become a flashpoint, and Eugene Roberts was tasked with keeping his eyes on a bewildering number of political groups within the African-American community. In 1969, while still greeted as Malcolm X's bodyguard, he was a trusted face at demonstrations and a familiar figure at street-corner leafleting. No one was aware that he was taping conversations and investigating the backgrounds of local militants. Roberts moved around Harlem with a tiny microphone strapped to his chest and wired to a transmitter in his coat pocket. He was, according to his own admission, 'a walking radio station'. Routinely, two detectives pursued him at a distance with a bulkier tape-recorder in their car, from where they recorded conversations and comments as Roberts worked his way through meetings, rallies and the private homes of targeted individuals. For several months in 1968 he followed teenagers Michael Tabor and Jamal Joseph, the young Black Panthers who had risen from the streets to become the party's newspaper street-sellers. Tabor worked central Harlem and Joseph the South Bronx. They delivered newspapers and Panther literature to bookstores and nightclubs. Tabor had already squeezed a lifetime into a few short years. He had first taken heroin as a thirteen-year-old, was a high school basketball star at fifteen, and a heroin addict at seventeen, before life as a Black Panther straightened him out and utilised his precocious intellect and towering self-confidence. Roberts had reasoned that if he followed in Tabor's footsteps he would sooner or later discover who was subscribing to the *Black Panther* magazine and who was a supporter of the cause. What he did not know was that a very crude form of counterintelligence was taking place in Tabor's bedroom. By night the young Panther – now known by his *nom de geurre* Cetewayo (or simply 'Cet'), a name he had taken from a nineteenth-century Zulu king – would scour through the papers he was selling and soak up the terminology and the arguments. Then he would cut up the articles and glue them into a scrapbook, much as he had done with basketball players as a child. In the course of clipping, Tabor filed the first few articles about police and FBI infiltration of the Black Panther Party, but in the main he laid the scrapbook out like a sports fan. He dedicated pages to each of the Panther leaders as if they were basketball stars – Bobby Seale, Huey Newton and Eldridge Cleaver in Oakland, Fred Hampton in Chicago, and Stokely Carmichael from the Bronx, who had recently left Howard University in Washington DC and returned to New York. Carmichael had been a militant student there, arriving on campus in 1964 along with soul singers Donny Hathaway and Leroy Hutson.

In January, despite fiercely cold weather, demonstrators had gathered on the sidewalks outside the Metropolitan Museum of Art to protest about a new exhibition. Its full title was *Harlem on My Mind:*

Cultural Capital of Black America, 1900–1968 and, staggeringly, it featured no work by black artists or photographers. A few days later, ten paintings in the museum's permanent collection were defaced. Small incisions of the letter 'H' – assumed to mean Harlem – were scratched into the varnish covering famous paintings, one of which was Rembrandt's *Christ with a Staff*, painted in 1661. Although all the paintings were successfully repaired, the furore became headline news and the Met's director, Thomas Hoving, had to publicly apologise for what he described as 'an error in judgment'. This incident was often linked to another weeping sore in Harlem community life, the so-called 'Gym Crow' controversy.

As Harlem churned with political unrest Roberts spent most of his days monitoring the Gym Crow demonstrations, a series of community disputes that pitted Harlem against the nearby Columbia University. Plans to build a student gymnasium in Morningside Park, a small green space used by the area's largely black and Puerto Rican residents, had been bought up by the university as part of an expansion scheme that targeted open spaces and low-income rental homes to the north and west of the university. For an educational institution so close to Harlem, Columbia University was seen as an enemy rather than a friend. At the time, there was only one full-time black teacher at Columbia and a tiny number of black students, very few from the surrounding areas. But 9,600 tenants, approximately eighty-five per cent of whom were black or Puerto Rican, were being thrown out of apartment buildings or single-room residential hotels in the Morningside Heights and West Harlem area. Insensitive to the growing resentment, Columbia University then purchased old property and either demolished it or converted it for its own institutional use.

The Gym Crow demonstrations had become a *cause célèbre* for students and anti-war revolutionaries, among them the militant drifter Sam Melville, who sold radical newspapers on the Columbia campus. Melville had been born in Buffalo, New York, but grew up with his father, a trade union activist, in an intellectually curious home in the Bronx. One of his father's friends was Paul Robeson, the legendary singer and political activist. Driving in convoy, Robeson and Melville's father often went down to Harlem, in part to educate the young Melville about families who lived in the ghetto but also to show him the vibrancy of the street life, the bustling shopfronts, the gushing fire hydrants and busking street musicians. According to Melville, it was a time of political discovery that instilled in him a long-standing love affair with the area and took him on a remarkable journey from disenchanted teenager to violent political extremist. As the turbulent months of 1969 unfolded, Melville stole dynamite and with a small cadre of hippie followers embarked on a bombing campaign across New York, earning himself the sobriquet of 'Mad Bomber Melville'.

The New York Times called 1969 'The Year of Bombings'. The rise of counterculture had given energetic voice to campus and coffee-house radicalism, and the spectre of bombings, armed resistance and opposition to the Vietnam War was growing. It was inevitable that Harlem soul music would find its own unique way of reflecting this mood of disenchantment. When Columbia University rented administrative office space in the famous Theresa Hotel on Seventh Avenue, the dispute intensified. The hotel had a special place in African-American folklore. Traditionally, major stars appearing at the Apollo stayed there, and it was Motown's preferred residence-in-exile when the Supremes, the Four Tops and the Temptations were in Harlem. In 1960 it was where Malcolm X arranged for a visiting delegation of Cuban politicians, led by Fidel Castro, to stay after the Shelburne Hotel in Midtown had refused to deal in cash. The Cuban delegation, dressed in paramilitary style and smoking rocket-like cigars, were in town for the United Nations General Assembly. Their presence fascinated Harlem, and Castro attracted a string of visitors, among them the playwright Lorraine Hansberry and her close friend Nina Simone. Steven Cohen, in *The New Republic* magazine, described the Cuban visit as a watershed moment: 'This notion that Third World revolutionaries and American civil rights activists were allies in the same essential conflict . . . that racism and global capitalism were part and parcel of a single oppressive system, presided over by the United States – was a source of tremendous fear in Washington. And the last thing anyone needed was for radical blacks to start getting ideas directly from the Cuban guerrillas.'

By 1966 the Theresa was facing its own tough times and the new owners began renting out entire floors for office space. Those who supported Columbia University's stealthy land grab pointed to the blight of poverty, arguing that the area around the gymnasium northwards could only improve under the university's stewardship. These were the first signs of the gentrification that would in time transform central Harlem and force out poorer residents. The Gym Crow issue further intensified when the local Harlem newspaper *Amsterdam News* raged against the university: 'If Mayor Lindsay permits Columbia University to grab two acres of land out of Morningside Park for a gymnasium it will be a slap in the face to every black man, woman and child in Harlem. Columbia University, one of the richest institutions in the nation, only admits a handful of Negro scholars each year and its policies in dealing with Negroes in Harlem have been described as downright bigoted . . . Why then should the parents of Harlem give up their parkland to Columbia? What has Columbia done to merit such favouritism?'

Gym Crow – the name redolent of old civil rights battles in the Deep South – became an emotional, combative issue. Students from the Afro-American Organization, supported by Students for a Democratic Society, argued for a more enlightened and racially sensitive student recruitment policy and staged a series of occupations that grew into a campus-wide strike. Officers monitoring the student unrest reported back to BOSS headquarters that one of the unit's worst fears was coming to life. The university demonstrations were amalgamating their two greatest sources of anxiety: the radical left-wing students from the vanguard of opposition to the war in Vietnam and local community groups from Harlem, in part backed by the Black Panthers. Gym Crow also attracted high-profile support from the Olympic Project for Human Rights, the athletics organisation that had masterminded the Black Power salutes at the Mexican Olympics four months earlier, and which was still engaged in a battle to desegregate the prestigious New York Athletic Club in Midtown. Columbia University was under attack from all sides. Then the roof caved in. Bob Feldman, a student and leading campus activist, had dug deep into the university's commercial dealings and uncovered a secret deal between the university and the Institute of Defence Analysis, a military think-tank that supported the war in Vietnam. His disclosure ignited a rash of student sit-ins, which attracted support from across Manhattan.

Sam Melville, the New York City militant who later in 1969 embarked on a bombing campaign against the Vietnam war effort, was living locally and earning a living by selling the new-left *New York Guardian* newspaper, which he hawked across the campus and up to the storefronts on 125th Street. It was while selling the paper that he met the Harlem Black Panthers and his future girlfriend, Jane Alpert, a student journalist at Columbia who joined him in his campaign. The couple eventually decamped to the Village where they formed a radical cell of militant anti-war activists intent on disrupting those military-industrial companies that profited from the Vietnam War.

In the early morning of Sunday, 9 February 1969, Harlem was not yet awake and the near-deserted streets hid beneath darkening clouds. The weather forecast predicted a day of slushy rain and cold winds. It was a serious misreading of what lay ahead. New York was about to be paralysed by a snow storm that, for three long burdensome days, would bring the city to a halt. Forty-two New Yorkers died during the storm and two hundred and eighty-eight people were injured. Thousands of passengers were stranded at airports and train stations. Most public workers had Sunday off, and mobilisation to clear the snow was slow; it took a further three days before the beleaguered mayor was able to announce that major highways, the subways and commuter rail lines were back to normal.

Harlem closed down for the duration but it was far from the worst-hit area. The blizzard dug deepest in Queens, where twenty-one people died and roads remained unploughed for days after the storm. Residents were outraged by what they saw as administrative incompetence, and inter-borough rivalries lurking just below the surface of New York life took on a tense racial dimension. Neglect had played a part, too: forty per cent of the city's snowploughs were not working and crucial equipment was in the wrong place at the wrong time. Housebound and unable to make his daily journey down to Harlem, Eugene Roberts was holed up in his safe house in the Bronx, quietly glad that the storm had given him time to update his ledger before it was handed over to his bosses downtown. Roberts sat at his Formica kitchen table drinking bitter black Nescafé and transcribing his notes. With his tongue protruding in a childlike state of concentration, he recounted the details of a core group of people whom he knew to be the nucleus of the Harlem Black Panther Party. He was scrupulous with the facts. Names, addresses and any piece of information that might help his superiors were recorded – former criminal records, pseudonyms, even their body shapes. It was on the basis of these notes that the NYPD's undercover BOSS team planned a series of dawn raids that further enraged the tense streets of Harlem.

What Roberts did not know and what remains truly remarkable were the secret machinations that had gone on behind his back. A prominent name on Roberts' ledger was one Ralph Wyatt, a Black Panther Party branch leader he had followed on several occasions. Roberts had even taped Wyatt's conversations in the Panthers' storefront office at 2026 Seventh Avenue. What Roberts was blithely unaware of was that Wyatt was in fact Patrolman Ralph White – also a 'deep' agent working undercover to infiltrate the Black Panthers. For reasons unknown only to themselves, the NYPD had decided to keep both officers unaware of the other's identity, and while this theoretically kept them safe, it led to a preposterous catalogue of errors. Sometime in early February, in a bizarre sequence of events, Ralph White – who had reached a position of power within the Panthers – 'promoted' Roberts into the Panther security detail, believing his background as Malcolm X's bodyguard was ideal experience. It was a moment of chaotic counterintelligence – an undercover police officer promoting another undercover officer within the ranks of a militant organisation that they were both separately targeting. Nor was it the only blunder. It transpired that at least six other undercover spies were in the pay of the FBI, too.

The intrigue deepened. On 25 February Ralph White masterminded a Panther detail to survey downtown department stores with a view to launching a bombing campaign. Roberts was dispatched to stake out Macy's, Korvette's and Abercrombie & Fitch. On his return, the two agreed that Abercrombie & Fitch 'would be the jackpot', offering the best opportunities to place sticks of dynamite on the first floor, to 'cause confusion and chaos'. It was an act of extraordinary conspiracy, implicating the NYPD's secret intelligence unit in inducing and planning a bombing campaign. It proved to a be a grievous mistake in the campaign to destabilise the Harlem Panthers and one that would bring BOSS's undercover operations into public disrepute.

The operation had its origins in a still-unexplained night on 17 January when, according to a police version of events, an explosion shattered windows of the Highbridge Police Station in the Bronx. A police patrol reported seeing a red Dodge Dart parked on Harlem River Drive immediately opposite the precinct station house. There was a black woman at the wheel, a nineteen-year-old trainee nurse called Joan Bird who was enrolled at Bronx Community College. Two unknown black men were with her in the car. When a motorcycle patrol approached, a shootout erupted, the men escaped, and Bird was taken in for questioning. Her mother – a Jamaican immigrant who at the time was working as a psychiatric assistant at Mount Sinai Hospital – was roused from her bed at the Bird family's five-room apartment in Harlem and taken to Wadsworth Avenue Police Station. The two women cried in each other's arms. Bird's left eye was bruised and half closed, her upper lip was swollen, and there was a cut on her right cheekbone. It was the beginning of a questionable investigation that led the police on a catastrophic pursuit of what became known as the Panther 21 trial, one of the longest and most contentious criminal trials in the history of New York.

On the night of the supposed explosion Roberts had been at a music event at Rockland Palace, a famous venue on the corner of 155th Street and Eighth Avenue which was hosting local soul groups. Visiting Black Power activist Ron Karenga of the Los Angeles-based Black Congress, a detested rival of the Black Panthers, also gave a speech. Armed with evidence, much of it from Roberts, the BOSS leadership spent much of February and March planning the biggest raids in the history of the NYPD, unaware that the actions of their own officers had already fatally undermined their investigations.

Just after midnight, on the morning of 2 April 1969, the jury room at the Criminal Courts Building was crackling with nervous excitement. Over one hundred police officers had gathered there, waiting to be briefed on a covert operation that few in the room knew anything about. It was a day that would permanently stain their reputation and leave them exposed to accusations of corruption, criminality and racial bias. Eyes darted around the room and papers were shuffled as scattered conversations about dynamite, explosives and a grand plot to bomb New York hung in the air. There was whispered talk about small units of radicals planning an atrocity: no policeman was safe. Uptown it was the Panthers; downtown it was a group of hippie radicals determined to bring 'Amerika' to its knees.

Inspector William Knapp and Captain Michael Willis of BOSS directed the gathering. BOSS was an open secret in New York and its origins stretched as far back as 1905 when it was launched as the 'Italian Squad', led by the first Italian-American detective in the NYPD, Joe Petrosino. He had been appointed to combat anarchist bomb plots by Italian immigrants and Sicilian gangsters. By February 1969 the unit's fixations had shifted with time; it was now obsessed with the anti-war counterculture and black revolutionaries.

The crowded room was sworn to secrecy as the suspects' names, addresses and images were circulated with dire warnings. Roberts' ledger was read out methodically and without exaggeration. It was only when the addresses were allocated that the majority realised that it was a mission across 110th Street, in the ghetto tenements of Harlem, Washington Heights and the South Bronx. Five-man details were assigned, each with a dedicated black officer and carrying one shotgun and two bulletproof vests. By 4.15 a.m. the units were dispatched north to Harlem and the South Bronx, fanning out in different directions and coordinated to the minute. Each had been told to arrest the suspects then drive them to pre-assigned police stations scattered across the boroughs. They were instructed that none of the suspects were to be alerted about each other's arrest and were to be kept apart at all times.

At 5 a.m. senior BOSS officer Sergeant George C. Abraham and two colleagues knocked on the door of Apartment 4D at 460 West

126th Street. Another officer had been assigned to the front of the building and was crouched down by a row of garbage bins beneath the rusting fire escape that zigzagged down the building like a metallic snake. A fifth officer was positioned to the rear of the apartment block, guarding a possible escape route via the side of the Apollo Theater onto 125th Street and Amsterdam Avenue. A voice inside the apartment asked who was there. To try to trick their way into the apartment, Abraham claimed to be a social worker investigating a welfare application. At exactly the same moment due north on 163rd Street, officers surrounded an apartment occupied by Michael Tabor and his girlfriend Rosalind Bennett. Again, the arresting officers had gained entry by a ruse, claiming this time that they had come to the apartment in response to a complaint of noise by neighbours. As soon as the door was partially opened the police stormed Tabor's home and gave chase into the kitchen. He was dragged outside and subsequently claimed that the arresting officer, Joseph Coffey, had screamed, 'I've got you, you black bastard.' Tabor's personal effects were seized, his scrapbooks logged and posters ripped down from his wall, among them one of Panther leader Bobby Seale and another of the athletes Tommie Smith and John Carlos raising their gloved fists on the podium at the Mexico Olympics. It was an image that had gone round the world only six months earlier and given international visibility to Black Power. Among the documents seized was an analysis of what Tabor told police was a statement of revolutionary humanism. It was a faded sepia document outlining the Ten-Point Programme of the Black Panther Party, which had been drafted on 15 October 1966 by Huey Newton and Bobby Seale.

1. WE WANT FREEDOM. WE WANT POWER TO DETERMINE THE DESTINY OF OUR BLACK AND OPPRESSED COMMUNITIES.
2. WE WANT FULL EMPLOYMENT FOR OUR PEOPLE.
3. WE WANT AN END TO THE ROBBERY BY THE CAPITALISTS OF OUR BLACK AND OPPRESSED COMMUNITIES.
4. WE WANT DECENT HOUSING, FIT FOR THE SHELTER OF HUMAN BEINGS.
5. WE WANT DECENT EDUCATION FOR OUR PEOPLE THAT

EXPOSES THE TRUE NATURE OF THE DECADENT AMERICAN SOCIETY. WE WANT EDUCATION THAT TEACHES US OUR TRUE HISTORY AND OUR ROLE IN THE PRESENT-DAY SOCIETY.

6. WE WANT COMPLETELY FREE HEALTH CARE FOR ALL BLACK AND OPPRESSED PEOPLE.
7. WE WANT AN IMMEDIATE END TO POLICE BRUTALITY AND MURDER OF BLACK PEOPLE, OTHER PEOPLE OF COLOR, ALL OPPRESSED PEOPLE INSIDE THE UNITED STATES.
8. WE WANT AN IMMEDIATE END TO ALL WARS OF AGGRESSION.
9. WE WANT FREEDOM FOR ALL BLACK AND OPPRESSED PEOPLE NOW HELD IN U.S. FEDERAL, STATE, COUNTY, AND MILITARY PRISONS AND JAILS. WE WANT TRIALS BY A JURY OF PEERS FOR ALL PERSONS CHARGED WITH SO-CALLED CRIMES UNDER THE LAWS OF THIS COUNTRY.
10. WE WANT LAND, BREAD, HOUSING, EDUCATION, CLOTHING, JUSTICE, PEACE AND PEOPLE'S COMMUNITY CONTROL OF MODERN TECHNOLOGY.

The pace of change in black music in 1969 is best described as a big bang, a sudden splintering and diversification of soul music. Three cities, especially – Detroit, Memphis and Chicago – could point to distinct styles, but the change in this year alone threw up new forms of music that would stretch decades into the future. The change was tangible in Michael Tabor's bedroom. A box of Motown hits, James Brown's funk anthems, obscure albums and private pressings on local labels, and a pile of albums he had bought or borrowed from a local militant music workshop called the East Wind. When Tabor resisted arrest in the dawn raid, it was said that neighbours could hear his protests echoing through the corridors. He had a sonorous and commanding voice, and he used it to become the most powerful orator of the Harlem Chapter of the Black Panthers. Born and brought up in an unforgiving ghetto, his life had ricocheted from street basketball to heroin, from self-taught political theory to Black Panther activism. He was regularly seen on the corner of 125th and Seventh Avenue selling the *Black Panther* newspaper or distributing leaflets, and he would often show up at the East Wind, sometimes just to listen to the performances, sometimes to drop off Panther literature.

He could have won a sports scholarship on his basketball prowess alone but, just as easily, he could have drifted into crime and chronic drug abuse. Like many other teenagers of his day, including Nile Rodgers, the legendary disco producer and brains behind the New York club band Chic, Tabor had seen the Panthers as a cool response to the social conditions of young African-Americans and a seductive and powerful alternative to a life of ghetto alienation. Throughout America's major African-American neighbourhoods young teenagers were queuing up to support the cause. In 1967, in Chicago's teeming South Side, Yvette Marie Stevens, then only fifteen years old, had joined the Panthers at the bequest of Chicago leader Fred Hampton. She assumed the name Chaka Adunne Aduffe Hodarhi Karifi, a significant step on her journey of self-discovery which transformed her into the epic R&B singer Chaka Khan. In the Southside ghettos of Philadelphia another teenager, Olympic-class swimmer James Foreman, joined the black nationalist group Ron Karenga's US Organization, and took the Swahili name James Mtume. Later in life he became a brilliant soul musician and Donny Hathaway's producer.

As Michael Tabor was handcuffed and bundled into a waiting police car another raid was under way. This time it was at an address downtown at 336 East 8th Street near Avenue C in Alphabet City where a man called James Collier was taken into custody. He was living with his wife and child and two homeless Puerto Rican boys to whom he had given temporary shelter. Meanwhile, in extraordinary circumstances back up in Harlem, Detective Francis Dalton crouched down outside an apartment at 112 West 117th Street and lit a petrol-soaked rag. When the other four officers yelled 'Fire! Fire!' residents Lumumba Shakur and his girlfriend Alice Faye Williams rushed to the door and straight into the trap. Simultaneously, on the sprawling Edenwald Projects, a public-housing neighbourhood off Laconia Avenue in the North Bronx, schoolboy Eddie Joseph was in bed at the home of his adoptive grandparents, both former members of Marcus Garvey's United Negro Improvement Association. This time the police raiding party banged heavily on the door claiming there was a gas leak and advising the residents to open up. The teenager was arrested. He was driven south in handcuffs to the Tombs, the NYPD's detention complex in Lower Manhattan – at the time one of the most overcrowded jails in the USA. With each raid, evidence or items of interest were carefully bagged and recorded, but another fundamental error had been made: the officers had been flagrantly dishonest, and in most cases had lied to gain entry. When John J. Casson's apartment was raided detectives seized a pistol, some bullets and a copy of the *Black Panther* newspaper with an article about bombs and grenades. They also took a decorative sword which, according to one detective, was incapable of being used violently. 'We were given these things to examine. I pulled the sword out of its sheath, ran the edge along my wrist, pressed my hand against the tip. Blunt! It couldn't have been used for shish-kebab.'

By the end of the synchronised police operation, twenty-one members of the Harlem and Bronx Sections of the Black Panther Party were charged with a bewildering array of supposed crimes – 156 counts of conspiracy to murder police officers and blow up the Bronx Botanical Gardens, a district school office in Queens, police stations, railroad sites and subway switching stations. They were further accused of plotting to bomb several Midtown department stores. Two of the Panthers – teenagers Lonnie Epps and Eddie 'Jamal' Joseph – were too young to be charged as adults, and so were treated as youthful offenders. Two others, William E. King (aka Kinshasa) and Lee Roper (aka Shaba), were subsequently arrested by the FBI while living under assumed names in Columbus, Ohio. That meant that a core of thirteen committed Black Panthers were being held in separate jails, awaiting trial. As 1969 progressed, their story was destined to become an international *cause célèbre* and the political show trial that followed would not only put the Black Panthers in the dock but American law enforcement and the justice system, too. The court proceedings that dramatically unfolded over the next two years gave the Panthers a public platform to challenge their arrest and exposed the extent of police infiltration into the organisation and the paranoia that Harlem – the 'politicised ghetto' – provoked in the minds of the NYPD and the FBI. Roberts had survived the dangerous double life of an undercover cop but his role in the conspiracies would eventually be the Achilles heel in the case against the Black Panthers.

*

A new generation of soul-infused music had sprung up in tandem with the mass arrests of the Harlem Panthers. Much of it was community-based and had its locus in the streets and tenement yards that spread out from 125th Street. Prominent among this new generation of Harlem groups were the afro-jazz band the Har-You Percussion Group, a collection of local youths aged from sixteen to nineteen who were funded by the Harlem Youth Opportunities Unlimited and trained virtually from scratch by a local music teacher Roger 'Montego Joe' Sanders. A Jamaican immigrant, Montego Joe had played with Art Blakey, Max Roach and Dizzy Gillespie in jazz clubs across Harlem and the South Bronx. Har-You Percussion released an album called *Sounds Of The Ghetto Youth*, the profits from which went to a Harlem scholarship fund, but it disappeared into long-term obscurity until it was discovered by crate-diggers decades later and elevated to elite status among aficionados of rare groove and underground funk. The music was significant for its range and its fusion of styles – Latin soul with raw funky bass, heavy drums, burning soulful horn lines and ghetto vocals. One track, 'Welcome To The Party', remains an all-time afro-funk classic.

Feeding off the febrile atmosphere, a generation of soul musicians were refracting the language of militant politics and heightened social tension. Harlem became the epicentre of a new kind of rebellious soul that included the Last Poets, the pioneering spoken-word ensemble; the secular gospel group the Voices of East Harlem; the razor sharp jazz poets Gil Scott-Heron and Brian Jackson; Jackie Early and her band Black Jazzoetry; Harlem's Grass Roots; the pan-African R&B groups like Vishnu and the African Rhythms West; local soul outfit the Black Vibrations; vocalists Ed Taylor and Joan Faulkner; and the avant garde jazz group Bob Moses and the Open Sky Trio. Meanwhile on the West Coast, the Oakland Panthers had formed their own in-house band, a Marxist-inspired funk quartet aimed squarely at the proletariat called the Lumpen. In the main they were a West Coast band who never travelled east to Harlem and remained for most of their short career a community soul group in Oakland.

The Last Poets had their creative home at the East Wind loft on 125th Street between Madison and Fifth Avenues, a distressed tenement that had become a black arts centre, a makeshift gallery, a rehearsal space for local talent and an illegal nightclub for the cognoscenti. Coffee houses and loft venues had sprung up across Manhattan. Most were downtown where beatniks, folk singers, jazz hounds and poets mingled in the warren of streets in and around Greenwich Village, or performed in the loft owned by the late John Coltrane's drummer Rashid Ali. The East Wind was its uptown equivalent. When it opened in the autumn of 1968, it drank from a powerful brew: local black poets, militant songwriters and arts activists improvised to the background beats of the loft's resident percussionist Nilaja Obabi. Felipe Luciano, an African-Puerto Rican and one-time member of the Last Poets, had just been released from jail. Many years later, he described his first visit to the East Wind to the Dutch author Christine Otten in her imaginative account of their lives: 'It was early evening and dusk was closing in. I found the East Wind easily enough. It was in a loft on the second floor halfway down 125th. You had to go up a set of narrow stairs and came out into a big empty space with timeworn wooden floor. There were low couches, pillows on the floor. An old-fashioned dark red and yellow carpet. It looked lived in. At the back was a small stage, a desk next to it, with a green glass lamp that shone onto the mess of papers and books. I remember it exactly. On the walls there were all kinds of posters, performance announcements. Amiri Baraka and the Spirit House Movers. James Brown at the Apollo Theater.'

A few records were on sale, among them copies of the proto-rap record 'Is It Too Late?' by Duke Edwards and the Young Ones, local records by Harlem indies like Carnival, Rojac and Tay-Ster Records, and a legendary album called *Black & Beautiful, Soul & Madness* by Amiri Baraka and the Spirit House Movers, a spoken-word/soul/jazz album recorded in a family home in New Jersey and originally released on the obscure Jihad label. Baraka, then known as LeRoi Jones, had self-recorded and produced the album at a pressing plant in his native Newark. It was a landmark recording that unleashed a passion for spoken-word soul. Earnest young record collectors carried the album around with them like a trophy. The opening track, 'Beautiful Black Women', is an anthemic love poem urging young women to join the movement for change. Baraka's tone is that of the angry romantic but his insistence is tempered by Bobby Lyle's gentle bass and, periodically, a stabbing saxophone or breezy flute by his brother Russell Lyle. This was groundbreaking music, the like of which many had never heard before, but it also had reassuring soulful backing vocals sung by the Spirit House Movers – Freddie Johnson, Leonard Cathcart, Gilbert Monk and Aireen Eternal. The backing singers supported the poem in a way that was familiar in soul and gospel music; they sang like a gospel chorus but deliberately refrained a recognisable chart hit from 1965 – Smokey Robinson and the Miracles' million-seller hit 'Ooo Baby Baby'. It was a piece of primitive DIY history – an early musical sample – with the familiar song being brought back again and again to support the revolutionary poetry. Critics have since claimed the album mimics doo-wop and bar-room R&B and so anticipates 'the mash-up genre by several decades'. By sampling the R&B hits of the past Baraka had laid down another plank of the foundations of hip-hop. But at the time it had a different name – 'spoagraphics' or spoken pictures. One of the original members of the Last Poets, Jalaluddin Mansur Nuriddin, (recording under the name Lightnin' Rod) put it more eloquently: 'We're just the speakers, the amplifiers for the people.'

From their base on 125th Street, the Last Poets spread out through Harlem, supporting local political causes and drawing crowds to street corners and community houses. This was the breeding ground of what became known as Afrocentric visions and opened up young minds to history. One of the incarcerated Black Panthers, the teenager Jamal Joseph, remembers seeing the Poets perform at a rally for the Harlem Tenants Council, in the dark heart of the Lincoln Projects, a warren of sixteen-storey buildings on Madison Avenue at East 132nd Street. It had become a community under the control of the tenants, virtually a no-go area for the police and a potential flashpoint for social disruption. Joseph described the night's gathering in his autobiography *Baby Panther* as 'more than a political rally – it was a cultural event.

There were African dancers, a jazz quarter and a concert by the Last Poets, a group said by many to have invented rap. Their lyrics and poems performed over jazz riffs and African drum beats were both incendiary and highly entertaining.'

The Last Poets first got together on 18 May 1968, at a festival in Mount Morris Park to celebrate Malcolm X's birthday, creating what *Source* magazine called 'a workshop of the mind'. The following month, PBS television executive and sometime jazz producer Alan Douglas turned up at East Wind and recorded the group. No significant distribution deal was ever struck but the album that emerged from the session defied logic: rather than disappear into obscurity, a staggering 800,000 were said to have been sold through word of mouth at political demonstrations, summer festivals and community networks across America's inner cities. Easily enough to take the Last Poets into the *Billboard* charts had the sales ever been quantified. Douglas subsequently negotiated a meeting with Jimi Hendrix – who he met at Woodstock later that year – and together they recorded the pioneering *Dorriela Du Fontaine* album with Hendrix's friend, the drummer Buddy Miles, and Lightnin' Rod. It was a project rich in cultural collision that again pointed forward to decades yet to come. The music critic Gene Santoro described the fiery collaboration as one that 'foreshadows the rap-meets-metal crossover of later artists like Run-DMC'.

The Last Poets had taken their name from a poem by South African revolutionary poet Keorapetse Kgositsile, the exiled anti-apartheid South African activist and Columbia University postgraduate student who was living in Harlem on a poetry grant. He published his first collection of poetry in 1969 and among his many contentions was the fatalistic thought that he was the 'last poet' and then there would be guns. African sensibilities had deep roots in Harlem jazz and academia but the opening of a local Black Panther office on Seventh Avenue at 112nd Street in 1968 brought African awareness into the main thoroughfares of Harlem youth culture. All three of the Last Poets had assumed African identities, and although the group's membership has changed over time, Jalal Mansur Nuriddin, Umar Bin Hassan and Abiodun Oyewole, along with percussionist Nilaja Obabi, are considered the core members of the group. Resplendent in West African dashiki shirts, they were a familiar sight at street corner gatherings, the bandstands in Mount Morris Park and tenants' group protests. They were friends of Lumumba Shakur, not so much in his guise as the leader of the Harlem Panthers, but in his paid role as an organiser of the Ellesmere Tenants Council, who regularly hired the group to headline at rent-strike meetings and protests against absent slum landlords.

Further east in the Puerto Rican-dominated Spanish Harlem, a group of young singers had formed under the banner of the East Harlem Federation Youth Association. Around twenty in number, featuring singers aged between twelve and twenty, they called themselves the Voices of East Harlem. The Voices drew on more familiar forms of soul music, mostly gospel and group harmony, and as their career developed they moved into fully produced studio backing. They were unquestionably from Harlem – not a mythologised Africa – and so dressed in an urban style, wearing matching denim jackets, Converse basketball shoes and trimmed afros. Initially put together by youth worker Charles 'Chuck' Griffin and his wife Anna, their debut performance was a benefit for the incumbent mayor John Lindsay, a far cry from the radical underground that had given birth to the Last Poets. Like the great Detroit soul groups, most notably the Temptations, the Contours and the masked members of the Masqueraders, the Voices of East Harlem had a dynamic opening routine. They would come through the audience, acting out the anger of a chain gang, clapping freedom songs and stomping the floor in workers' boots as they took to the stage. And unlike the Last Poets, who performed a capella, the Voices of East Harlem were backed by a funk band and considered themselves to be a soul choir rather than proselytisers. As their act attracted more and more attention, they strengthened the group with new talent from across Harlem and recruited the accomplished vocalist Bernice Cole from Philadelphia's Angelic Gospel Singers as a musical director. It was impossible not to be moved by the Voices of East Harlem's chaotic joyousness and goodwill. They appeared at the Metropolitan Museum of Modern Art's jazz garden in part to placate black audiences who were boycotting the museum after its pitiful all-white *Harlem on My Mind* exhibition. They also shared the stage at the Winter Festival of Peace at Madison Square Garden with countercultural giants Jimi Hendrix, Blood Sweat and Tears, and Richie Havens. The event was a fundraiser for the Vietnam Moratorium movement and became a historic concert for the wrong reasons. Suffering from exhaustion and the effects of a drink laced with acid, Hendrix managed only two songs before stumbling off stage incapable of continuing. By 1970 the Voices had signed to Elektra Records and released their first album *Right On Be Free*, which, in keeping with the times, had the entire choir carrying a strip-banner and marching as if at a political demonstration. They attracted support from civil rights influencers, sharing a stage with Carlos Santana at the Fillmore East and with Harry Belafonte and Eloise Laws at the Westbury Music Fair.

Within a few months of their breakthrough, the Voices of East Harlem had headlined at the Apollo and were a stand-out hit at the 1970 Isle of Wight Festival, a pop concert which far outstripped Woodstock and attracted 700,000 people to a small island four miles off the English coast, where they shared a bill with The Who, Sly and the Family Stone, and the quixotic Jimi Hendrix again. It was their biggest audience, but triumphantly their greatest show was with B.B. King and Joan Baez live at the notorious prison known as Sing Sing in upstate New York. There they entertained one of the most intimidating audiences ever gathered together, including members of the Harlem Black Panthers still awaiting trial.

After appearing on an Atlantic Records compilation album *Soul To Soul*, filmed at a beach celebration concert in Ghana where they shared a stage with Wilson Pickett, Ike and Tina Turner, the Staple Singers and Roberta Flack, Flack made some calls to her college friends Donny Hathaway and Leroy Hutson. As a consequence Donny Hathaway produced tracks on the group's second album *Brothers And Sisters* while Leroy Hutson produced the Voices of East Harlem's eponymous third album and their fourth, *Can You Feel It*. What Hathaway and Hutson gave them was a musicianship that was missing in their more primitive community soul days, leaving them with at least one outstanding single, the remarkable

'Cashing In', a morality tale about love and economics, which became one of the great Harlem soul records of its era.

Three different strands of thought were influencing this new moment in black music – black pride, raised awareness of African history and community resistance forged by successive years of social rebellion. James Brown's 'Say It Loud, I'm Black And I'm Proud' had been released the previous year and become a crossover clarion call for ghetto self-awareness. African nationalism now threatened to dislodge the civil rights establishment that had grown up with Dr King's non-violent protest campaigns of the fifties. Soul groups such as the L.A. funk band Arlene Bell and the Kenyattas and Philadelphia's African Echoes, whose debut record 'Zulu Lunchbag' was a clever soul instrumental, were tentatively embracing African names and terminology. It was superficial at first, but the trickle became a flood.

Meanwhile, a disillusioned but sharply articulate university dropout with links to the South Bronx and Harlem was convinced he could bring his ghetto jazz poetry into song. Gil Scott-Heron shopped around a few independents until he struck lucky with the newly launched jazz label Flying Dutchman Records. The green shoots of a very new kind of black music were springing up through the cracked sidewalks of Harlem. It merged the spoken word with gospel, jazz and a sparse propulsive percussion, challenging the orthodoxy of Motown and its teenage love affairs with a new socially conscious kind of music.

Small Talk At 125th And Lenox was Scott-Heron's first significant step on a ladder of outstanding creativity that eventually led to the great heroin abuse song 'Home Is Where The Hatred Is' and the ghetto anthem 'The Bottle'. As a child, he had lived with his maternal grandmother, Lillie Scott, in Jackson, Tennessee, before moving to the Bronx, aged thirteen, when she died. The first song on his final album from 2010, *I'm New Here*, is the ironically titled 'On Coming From A Broken Home', an ode to his grandmother. 'Womenfolk raised me,' he claimed, 'and I was fully-grown before I knew I came from a broken home.' Scott-Heron was as interested in personal testimony as political discourse but it was the latter that made him famous. In an article in the *Observer* newspaper, the

Irish cultural critic Sean O'Hagan wrote that he 'made music that reflected the turbulence, uncertainty and increasing pessimism of the times, merging the soul and jazz traditions and drawing on an oral poetry tradition that reached back to the blues and forward to hip-hop. The music sounded by turns angry, defiant and regretful while Scott-Heron's lyrics possessed a satirical edge that set them apart from the militant soul of contemporaries such as Marvin Gaye and Curtis Mayfield.'

With his forceful mother at his back, he won a writing scholarship to the prestigious Fieldston School in the Bronx, a place where only the most fortunate and gifted ghetto kids ever studied. But by his late teens Harlem had become his spiritual home. Like his collaborator Brian Jackson, he had chosen to attend Lincoln University, Pennsylvania, because it was the place that their mutual hero, the Harlem poet Langston Hughes, had studied. Hanging out in Lincoln, Scott-Heron befriended the brother of one of the Last Poets, Abiodun Oyewole, and connected with the group through him. In his memoir *The Last Holiday* he wrote, 'I hung out with the jazz heavies, the ones you didn't hear too often on the radio. We spent a lot of our time supposedly doing our homework, but really in our rooms checking out the jams – Coltrane, Dexter Gordon, Herbie Hancock.' Once a month the young Lincoln University crew would travel to Harlem to the Last Poets' East Wind loft where they joined in the freeform workshops or stood back frozen in youthful awe simply watching who was about: the radicals, the intellectuals and a roomful of musicians from old jazz and from new soul. It's where they first met the percussionist Bernard 'Pretty' Purdie, who had already worked with James Brown and recently joined King Curtis and the Kingpins. Purdie endeared himself to the Lincoln students by telling them he had faked his age to get a licence to be able to drum in Harlem nightclubs, and was at least three years younger than his ID claimed. It was during those visits to Harlem that Gil Scott-Heron saw an opportunity. With the loyal Brian Jackson driving the musicianship, he began to pursue the prospect of a new kind of jazz poetry, and so all but abandoned formal education to become a writer, winning a $5,000 advance from a New York publisher for his first novel, *The Nigger Factory*. Jackson was a classically trained keyboard player, and with his musical brains as their calling card, they hawked an idea for a jazz poetry LP around New York indies. Bernard Purdie, who had already recorded extensively for the Columbia subsidiary Date Records and who was fighting to build his own solo career with the single 'Fickle Finger Of Fate', suggested they talk to Bob Thiele, a jazz industry veteran and one-time producer of John Coltrane and Archie Shepp, who had reached a point of crisis in his career. He was feeling disengaged with the senior management at ABC Records, who had a vice-like grip on the venerable jazz subsidiary Impulse Records, and was planning his escape. He had contacts galore – he claimed to have discovered Buddy Holly and played a key role in the development of Detroit vocalist Jackie Wilson's career – and was in the process of setting up his own label, Flying Dutchman Records.

Gil Scott-Heron took a gamble. Uninvited, he turned up at Thiele's office, convinced that he would be blocked at reception, but the opposite happened. 'When I opened the door to the Flying Dutchman office, Bob was standing there at a desk that faced the door, talking to his secretary and leafing through some papers. The surprise grabbed my throat and lungs, and fright held me for a second and a half. I hadn't expected the president of the company to be standing at the door but I quickly gave Bob my spiel.' His spiel was that he was a songwriter and had an idea for an album. Thiele surprised him by saying he knew his work but preferred his poetry, and if they made money from a spoken-word album then they could talk about recording a music album. Brian Jackson remembers it differently: 'Bob's office had this typical Tin Pan Alley set-up. He's got the pipe and the mounds of papers all over his desk. There's nowhere you can step. Albums on the floor, you know. Off in the corner, there was a little Spinet piano, badly out of tune, but it was there. He opens it up and says, "Okay, Brian, Gil, do your thing. Let's see what you got." We played "Pieces Of A Man", "I Think I'll Call It Morning" – all of these songs we had worked on over the last year or two. He's smoking the pipe, nodding.'

Whatever the real version of their meeting, it was transformative. One of Black America's most challenging and inventive soul poets stood face-to-face with a man from a different generation, a record company executive who had written one of the greatest pieces of jazz poetry ever, 'What A Wonderful World', which had been popularised around the world by Louis Armstrong. It was as if two different notions of jazz poetry had met: Thiele's 'bright precious days and dark sacred nights' confronting Scott-Heron's more angry dystopian vision of a society beholden to consumerism – a world of glib slogans, false promises and crass commercialism. Thiele liked the brainy arrogance of the words and the underlying cadences of jazz, and so took a major risk. He agreed to put Scott-Heron's streetwise soul on vinyl.

To create the impression of a live atmosphere, the record label borrowed some folding chairs and invited around fifty people to join them in the studio, which had been arranged much like a coffee shop. The outcome was the album colloquially known as *Small Talk* – its full title was *A New Black Poet: Small Talk At 125th And Lenox* – and among its many surprises was the now legendary poem 'The Revolution Will Not Be Televised'. Unexpectedly, the track, which has minimal music accompaniment and the background crackle of a live audience, attracted radio play in urban stations across America and has since become a landmark track in the story of radical soul music.

The deal with Bob Thiele was done when the two students were still officially enrolled at Lincoln University. 'I was nineteen, so I actually had to have my mother sign the papers,' Jackson says. 'Gil had just turned twenty-one so he was just able to sign the papers. We get in the studio. They're all there; Ron Carter, Johnny Pate was the conductor. I'm sitting there looking at all these guys and saying, "Why am I here again?" I was there because I wrote the songs and because I knew the songs better than anybody. Johnny, realizing at some point that I did know what I was doing, didn't try to run the session or anything. He just kind of sat there for me if I needed him.'

Gil Scott-Heron's career took off and, with his college friend Brian Jackson, he blazed a trail for pop and politics, scything through nearly every major political issue – the social conditions of America's urban ghettos ('The Bottle'), the heroin epidemic ('Home Is Where

The Hatred Is'), the anti-apartheid cause ('Johannesburg'), Watergate ('H20gate Blues') and nuclear meltdown ('We Almost Lost Detroit This Time').

Throughout the early months of 1969 the national media was fascinated by two overwhelming subjects: the failing war in Vietnam and the momentous hope that the US lunar mission Apollo 11 would make interplanetary history and land a man on the moon. Every detail of the space mission was fretted over in forensic detail. Pages of print were devoted to the astronauts and the complex scientific instruments they had at their disposal. But one fundamental question remained unanswered at a time when the war effort in South East Asia was draining money from the inner cities: how could America reasonably afford its journey into the unknown? It was a contradiction not lost on the quick-witted Scott-Heron. Sometime in the spring of 1969 he began to work on a new composition for his debut album and he called it 'Whitey On The Moon'. The lyrics juxtaposed ghetto life with the moon mission, boldly comparing life in a rat-infested ghetto tenement with the cost of the lunar explorations. It was a view shared by many on the countercultural left of politics and was backed up by the Black Panther leader Eldridge Cleaver, who was now exiled in Algiers and acting as the international editor of the glossy new-left magazine *Ramparts*. 'I don't see what benefit mankind will have from two astronauts landing on the moon while people are being murdered in Vietnam and suffering from hunger even in the United States,' he told a US press agency, describing the mission as a flagrant misuse of public funds.

Scott-Heron was never a member of the Panthers, and throughout his life tended to avoid organised political parties, but he lent an insightful and often challenging voice to their policies. He arrived with the 'shock of the new', no one had heard music quite like it before, and he was someone who was wilfully difficult to pin down and resisted classification. In one review in *The New York Times*, he was described simultaneously as an 'insurrectionist firebrand' and in the next sentence as a 'mellow protest singer'. He self-consciously shifted from anger to love and back to comic observation, often in the same song, and more than anything loved wordplay. For all his success as a radical songsmith, he was reluctant to see himself as a strident political voice. He once told British journalist Rob Fitzpatrick of *The Telegraph* that he was first and foremost a satirist: 'I learnt early on that your audiences take the songs in the way they want to rather than the way you might want them to. "The Revolution Will Not Be Televised" – that was satire. People would try and argue that it was this militant message, but just how militant can you really be when you're saying, "the revolution will not make you look five pounds thinner"? My songs were always about the tone of voice rather than the words. A good comic will deliver a line deadpan – they let the audience laugh.' It was his effortless wit that had first drawn Brian Jackson to work with him. 'What initially stood out to me about Gil was his sense of humour,' he told New Orleans journalist Kalamu ya Salaam. 'This guy had the oddest way of looking at things. He could say more in five words than anyone else, and it always just tickled me. He incorporated that same sense of timing and economy in his writing, particularly in his lyrics.'

Scott-Heron knew his limitations, too. He frequently put up barriers to defining his work and preferred, if pushed, to call himself a 'bluesologist'. Surrounded by much better vocalists all his life, he was blessed with a deep full-bodied voice. The master bassist Ron Carter, who had previously been part of the Miles Davis Quintet, played on 'The Revolution Will Not Be Televised' and once said of Scott-Heron, 'He wasn't a great singer, but, with that voice, if he had whispered it would have been dynamic. It was a voice like you would have for Shakespeare.'

The inauguration of President Richard Nixon in January 1969 was fertile ground for the new generation of radical soul poets. Here was a president who was widely disliked uptown and whose inaugural address seemed to point an accusatory finger at the rising tide of Black Power. 'In these difficult years, America has suffered from a fever of words; from inflated rhetoric that promises more than it can deliver; from angry rhetoric that fans discontents into hatreds; from bombastic rhetoric that postures instead of persuading,' he proclaimed from the east portico of the Capitol Building. 'We cannot learn from one another until we stop shouting at one another – until we speak quietly enough so that our words can be heard as well as our voices.' His call for quiet restraint was not reflected in policy and the continuing war in Vietnam and its economic toll on welfare funding cast the president in a dim light. Nixon's first inauguration cost $2.3 million and was attended by about 200,000 people. Commentators looked keenly at the invite list for the most significant event, the inaugural ball, and noted that it reflected, perhaps predictably, the power relationships across the nation: captains of industry, famous faces and wealthy political donors dominated. And of the 30,000 invited to the series of parties and inaugural balls only 400 at most were from the black community. Few soul singers answered Nixon's invitation. Motown – a fiercely Democratic Party corporation – politely declined, and the only singer of any significant note to rally to Nixon's cause was James Brown, who appeared on the stage of the DC Armory resplendent in an iridescent electric-blue suit. He had the balls to sing his 1968 hit 'Say It Loud, I'm Black And I'm Proud' to an audience largely composed of Washington's white political elite but it was a moment of incongruity that even the irrepressible Brown was embarrassed by.

Political speeches and street corner rap were intertwined, and many of those who flocked to join the Panthers had gathered together on Seventh Avenue and 125th Street in the summer of 1968 to listen to Bobby Seale speak. Alice Faye Williams, the Panther who became known as Afeni Shakur, had a sensation of being swept up by history and described a street corner crammed with the curious. 'There are all kinds of folk there – mothers, hustlers, teachers, gangsters, domestics, and kids all of them on that corner listening to Bobby Seale,' she remembered in her autobiography, *Evolution of a Revolutionary*. 'He says the Panther party is opening offices in New York, that they are coming and bringing change and order to our community, coming to heal the wounds of slavery and Jim Crow, coming to take arms against the aggression. They will not beat our ass any more.'

Jamal Joseph, just fifteen years old, and the youngest recruit to the Harlem Panthers, was also there to hear Seale. He described the street corner outside a branch of Chock Full o' Nuts as 'a cultural explosion' and 'a vibrant sea of black energy' surrounded by noisy record stores, cheap food and gangster style. In *Panther Baby* he described the emotions as 'lightning in our veins, rockets in our feet'. He told *Time* magazine: 'I was one of these kids who was in the church choir; I was in extracurricular activities, and I was in the NAACP. Martin Luther King's death changed that. It sparked something in me, some rage and some anger. I went down to Harlem, snuck down there, was on the fringes of the riot. Threw a couple of bricks through store windows, ran from a cop and got shot at by the cops. And then discovered the Black Panther Party, at first just through television, through looking at the images of the Panthers, with their leather coats and their berets and their guns, talking about black revolution. Not turning the other cheek. Those were some bad guys; I wanted to check them out.'

On the day of Bobby Seale's powerful call to arms, Michael Tabor was also in the crowd, unsure of what to do with his life. Always an obsessive music fan, who periodically tried to break into music journalism, he had abandoned the prospect of a basketball career and was drifting into crime and heroin addiction. But after Seale's speech he described feeling a surge of energy more powerful than any drug. In a flash of perception, he came to realise that heroin was suffocating the life out of him, and the next day he signed up as a Black Panther. Paradoxically Eugene Roberts was already sitting there, taking the name of new recruits; still deep undercover but hiding in full view. By now Tabor was a self-taught intellectual with a fearsome grasp of black history, a unique understanding of street politics and a hotline to young community soul groups across Harlem. He was a formidable new recruit but as soon as he put pen to paper his name was known to the offices of BOSS and marked out for special attention.

With Roberts acting as its secretary, the Harlem office identified two men who it was thought could lead the Harlem and Bronx sections of the party. Both were ex-prisoners who had been converted to Islam behind bars and were now known as Lumumba

Shakur (Harlem) and Sekou Odinga (Bronx). Both were from Queens and had met each other as young gangsters while attending the Andrew Jackson High School in Cambria Heights where they were known by their birthnames Nathaniel 'Shotgun' Burns and Anthony 'Beanie' Coston. It was a school mired in notoriety. Hip-hop trailblazers LL Cool J, Jam Master Jay and 50 Cent were students there before it was eventually closed down when a heroin-processing factory was discovered in the basement. By the mid sixties, the two met again, this time at the Great Meadow Correctional Facility in Comstock, a male prison described candidly in one hypercritical New York State report as 'the garbage heap of the state prison system'. Radicalised in prison, they returned to the streets of New York as prison-educated militants, and for all their troubled backgrounds both proved to be competent leaders who busily went about delivering on the Panthers' Ten-Point Programme with enthusiasm, running breakfast clubs, setting up soup kitchens and organising drop-in information services for tenants and drug dependents. Joan Bird, the jailed teenage Panther awaiting trial, had the job of running neighbourhood Christmas parties for impoverished children. She lent on the services of the Voices of East Harlem to sing festive community songs, but within a few short years that group had disbanded; the burden of touring with an entourage of over twenty people, the cost of hotel accommodation, transportation and flights to European festivals, and the necessity of hiring chaperones for the younger members proved beyond the budgets of many community groups and venues. Despite their infectious talent, their 1974 album *Can You Feel It* was their last, and they simply faded away.

It would be demanding a lot to expect the close friendships forged in the politically volatile atmosphere of Harlem in 1969 to have survived, but the extent of their disintegration was remarkable. The Last Poets went through a series of personnel changes and, despite their loyalty to political expression, struggled to be loyal to each other. By 1971 the original Poets had all but broken up: Abiodun Oyewole was in jail and Jalal Mansur Nuriddin was using the pseudonym Lightnin' Rod to blaze a trail for what became gangsta rap. In a visionary move by producer Alan Douglas, Jalal's jail toasts and street rhymes were paced out by metronome on vinyl and *Hustlers Convention* (1973) became the Holy Grail for the rappers who followed. (Kool and the Gang, who at the time were living in Harlem and signed to the indie De-Lite Records, added a cool street-funk backing track to the album.) Chuck D of Public Enemy claims: 'It was probably the most influential record to set off all those early Bronx MCs, but very rarely does *Hustlers Convention* get mentioned in the annals. It's a missing piece of culture.' The Last Poets splintered, regrouped and only came together again on rare – and fraught – occasions, although they now seem to have reunited in later life and regularly tour the literary and political festival circuit.

Personal disaffection mired what were already political schisms. None more so than in the case of Gil Scott-Heron and Brian Jackson. Having met as teenagers on the Lincoln University campus, enjoyed a successful career for over a decade, and managed to suppress disagreements for many years, the publishing company they co-owned imploded when Scott-Heron succumbed to a serious crack cocaine addiction. In 2001 he ended up on the 'rock' – New York's Rikers Island penitentiary. Writer Alex Wilkinson described Scott-Heron's decline in *The New Yorker* magazine, calling him a ghost of his former self: 'He is bald on top, and his hair, which is like cotton candy, sticks out in several directions. His cheeks are sunken and deeply lined. Dismayed by his appearance, he doesn't like to look in mirrors. He likes to sit on the floor, with his legs crossed and his propane torch within reach, his cigarettes and something to drink or eat beside him. Nearly his entire diet consists of fruit and juice. Crack makes a user anxious and uncomfortable and, trying to relieve the tension, Scott-Heron would sometimes lean to one side or reach one hand across himself to grab his opposite ankle, then perhaps lean an elbow on one knee, then maybe press the soles of his feet together, so that he looked like a swami.' After ten days on remand, the fifty-two-year-old singer pleaded guilty to felony possession of cocaine and agreed to enter a residential centre, but he failed to fulfil the conditions of his drug rehabilitation treatment and was jailed. When the man who was frequently called 'the black Bob Dylan' died in 2011 his greatest collaborator Brian Jackson declined the invitation to his friend's funeral, saying, 'I've already said my goodbyes to him a long time ago.'

Although the media focused almost exclusively on the Panthers' super-cool street look – the shades, the black berets and the leather-fisted salutes that were to pass into the iconography of soul music throughout the seventies – a much more complex pattern of membership had emerged. There were disaffected teenagers such as Jamal Joseph, Nile Rodgers and Michael Tabor who saw the Panthers as their generation's extension of the civil rights movement. There were young women like Alice Faye Williams, Joan Bird and Kathleen Cleaver of the Oakland Panthers who recognised the roots of a new kind of streetwise feminism. There were former criminals like Lumumba Shakur, radicalised in prison where he converted to Islam, and the ex-Marine Kwando Kinshasa who had rebelled against the military system in Vietnam. Most disturbing of all, for the ailing fanatical director of the FBI, J. Edgar Hoover, the Panthers could count among their numbers a highly educated generation of young African-Americans that included Dr Curtis Brown and Professor Angela Davis. The latter was the Black Power communist leader who, in 1970, was on the run and on the FBI's Most Wanted list, accused of purchasing the weaponry used in a courtroom shootout in California. She had been born and raised in Dynamite Hill, an area of Birmingham, Alabama, so named because Ku Klux Klan members regularly bombed its streets during the civil rights era. There she attended school with the city's most celebrated soul singer and producer Sam Dees.

Even in 1968, there had been many signs that the Black Panthers were being targeted by the police and the FBI, and that a strategy of deep penetration intended to derail the organisation. Although the full extent of the surveillance and Eugene Roberts' malign role in their activity had yet to surface, most members instinctively felt that they were being monitored by covert government forces. In December Dave Hilliard, a twenty-six-year-old captain at the Panthers' national headquarters in Berkeley, California, had claimed that the Panthers were being 'set up' and lured into traps by the police. It was dismissed as fanciful at the time but was in fact a huge understatement of the forces that were gathering against the militant group. Michael Tabor had not only read the story of infiltration, he had clipped it and glued it into his scrapbook. Arrests came daily. Huey P. Newton, the Panthers' Minister of Defence, was imprisoned in November 1968; Eldridge Cleaver, their Minister of Information, was in hiding and had spent six months as a fugitive in Cuba; and party chairman Bobby Seale was by the beginning of 1969 on probation after gun law violations. J. Edgar Hoover claimed openly that the Panthers were 'the greatest threat to the internal security of the country'. The FBI's COINTELPRO programme and BOSS's undercover infiltration of the Harlem Panthers were conspiracies that were never fully exposed for decades, by which time many of the key schemers were retired or dead. The life of undercover officer Eugene Roberts drifted ignominiously towards a sad and alcoholic end. He died anonymous and alone in Virginia in 2008. The pastor who conducted his funeral service knew him only as Mr Roberts and could not remember his first name.

The arrest of the Harlem Panthers and the preparation for the forthcoming trial finally blew Eugene Roberts' cover. Cited as a prosecution witness, his role as a 'deep' was exposed. By mid April 1969, the NYPD had captured the last remaining members of the Harlem Panthers. Lonnie Epps, one of the wanted teenagers, gave himself up after he was taken to a police station by his father. Another wanted man, described in melodramatic press reports as 'The Scientist', was in fact Dr Curtis Powell, a Black Panther member who had been born in East Orange, New Jersey. On leaving school at eighteen, he had joined the Marine Corps, then studied chemistry at Seton Hall University, followed by postgraduate study at the Albert Einstein College of Medicine and the University of Paris, where, unusually for a wanted felon, he had studied brain enzymes and carcinogenesis. Powell finally received his PhD from the University of Stockholm in 1968. During his time studying in Paris he had met Malcolm X at a lecture at the Maison de la Mutualité on rue Saint-Victor, and his journey to radicalism began in earnest. It was presumed by the FBI that Powell had been planning low-level chemical warfare. The NYPD raiding party found a small stock of hydrochloric and nitric acid in his apartment together with an incriminating book, *High Explosives and Propellants*.

The police identified their biggest target as Kwando Kinshasa. He was a former sergeant in the Marines and a Vietnam veteran (and is now an ethnic studies professor at the John Jay College of Criminal Justice). He had become a target when the FBI's COINTELPRO operation identified him as the author of an infamous Black Panther training manual, 'Urban Guerrilla Warfare', a copy of which had been found in Michael Tabor's possession.

The arrest of the last member of the Panther 21 happened in circumstances that defied expectation. Lee Berry was arrested at the Manhattan Veterans Hospital, where he was being treated for epilepsy, a condition that had worsened during his period of active service in Korea. The arrests of Powell, Berry and Kinshasa challenged orthodox thinking and seemed to indicate that the ranks of the Panthers and their ghetto militants had been swollen by disillusioned, radicalised military men from the war zones of South East Asia. It was a trend that had yet to be fully understood. Further south, in Memphis, a local militant group who called themselves the Memphis Invaders replicated the pattern. Among their prominent members were Vietnam veterans – the group's leader John Burl Smith and the outstanding Stax soul singer John Gary Williams – both of whom had recently returned from active service.

Rather than put the convalescing Berry on security watch at his hospital bed, the arresting officers made the catastrophic error of dragging him from the hospital and imprisoning him in the Tombs at the New York Detention Centre. He was placed in solitary confinement with a diet consisting solely of bread and tea. Due to clerical confusion at the time of his arrest, his medication was withdrawn. His health deteriorated so dramatically he was unable to stand trial. The circumstance of Berry's arrest was not symptomatic of the treatment meted out to the Panther 21, but it was just another in a string of mistakes that were to turn the spotlight away from the Panthers and on to the conspiratorial role that the police and the secret state had played in the mass arrests of 1969. Michael Tabor was initially taken to the Tombs, too; shortly after, he was driven under escort to Rikers Island where he waited for the trial that would bring him to the front pages of every newspaper in America.

Two New York models honour King Curtis at a mock coronation staged by Atlantic Records. The idea had its origins in Sweden when a group of soul fans turned up at a King Curtis show with a fake crown.

MARCH

King Curtis and the Ghetto Odyssey

On a midweek night in March 1969, Curtis Ousley was ensconced in a darkened bar cradling a whisky sour. Each night, after his show, he would delay going home and dive into a bar. He had been there a hundred times before. His silver pinky ring glistened against the whisky glass, and he held a cigarette between his middle fingers, a technique he had adopted from old jazz men, who smoked while they played. He was alone and determined not to be noticed. A brown velour bucket hat sat next to him on the bar and tucked inside its bowl, hidden from view, was a pair of round prescription glasses that he was not yet accustomed to wearing. When he placed the hat jauntily on his head, he had the street-smart look of a Harlem gangster, but the glasses put years on him, rounding out his features and giving him the demeanour of a studious theology professor. He was in fact a man immersed in music, magnetically attracted to Harlem nightlife as if it held a magical power. His marriage was at breaking point and in the hands of lawyers, but he hid his feelings behind a taciturn smile, nodding periodically at the barman and the line of liquor bottles behind him as if they knew how he really felt. Oddly, for a man so immersed in music, he never glanced through the fug of smoke to the jazz quartet on stage. He was there to listen, not to watch. Periodically, he would tap out percussion on the walnut bar with the edge of his beer mat, keeping time with the drummer, rarely letting the syncopation falter, and then, suddenly, with a flash of his plump right hand he would work brief routines up and down his dimpled glass, his fingers following the notation of a tenor saxophone.

Curtis Ousley was better known to the record-buying public as King Curtis, one of the most prodigious musicians in America and one who had managed successfully to span jazz and soul and all its many variants. In 1969 he was at the height of his considerable powers, and although he still had the energy to form another great band, inside he felt bereft – deadened by the shouting and screaming at home, unwilling to face up to his own shortcomings, and staring divorce sullenly in the face. Curtis was seriously over-stretched but incapable of letting a job opportunity pass him by. He was contracted to provide musical-director services to Atlantic Records, he had signed up to tour with Aretha Franklin, he had a residency at Club Baron on the corner of 132nd Street (sharing alternate nights with the promising young jazz guitarist George Benson), and he had agreed in principle to take on a new role as musical producer and bandleader at a fledgling television show called *Soul!* on Channel 13. And he had just returned from a European tour with the Sweet Inspirations and Detroit soul singer Deon Jackson. He was flat-out exhausted.

To try to buy himself more hours in the day, he had impulsively bought Cannonball Adderley's customised railway carriage with the hope of saving wasted time at airports by travelling to distant venues hitched to a Pennsylvania Railroad train. But the train was old and needed constant repairs, and the time he saved on journeys was eaten up with endless phone calls to railway engineers in the Bronx. Infamously King Curtis had once waved away James Brown's claims to be 'the hardest working man in show business' by saying dismissively, 'He can't be that busy if he has time to boast about it.'

King Curtis knew Harlem better than an old friend. He could map it out in his mind – the cornershops, the liquor stores and the laundromats – and he could check them off like an octave as they hugged the road north on Lenox and across 110th Street. His midnight odysseys – searching the nightclubs for the next great instrumentalist – meant he knew every Rabelaisian character who populated those streets: the gregarious label-owner and *bon viveur* Fat Jack Taylor; the 'polyunsaturated pimp' Fast Eddie; the exuberant and super-talented Allen twins; the wayward basketball star Earl 'The Goat' Manigault; the bootlegger and record-store owner Paul Winley; the effervescent radio DJ Frankie 'Love Man' Crocker; and Mademoiselle Mabry, the statuesque ultra-glamorous fashion model who had recently married jazz legend Miles Davis. Through a mixture of talent and dogged professionalism, he had surfed the many changes that music had thrown at him, and in a world of casualties had survived. Still in his mid thirties, he was one of a minority of musicians who had successfully clung to the roller-coaster of black music as it rattled noisily from big band, to bebop, to doo-wop, to rhythm and blues, and triumphantly into sixties soul. Something deep inside him sensed it was all about to change again, but this time the change would leave many victims in its wake. And so he braced himself for a time when soul music would fragment into jazz-funk, psychedelic soul, underground disco and the mighty messages of a more political ghetto.

King Curtis had navigated the dangers for decades and resented those who exaggerated them. He could physically defend himself, but more importantly he had found ways of controlling his volcanic temper and concealing his true feelings. As he passed crowded street corners, he often took off his glasses and hid them in his coat pocket, aware that looking studious also made him appear vulnerable. After climbing the brownstone stoop and reaching the sanctuary of his apartment, he would check the corridor carefully before closing and locking the door of his apartment. His last ritual of the night was the most important. He would hang his leather coat on a peg by the door and pull out a small sheaf of hand-written notes – usually scribbled on the torn edges of telephone directories – and printed business cards. If it was a good night and his efforts had borne fruit, he would have the details of a trumpeter or an organist hidden amongst the hieroglyphics of Harlem's dark sacred night.

Since he had been taken into care as an infant, he had developed a powerful will to survive. He was born Curtis Montgomery in Fort Worth, Texas, in the 'Negro Ward' of St Joseph's Catholic Hospital, and briefly lived in a shack near Hell's Half Acre, an old slum on the lawless side of town that would become known as the Butler Projects. His mother had struggled to cope, and he and his sister had been adopted by a young newly married couple, Josie and William Ousley of Mansfield, Texas. His new parents – a huge influence on his later career – taught Curtis the basic economics of life. He was careful with money, mindful of its value, but was never someone who could be described as mean or avaricious. They spoiled him, the way adoptive parents often do, and when his fascination with brass instruments surfaced at the age of ten, he was given his first saxophone. His skills blossomed, and by the time he left high school he was an accomplished musician who could sight-read and play confidently across the entire brass section. He was too old to be described as a child prodigy but too young to go on the road unaccompanied. When he was eighteen his parents finally relented, and in 1952 he joined the Lionel Hampton Band and embarked on an eventful career, performing on the same stage as Charlie Mingus, Wes Montgomery, Dinah Washington and Dizzy Gillespie. It was during his period watching the jazz aristocracy close-up that Curtis came to realise that the very best were neither showy improvisers nor self-obsessed soloists but literate musicians who could read scores with ease, and know when it was time to slip into the background. Sometime in the hot summer of 1955 Curtis began to fret about his future as a jazz musician; according to those close to him, it was a scab of doubt that he picked at for months. It was never due to a lack of self-belief, more an anxiety about the economic viability of the music. He knew too many musicians strung out on heroin, barely existing from one impoverished day to the next. Although his journey away from jazz alienated him from the purists who occupied Harlem's jazz haunts, he shrugged them off and embarked on a restless period of work, searching for a new direction and, more importantly, trying to make enough money to live. Musicologists have described his journey as 'versatile' and 'diverse', but it was more accurately a deep-rooted survival instinct. He recorded for ATCO Records as a nascent R&B musician and then for Prestige as a jazz musician, working by day as a session guy and by night fronting his own band in nightclubs throughout Harlem. After a period with Capitol Records, he threw the dice again, and in 1961 signed a scrappy contract with Enjoy Records, a Harlem indie owned by the streetwise entrepreneur Morgan Clyde 'Bobby' Robinson. The makeshift label was run from the back of his shop, Bobby's Happy House, on 125th Street near the Apollo. Robinson, the grandson of a slave and a man of outrageous fashions, had bought a bankrupt hat store and converted it into a shoe-shine business, which sold records in the rear. Eventually the vinyl took over and Bobby Robinson's became a Harlem landmark, a cluttered place where gospel, R&B and soul were traded with the same screeching urgency as hot stock on Wall Street. Robinson launched some of Harlem's most revered local indie labels, among them Fury, Fire and Whirlin' Disc, but it was his most enduring label Enjoy that came to define Harlem's musical odyssey, linking R&B to old-school hip-hop and recording an extraordinary journey from King Curtis and the Noble Knights to Grandmaster Flash and the Furious Five. Record executives from downtown queued up at the Apollo and crowded into his cluttered shop to get a handle on what was going on with the latest independent R&B records. Robinson sold them hot new singles and age-old cons such as selling old overstocks as new releases.

The Enjoy contract resulted in King Curtis's most successful solo single 'Soul Twist', a helter-skelter instrumental which cashed in on the early days of the twist dance craze. It spent two weeks at the top of the R&B charts in April 1962, reaching the Top Twenty of the crossover pop charts. At the time, King Curtis was in residence at Small's Paradise, the basement club that had been a jazz focal point since the thirties, and which after several generations of local ownership had been acquired by the basketball star Wilt Chamberlain, who transformed the club into a haven for independent soul music, a basketball theme bar and the authentic home of the twist dance-craze competition. On Tuesdays nights – the dedicated twist nights – people flocked to Small's Paradise from all over New York. The Peppermint Lounge, a more famous rival ballroom downtown in the safety of Midtown Manhattan, attracted the glamorous – the likes of Audrey Hepburn and Marilyn Monroe – but it was Small's that had the kind of ice-cool reputation that only dangerous Harlem could bestow. King Curtis kept the floor gyrating by performing extended versions of 'Soul Twist', building up the kind of kinetic atmosphere that became synonymous with New York's disco underground in the eighties. 'Soul Twist' was credited to King Curtis and the Noble Knights but Curtis soon changed the name of his supporting musicians to the band name that made him renowned throughout Harlem. At their height King Curtis and the Kingpins' line-up consisted of Ernie Hayes (organ), Billy Butler (guitar), Jimmy Lewis (bass) and Ray Lucas (drums), and among their catalogue were 'Soul Serenade', 'Memphis Soul Stew', 'Instant Groove', 'Teasin'' and 'Soulful 13', none of which could honestly be called soul standards. But it was not half-remembered records that built their reputation; success was forged in the hottest furnace of them all, the legendary Apollo on 125th Street where they were the house band.

For several years in the mid sixties King Curtis commandeered space at the Lenox Lounge on Lenox Avenue, where Billie Holiday, Miles Davis and John Coltrane had famously played. It was in the shadows of the daytime nightclub that King Curtis tested out aspiring musicians, demanding that they perform impromptu in the Lounge's atmospheric Zebra Room, amidst the black-and-white striped walls and kitsch Africana. It was a time of flux in Harlem's live music scene as jazz gave way to R&B and street funk. 'I saw the music was dividing,' Curtis once said. 'I had the commercial business sense to realise that "way out" jazz wasn't getting to the public. Good as those big name jazz musicians were, they'd always come over to where I was working. That meant they didn't have jobs themselves. I wasn't as good as they were, but I wasn't going to be asking anybody for two bucks.' He listened intently as hopeful musicians worked their way through the scales. The decision was instant: they were in or out.

For ten eventful years King Curtis recruited new faces, or replaced musicians who had fallen short of his quietly demanding standards. For a spell, as bandleader at the Apollo, he provided the backing for Otis Redding, James Brown, Marvin Gaye, Aretha Franklin and Stevie Wonder. Curtis stuck to one immutable rule: that visiting musicians must come prepared with sheet music. In a world known for gifted amateurism, he was the ultimate professional. Otis Redding had made his first appearance at the Apollo when he was still a relatively unknown vocalist, and was taken aback when King Curtis refused to support him unless he could provide professional sheet music. He scared the young singer into a panicked retreat. Redding spent the entirety of his $400 dollar fee having sheet music hurriedly printed at a store in Harlem and returned home to Macon, Georgia, chastened, out of pocket and determined never to be exposed as an amateur again.

Curtis had worked the Apollo more often than anyone and knew every ruse in the book, and although he relished the regular work and local prominence it gave him, he often bristled at the constraints – and the con men – that sometimes dragged the Apollo down. It was a decrepit venue, suited to a previous big band era, and located in a thoroughfare that was now at the epicentre of a troubled neighbourhood. But despite its woes, the Apollo had refused to go gentle into that good night: it stood erect in the middle of 125th Street like a Marine Corps recruiting sergeant, proud of its heritage and fearless of its future.

Like many of his jazz forefathers, King Curtis had played most of the nightclubs, worrying away at detail and aspiring to bring together the greatest band ever. For a few short months in the mid sixties, he came close to achieving his ambition when he played and recorded as King Curtis and the Kingpins. Now a long-forgotten 'supergroup', they featured jazz drummer Bernard 'Pretty' Purdie, guitarist Cornell Dupree – described by Atlantic-boss Jerry Wexler as 'the finest guitarist ever' and who generously adapted his style to accommodate the more flamboyant and unpredictable Jimi Hendrix. Despite the rough, drunken and chaotic instrumentation that defined early R&B, King Curtis and the Kingpins, through sheer bloody-minded professionalism, became one of the most significant if unsung groups in the history of soul music. Conscious of Curtis's low profile in the mainstream, Atlantic had happened on a unique promotional idea that brought him press attention beyond Harlem. If he was announcing a new tour or launching a new album, he would be introduced to the press sitting on top of a red velvet throne, flanked by two glamorous assistants who would produce a gold crown and sit it on top of his head. It was a popular routine with celebrity photographers, who were guaranteed to return to their editors with an eye-catching shot.

But press stunts alone never seemed to raise his profile quite high enough, and despite a towering reputation within the cognoscenti and a prodigious output, King Curtis and the Kingpins remain comparatively unknown, overshadowed by the Funk Brothers, the studio musicians at Detroit's 'snake pit' who built the rhythmic undercarriage of the instantly recognisable Motown sound, and Booker T. and the M.G.'s, the multiracial band who supported most of Stax's greatest hits. One possible explanation is that King Curtis and the Kingpins were never associated with a distinctive sound; they worked largely unheralded as the freelance nucleus of Atlantic Records' studio musicians and for a time in the late sixties as the backing band of choice for Aretha Franklin. After a lowly-paid period as session musicians accompanying Atlantic stars like Ruth Brown, LaVern Baker and Clyde McPhatter, King Curtis and the Kingpins embarked on a punishing schedule of singles and compilation albums, bringing an R&B edge to pop hits, or rush-releasing cover versions of songs already familiar on the transistor radios of America.

King Curtis's musical literacy was legendary and he could scan sheet music like a barcode, getting beneath the skin of a song in seconds. Between 1967 and 1969 his capacity to replicate and adorn the work of others intensified and he released instrumental versions of a string of sixties hits, among them Bobbie Gentry's suicidal narrative 'Ode To Billy Joe', Stevie Wonder's 'I Was Made To Love Her', Jeannie C. Riley's 'Harper Valley PTA', Dionne Warwick's 'Valley Of The Dolls', Otis Redding's moody requiem '(Sittin' On) The Dock Of The Bay;' and Procol Harum's psychedelic classic 'A Whiter Shade Of Pale'. Each one, different in genre and style, is laced through with King Curtis's signature saxophone solos, his imprimatur unmistakable even in already familiar tunes. Paradoxically, the more the pace of releases grew, the less King Curtis was known to the wider American public. He had an avid following in Europe and his Swedish fans once crowned him King of Soul at a kitsch ceremony where he appeared flanked by bathing-costume beauties drawn from the ranks of his Mod fans in Scandinavia. One possible reason why he flew so consistently below the radar in America was his extraordinary range. In his decade at the Apollo, he mastered every sub-genre of sixties soul music. His outstanding 'Memphis Soul Stew' deconstructs every instrument in the Stax studio system and fashions them into a furious piece of southern soul music. 'Soul Serenade' was a plaintive, softer song capable of being the backing track for the great balladeers of the era from Sam Cooke to Solomon Burke, while the impudent 'Soul Twist' had all the lively chutzpah of Chubby Checker.

According to rockabilly folklore, King Curtis had made his first substantial mark on music in March 1958, when he provided the distinctive saxophone refrain for the Coasters' song 'Yakety Yak', the record that introduced the staccato-led 'chicken scratch' saxophone sound to a mass audience. The hectic, borderline comical saxophone sound became known as the 'yakety sax' and paved the way for more mayhem to come – Boots Randolph's response tune 'Yakety Sax' (1963), Bill Black's Combo's 'Little Queenie' (1964), Ace Cannon's 'Sea Cruise' (1965), Willie Mitchell's 'That Driving Beat' (1965) and 'The Champion' (1966), and, in time, more fully rounded soul songs like Junior Walker and the All Stars' 'Shotgun' (1965) and 'I'm A Roadrunner' (1966). It was the distinctiveness of 'Yakety Yak' that initially brought Curtis to the attention of Atlantic Records boss Jerry Wexler, smoothing the way for him to become a fixture at the company's Manhattan headquarters where he became a label-mate of the Coasters, Ben E. King and Arthur Conley. At Atlantic, his friendship with Wexler deepened, and as tensions within the recording industry grew with the reverberations of the Black Power movement it became a matter of life and death. At the now infamous National Association of Television and Radio Announcers (NATRA) convention in Miami, Wexler and Curtis were sitting together during dinner when guest-speaker Bill Cosby fanned the flames with some ill-timed comments. A gang surrounded the Atlantic table and Wexler's life was openly threatened. King Curtis, who was there to collect an award as instrumentalist of the year, took control and secured his boss's safe passage out of the venue as threats intensified and guns were brandished. Wexler has since claimed that his effigy was hung over the balconies of the convention hall.

Two records released at opposite ends of the sixties underlined the scale of the shifts in soul music. Bob and Earl's evergreen dance-craze record 'Harlem Shuffle' (1963) is one of the most instantly recognisable soul records of all time and Donny Hathaway's 'The Ghetto' (1969) was one of the great transformers: a masterpiece in its own right, it created new openings for black musicians to present their communities in all their rich and ravaged diversity.

'Harlem Shuffle' was a pitiful failure when it was first released. But its popularity grew on the turntables of nightclubs across Europe. With time, it was released in every major territory across the continent, and then in 1969 it was reissued in the UK, where it careered up the charts, taking the vocalists and their producers by surprise. Its meteoric achievements did not end there. In 1986 it was resurrected by the Rolling Stones, featuring Mick Jagger in a duet with Bobby Womack. It was a song that never seemed to date, and for almost twenty years it featured in pop charts somewhere in the world. Donny Hathaway's 'The Ghetto' never reached the same heights of recognisable popularity but it brought the urban crisis into musical form. Produced by King Curtis, it is longer, more reflective and jazzier than most sixties hits, and even today stands out as a gigantic moment in the evolution of soul music. Despite their differences, both records are intimately tied up in the history of Harlem and represent two contrasting facets of the neighbourhood: the vibrant exuberance of nightlife and dance, and the brooding realities of a socially dysfunctional America.

Strangely, for a record that became synonymous with Harlem, 'Harlem Shuffle' was produced thousands of miles away in Los Angeles. Written by Gene Page and Fred Smith, the song has often been wrongly credited to the then unknown Barry White, a talented pianist with a seductive growling voice. He was, then, a small-time gangster from South Central L.A., who would transform his life to become the great romantic bear of the underground disco era and the most unlikely sexual soul singer ever. It is now accepted that White played no role in the song's composition since, at the time of its writing, he was serving a jail sentence for receipt of stolen goods – the theft of $30,000 worth of Cadillac tyres. 'Harlem Shuffle' was sung initially by Bobby Byrd and Earl Lee Nelson. When Byrd became distracted by a solo career, Earl Nelson hired another Bob – this time a local singer Bob Relf, who had recently graduated from Fremont High in South Central, a public school that in the past had produced the doo-wop group the Laurels and in the future would become the home turf of the Crips gang and the rap producer Dr Dre. Relf was a singer gifted beyond his success. He had a couple of singles that disappeared without trace and moved around L.A. soul groups with the speed of a pinball, eventually finding a modicum of success in Europe with an outstanding double A-side dance release, 'Blowing My Mind To Pieces/Girl, You're My Kind Of Wonderful' (1968). Relf has since claimed that Harlem only entered their minds because of its reputation and that their record was a derivative of a pre-existing release by Round Robin called 'Slauson Shuffletime'. Bob and Earl intuitively felt that a song about the Slauson thoroughfare was too local and lacked status so they relocated the setting to Harlem, the capital of black America and the unrivalled home of jazz dancing.

King Curtis could play 'Harlem Shuffle' in his sleep, having played it maybe 4,000 times on stage, twice nightly at the Apollo and often as part of a ferocious medley of instantly recognisable soul songs. It was frequently chosen by naïve hopefuls at the amateur night, or by visiting acts trying to ingratiate themselves with the theatre's notoriously demanding audiences. Ironically, for all the late hours he spent trawling Harlem clubs for talent, King Curtis found his greatest discovery while backstage at the Howard Theatre, where he struck up a conversation with a local music student called Donny Hathaway. By then, Curtis was a producer and talent scout who was remunerated either by a finder's fee or a revenue share in any new acts he brought to Atlantic. He met

Hathaway again at a music industry convention where they bonded over their mutual obsession with jazz and a near-neurotic interest in the future direction of black music. According to Hathaway's wife, Eulaulah, Curtis shared an elevator with her husband, and as the elevator descended Hathaway picked up the sound of its whining motor and sang a song in perfect pitch with the elevator as his backing band. It was the moment that King Curtis realised he had discovered the most talented soul musician ever. It was a bold claim but one he sincerely believed.

Donny Hathaway and his fellow student Leroy Hutson from New Jersey, who subsequently replaced Curtis Mayfield as lead singer with the Impressions, had by then sketched out an early version of a song called 'The Ghetto', which they co-wrote while sharing an apartment near the campus of Howard University in Washington DC. Hutson remembers the day the song first flickered into life. They were sitting in their apartment in the midst of a thunderstorm watching the sun burning through dark ominous clouds when suddenly the heavens opened. Rain fell like a drum solo. 'There was thunder, rain and sunshine all at once,' Hutson reminisced, 'and the two of us knelt at the windows of the apartment and looked out, and it was like the traffic was synchronised to the movement of the song. It was all so magical and a very wonderful occasion.' 'The Ghetto' was revolutionary in its sheer beauty. According to the writer Emily J. Lordi, it broke with expectation, challenged orthodox thinking about poverty and was 'a song meant to counter dire portraits of urban black life'. 'When I think of music,' Hathaway once said, 'I think of it in its totality, complete. You know, from the lowest Blues to the highest symphony.' What set him apart was this unashamed academic approach. Most of his contemporaries viewed soul as music of the streets or the dance floor; Hathaway was unafraid to see soul as the music of the conservatoire, unafraid to connect soul music to classical scholarship. Even at high school in St Louis his teachers were mystified at how he could play Grieg's piano concerto without a single error. Composer Edward Howard commented that 'Donny could write music like you write a letter. He would sit in a club and write different arrangements of a song between sets.'

To fully understand Hathaway and Hutson's vision for a new kind of soul music, you have to understand Howard University and the cradle of creativity that surrounded them. Inner-city Washington was still smouldering with the riots that followed the assassination of Martin Luther King. Buildings were charred into rubble or surrendering to neglect, and the white middle classes, particularly the political establishment, were fleeing to the suburbs or deeper into the leafy enclaves of North West DC. Standing proud amidst the ghetto's many social problems was Howard University, the historically black university whose campus stretched from decaying ghetto streets around 14th and up the vertiginous acres of Rock Creek Park. The campus had one of the greatest concentrations of soul music talent ever. Carla Thomas, the Stax recording star and daughter of the irrepressible Rufus Thomas, was majoring in English Literature; Jessye Norman, the classical vocalist, was studying a Bachelor of Arts in Music; and Twinkie Clark of the gospel group the Clark Sisters was studying Divinity. Hathaway met his future wife Eulaulah, the mother of quiet storm soul singer Lalah Hathaway, at choir practice. Responding to student unrest that criticised the faculty for only teaching European classical music, the university was in the reluctant process of establishing a jazz studies curriculum, which would be led by Professor Donald Byrd. Herbie Hancock was already studying there and Byrd's new intake of students became the successful jazz-funk group the Blackbyrds.

Hathaway and Hutson's apartment was near the corner of 14th and T Street where the riot had hit hardest. It became a hive of improvisation; their classmate Roberta Flack, who had been the youngest student ever to enrol at the university when she won a piano scholarship aged fifteen, provided guest vocals and soon became Hathaway's recording partner in a series of stunning love duets including the quiet storm classics 'Where Is The Love' and 'The Closer I Get To You'. A sister record to 'The Ghetto', the powerful 'Trying Times' had the same depth and social anger, and it, too, was co-written with Leroy Hutson. After Roberta Flack signed to Atlantic, it was given to her for her debut album *First Take* in 1969.

Hathaway had been adopted by his grandmother and raised in St Louis where he became a gospel prodigy. For a period in his childhood he toured America as Little Donny Pitts, a four-year-old singer dressed in a white sailor suit, sharing stages with Mahalia Jackson and Aretha Franklin. At university he became obsessed with the history of jazz, studying voraciously and learning about Harlem's forbidden jazz clubs. He had a party piece that regularly astounded his fellow students. He could sit at a piano and play out the history of twentieth-century black music from ragtime to jazz-funk. Bewitched by that evolution, he once admitted to a European journalist that he could sit for hours listening to King Curtis as his mentor picked his way across the late night geography of Harlem to after-hours nightclubs where the sorcerers of bebop played a form of jazz that baffled the outside world. Hathaway believed that in order to make an impact on the reinvention of soul music he had to move there, but in his student years he was under financial pressure. Eventually he drifted away from college, his wife claiming that they had nothing more to teach him.

For a while Curtis Mayfield tried to convince him that Chicago could offer the best guarantee of employment. It was where his birth mother lived and Mayfield briefly won the battle for Hathaway's attention. Hathaway left university for the Windy City and remained there for a year, joining the Mayfield Singers and briefly becoming an A&R producer for Mayfield's newly established Curtom Records. He stayed long enough to sign his friend Leroy as a vocalist and produced studio sessions for local vocalists Garland Green and Syl Johnson.

Throughout Hathaway's spell in Chicago, Curtis remained in touch, often whispering sweet poison in his ears. It worked. Hathaway fell out with Mayfield. They disagreed about the musical direction of the company and the extent of Mayfield's creative control. Fully aware of the tensions at Curtom, Curtis did everything in his power to attract Hathaway to Harlem and bounced Jerry Wexler into guaranteeing Hathaway a solo deal and producer's contract with Atlantic Records. To ease his passage out of Chicago, Hathaway told Mayfield he was quitting music altogether and taking up work as a teacher. It was an unnecessary deception, and when

Mayfield read of the Atlantic deal in the trade press, he went nuclear, vowing never to speak to Hathaway again. He even banned his family from continuing their friendship with Hathaway's pregnant wife. It was a bitter end to one of soul music's most promising collaborations but it opened up a world of possibilities. By the end of 1968 the myth and lure of Harlem had proved too powerful for Hathaway to resist. Along with a few of his Chicago associates, including Hutson and the arranger Johnny Pate, he gravitated to one of soul music's main thoroughfares, the bustling 125th Street.

Just as Hathaway was on the brink of leaving Chicago, Curtis Mayfield cut a duet that paired him with Chicago singer June Conquest. June and Donnie's 'I Thank You Baby' (1969) remains one of soul music's unheralded classics and is in every respect as good as the gold-standard duets by Marvin Gaye and Tammi Terrell or Maxine Brown and Chuck Jackson. But something about the song underlines Hathaway's impatience. It was a powerful love song with all the familiar cadences of mid sixties soul – which by 1969 was a conventional but somewhat dated sound – but it spoke of the past. Hathaway was a dreamer and an innovator, a young man determined to revolutionise soul, to take it forward, not back. Hathaway's epic composition 'The Ghetto' hinted at a form of music yet to come, anchored in jazz, a longer and more political kind of soul music that captured the tension of modern urban life. Hathaway's style was more 'symphonic'. The vocals were stripped back and street-like, and the style of composition was more classical. It would be no great exaggeration to say that 'The Ghetto' irrevocably changed the direction of soul music and mapped out its future direction, one that influenced Marvin Gaye's stellar *What's Going On* (1971), which became arguably the greatest album of its era.

The title alone brought a word synonymous with Harlem and social deprivation into widespread use. The term 'ghetto' had been in use in a European context as far back as 1516 when Venetian Jews were confined behind the high walls of the Ghetto Nuovo, an island which had once housed a copper foundry and its industrial waste, therefore a *geto* in local dialect. For centuries the word was associated with Jewish persecution until, in 1931, Harlem's most revered poet Langston Hughes wrote a short poem simply titled 'Harlem Ghetto'. It reflected a demographic shift in the history of the area, as Jews left for the wealthier boroughs and Harlem became associated with black immigrants from the West Indies and the Deep South. Hughes looked around him and saw a world that was crueller and more impoverished: the ghetto as a prison.

By the end of the Second World War, and the subsequent Nazi war trials, the word 'ghetto' simultaneously described a place of sanctuary and an overcrowded area of a city occupied by incomers or low-income families. Ralph Ellison, the author of *Invisible Man*, wrote in 1948 that to 'live in Harlem, is to dwell in the very bowels of the city, it is to pass a labyrinthine existence among streets that explode monotonously skywards with spires and crosses of churches and clutter underfoot with garbage and decay'. And in the same year, one of Harlem's most eloquent literary witnesses, the internationally acclaimed author James Baldwin, who had been born and raised there, looked back on Harlem's bleaker housing projects as cursed by spiritually impoverished social housing. 'The projects are hideous,' he wrote in *Nobody Knows My Name*, 'there being a law respected throughout the world, that popular housing shall be as cheerless as prison. They are lumped all over Harlem, colorless, bleak, high and revolting. The wide windows look out on Harlem's invincible and indescribable squalor: the Park Avenue railroad tracks, around which, about forty years ago, the present dark community began; the un-rehabilitated houses, bowed down, it would seem under the great weight of frustration and bitterness . . .'

By 1969 'ghetto' had come to mean urban areas inhabited by poorer black families and the term was applied to inner-city African-American neighbourhoods, which in New York meant Harlem, the South Bronx and Brownsville in Brooklyn. With its decaying buildings, metal fire escapes, crowded stairwells and fire hydrants, Harlem became synonymous with the word increasingly celebrated in the evolving culture of soul music. Yet, curiously, 'ghetto' was a relatively late entrant into the vocabulary of soul. Motown, the most successful soul label, tended to focus on teenage romance and resisted any intrusion from outside the bubble of young love. It was not until 1969 that a harder-edged social realism began to shape soul and it was in no small part helped by the success of Donny Hathaway's song and the reach that Atlantic Records had into the mainstream market. Within a few short months of the song's release, the word 'ghetto' erupted – like a riot of sorts – and suddenly became commonplace in song titles, lyrics and in the names of the artists themselves.

Meanwhile, in Memphis, the creatively rejuvenated Elvis Presley recorded his hit 'In The Ghetto', a song originally written for Sammy Davis Jr by country singer Mac Davis. Davis had imagined the story unfolding on a winter's day in Chicago's South Side. Although neither of these landmark songs were actually set in Harlem, Harlem's associations with the word 'ghetto' came to dominate the popular imagination. Hathaway's record coincided with other ghetto-related releases, including James Brown's novelty funk record 'Santa Claus Goes Straight To The Ghetto' (1968) and Marlena Shaw's proto-feminist song 'Woman Of The Ghetto' (1969). Artists were suddenly keen to associate themselves with the term – a group called the Ghetto Boys had already recorded 'Handwriting On The Wall' (1966) and soon new ghetto sounds were hitting the streets: Tony Clarke's 'Ghetto Man' (1970), The Luv Bug's 'Soul In The Ghetto' (1970), Carlos Malcolm's 'Bustin' Outta The Ghetto' (1970), Vernon Garrett's 'We People In The Ghetto' (1971), Luther Ingram's 'Ghetto Train' (1971), Getto Kitty's 'Stand Up And Be Counted' (1972), and then Candi Staton's gospel-tinged 1972 cover version of Elvis Presley's hit. Within a matter of a few years, the ghetto and social deprivation were mainstream within African-American music. Love and romance still thrived but a barrier had been broken. For the first time in the history of soul music, it became possible to secure global hits that focused on the lives of the disadvantaged: Marvin Gaye's epic 'What's Going On' (1971), War's 'The World Is A Ghetto' (1972), The Spinners' 'Ghetto Child' (1973), and the Philadelphia International All Stars 'Let's Clean Up The Ghetto' (1977).

Soul music was at last providing King Curtis with a reasonable living, and as the trickle of money began to flow, he found himself on the horns of a new kind of dilemma: to stay in Harlem or move to a new home closer to his record label in Midtown Manhattan. He rented an apartment in a crumbling brownstone at 150 West 96th Street and then bought a stake in a second apartment at 50 West 86th Street, strategically placing himself between the two landmarks of his life – the Apollo Theater and the offices of Atlantic Records on Broadway. In part, this was to prepare for his divorce and escape an acrimonious home life. Yet the decision troubled him. Wexler comforted him with an extended contract at Atlantic, but Aretha Franklin, among others, insisted that Harlem was more dangerous now and in the grip of crime and a spiralling heroin epidemic. In her mind it was time to move. Curtis was keen to move up in the world but he was equally anxious not to be cut off from the place that had electrified his younger life. Paradoxically, his venture into property and his carefully planned move away from Harlem proved to be a fatal mistake. On 13 August 1971 he was adjusting an air-conditioning unit in his new apartment, which was accessed via the basement, when an argument broke out between himself and a man hanging around the entrance. In the altercation, a twenty-six-year-old Hispanic drug addict called Juan Montañez stabbed King Curtis to death. There are conflicting reports of his final moments. Some newspapers claimed that Curtis died in an emergency vehicle en route to Roosevelt Hospital while those close to the dying musician claimed he was still alive and held on for many more hours as emergency doctors tended to him. They said that on his arrival at the hospital, he was gasping for breath and medics fought to repair a series of deep knife wounds to his upper body. The windpipe that had served so majestically on stage had been punctured beyond repair, and even if he had survived it was highly unlikely he would have been able to return to music. As doctors worked on the famous saxophonist another victim was rushed to the hospital. It was his attacker, drenched in blood and bent double with four stab wounds to his abdomen. Even in death Curtis had not been easily beaten. In the furious fight between the two men, Curtis had somehow disarmed the younger man and used his assailant's knife to fight back.

Radio stations across Harlem devoted their day's schedule to a man who had become a local celebrity. Michael Cuscuna of Radio

Station WABC simply said, 'He was one of the best,' and Tex Wishik, sales manager at the Colony Record Shop, downtown at Broadway and 52nd Street, a popular gathering place for musicians, said, 'He worked all the time. Every musician knew him, white and black. He sold well on records and tapes. He was a nice guy. But he had a temper and he wouldn't take any nonsense from anyone.'

King Curtis's body was laid in public view at St Peter's Lutheran Church, on 54th and Lexington, and his funeral was attended by Harlem's late night elite. The Reverend Jesse Jackson flew in from Chicago to deliver the eulogy. The mourners included songwriter Brook Benton, singer Arthur Prysock, Dizzy Gillespie, King Coleman and the Isley Brothers. Stevie Wonder, then on the cusp of becoming an international superstar, and an emotionally bereft Aretha Franklin, who had often relied on her musical director to lift her own depressive spirits, both sang dedications. When Stevie Wonder took to the microphone, he delivered a moving version of 'Abraham, Martin And John', a eulogy to Lincoln, Martin Luther King and John F. Kennedy, which at the time was a Top Forty hit for Smokey Robinson, and about to be more famously covered by Marvin Gaye. Stevie Wonder improvised a new and final verse, adding King Curtis's name to the roll-call of the dead. The Kingpins, who were all musicians handpicked by the deceased, delivered on one of his final wishes, a one-hour unbroken version of his biggest hit, 'Soul Serenade', an improvised soul jazz requiem which continued until the last mourner had drifted away. But as with almost every funeral, a family dispute lingered long after the requiem ended. The bitterness of his divorce, which had so troubled Curtis over the previous three years, erupted in an unseemly stand-off. Curtis's estranged wife Ethelyn resented the presence of his new girlfriend, Modeen Broughton, a staff writer at Chess Records. She was escorted into the church by the Reverend Jesse Jackson, in a manner that his former wife considered demeaning and disrespectful.

Perhaps the greatest tragedy of all was that King Curtis – a legend within his industry – died comparatively unknown. For all his hundreds of recordings, he had only ever delivered one hit – 'Soul Twist', a saxophone paean to the early sixties dance craze – but even that had failed to secure him a gold disc. Beyond the cognoscenti and the music scene itself, his name had all but faded from history; King Curtis had devoted so much of his time to supporting and endorsing others. There were his cover versions of McCartney-Lennon's 'Hey Jude' and Jimi Hendrix's 'Hey Joe'; his virtuoso homage to the music of Sam Cooke; his subtle interpretation of Marvin Gaye's 'I Heard It Through The Grapevine'; and his elegant reworking of Ben E. King's 'Spanish Harlem', an instrumental which takes the song and its neighbourhood on a reverse journey away from soul and back on a wandering pilgrimage to its roots in Latin jazz. Most of all, there was his early endorsement of Donny Hathaway and his determination to bring 'The Ghetto' to wider audiences.

King Curtis had left another significant legacy – a live album with Aretha Franklin and the Memphis Horns recorded at the Fillmore West in San Francisco. By then, Curtis's ruthless pursuit of perfection, which he shared with Hathaway, had led him to recruit a new generation of Kingpins, including jazz guitarist Cornell Dupree, master drummer Bernard 'Pretty' Purdie and the then unknown Billy Preston on the organ. Although the concept of the supergroup was a phenomenon known largely to rock music, Curtis had studiously pulled together his own perfect combination, drawn selectively from the great river of talent flowing through black America, and, to top it all, the legendary Aretha Franklin featured on vocals.

One of Curtis's closest musical allies was the exiled Beatle John Lennon, who in 1980 was shot by Mark Chapman in the doorway of the Dakota apartment block on the Upper West Side. His body was delivered dead on arrival to the same Roosevelt Hospital that had tried to save Curtis's life. Lennon and Curtis had stayed in touch since August 1965 when King Curtis and the (original) Kingpins performed a virtuoso version of 'Soul Twist' as a warm-up act at the Beatles' historic concert at Shea Stadium. When Lennon broke with the Beatles and relocated to New York the pair reconnected. Lennon viewed King Curtis as the gold standard of saxophone players and invited him to come to the studio as he worked on a solo album. By then, Curtis had left the Apollo but was still working intensely, juggling a crowded diary of live shows, session work and guest appearances. Since its opening in 1968, he became a familiar face at the Record Plant, the 12-track studio at 321 West 44th Street which was then the 'living room' for many of New York's most creative pop stars. Lennon had booked time there to rehearse and record tracks for his *Imagine* album. King Curtis acted as guest saxophonist and Lennon's trusted advisor. There are two extant photographs of the sessions. One captures an unusual look of awe on Lennon's normally impudent face as he fixes his gaze on Curtis's chubby fingers dancing balletically across the saxophone keys. Another shows the ex-Beatle looking up respectfully at Curtis's face as a child might regard a favourite teacher. Lennon had first heard of him on records imported to Liverpool in his art school years and had cherished the saxophone – not so much as a sound but as a signifier of the giants of black American music – ever since.

The murder of King Curtis was solved within hours of his death in a city where murder rates were escalating and a badly stretched police force were failing to meet their annual targets. For the first time since records began, the murder rate had broken through the 1,000 mark: 1,043 people were murdered in 1969, up from a total of 390 in 1960. Over sixty per cent of victims knew their killer, but a growing number were random, opportunistic, or the product of crime-infested neighbourhoods blighted by heroin. Rising crime was one of many problems that confronted New York City's increasingly beleaguered mayor John Lindsay, in what social historians were beginning to call his 'ungovernable city'. Arrests in the city rose by just under fifteen per cent with the sharpest increase among teenagers. The majority of arrests were felonies: possession of dangerous drugs (a thirty-seven per cent rise), possession of dangerous weapons (seventy-two per cent rise) and robbery (twenty-three per cent rise). Although escalating crime statistics were widespread across the city, the rates in the hardened ghettos of Harlem, the South Bronx and the Fulton Street area of Brooklyn's Bedford-Stuyvesant neighbourhood outstripped other parts of the city. The social historian Michael Javen Fortner claims that from 1968 onwards New York 'became a dangerous place', and in his challenging book *Black Silent Majority* he charts crime rates skyrocketing in the city: 'the rate for murder and non-negligent manslaughter was nearly double the national average; the robbery rate was more than five times the national average and the burglary rate was double the national average'. The odds were stacking up against the mayor and his administration. Every blocked drain, every discarded paper wrapper swirling in the wind, and every overturned garbage can was a stark reminder of the divisive sanitation workers' strike of 1968 and the bitterness that resulted from failing public services.

John Lindsay had been a triumphant appointment when he won the mayoral election of 1965. A confident and handsome man, he was frequently compared with President John F. Kennedy and congratulated for his film-star good looks, his popular touch, and the ease with which he understood the emergent trends in society, especially youthful and urban attitudes. The telegenic liberal Republican stumbled on one of his most popular postures by sheer chance. On his first day as mayor, there was a transport strike which crippled the bus and subway system. Rather than chastise the strikers from his mayoral perch, Lindsay took to the street and walked four miles through New York to his office. People liked his approachability and the cheery way he greeted passers-by, shopkeepers and school children. The mayor's casual walkabouts became a powerful signifier of his openness and, unlike many men of his generation, he was intellectually curious enough to try to understand the many variants of youth culture that were sweeping the world. Much of Lindsay's first two years in office were focused on the city's most deprived areas and keeping a lid on urban tension. He had been the uncredited author of the introduction to the Kerner Report, in which President Johnson's taskforce looked at the underlying problems of race riots, and he wrote the report's most damning words: 'Our nation is moving towards two societies, one black and one white – separate and unequal.' Then, in a powerful piece of prose, he pointed the finger at white complacency and the burdens that slavery had bequeathed: 'What white Americans have never fully understood – but what the Negro can never forget,' the report asserted, 'is that white society is deeply implicated in the ghetto. White institutions created it, white institutions maintain it, and white society condones it.'

On the night of 4 April 1968, Mayor Lindsay and his wife had been attending the opening of a play on Broadway when a call from his media team alerted him to the assassination of Dr Martin Luther King in Memphis. Lindsay left his seat in the stalls and contacted police commissioner Howard Leary and civil servant Barry Gottehrer, who the mayor had installed as head of an urban taskforce. They were informed that crowds were already gathering in Harlem and around Bedford-Stuyvesant. According to an eye witness, 'there was a lot of running and yelling and smashing of windows and throwing rocks and stuff'. Although the police told Lindsay it was too dangerous to travel to Harlem, he overruled them and said that 'somebody just has to go up there. Somebody white just has to face that emotion and say we're sorry.' The convoy arrived at 125th Street and Eighth Avenue with a righteous mission and with a sense of political theatre. The mayor emerged from his car and was immediately surrounded by mobs of young protestors. Making space for himself and using a police bullhorn, Lindsay gave an impromptu speech denouncing the assassination. It was a far from comfortable experience. A group of militants, the infamous Five Percenters – a breakaway faction from the Nation of Islam – surrounded the mayor, either protecting him or intimidating him depending on which version you believe. But the majority of the crowd responded to his words, and although there was violence and storefronts were destroyed, compared with the mass rioting in Memphis and Washington DC, trouble in Harlem was contained. Jack Newfield, a journalist with the New York weekly *Village Voice*, likened the mayor's intervention to *High Noon* and described a scene in which 'tall, grim Lindsay strides down Lenox, into a subsiding storm of bricks'. It is a comforting fantasy, Newfield wrote, that 'Lindsay has earned because he is the only white mayor in America . . . to have the grudging trust of the black underclass.' In the early hours of the tense morning, Lindsay pulled off a masterstroke. He instructed the city's sanitation department to pile resources into Harlem and clean up the debris of the sporadic looting, and insisted that there should be no press photographs of the riots or the aftermath. It was manipulating the truth, but his actions showed both himself and Harlem in a good light: rioting had supposedly been averted.

The following day Lindsay returned to Harlem and took to the studios of Radio Station WLIB at 310 Lenox Avenue to take part in extended broadcasts with Harlem jazz pianist Billy Taylor. They talked about King's life and death and his civil rights campaigns, and took calls from the mournful, as well as interspersing the show with gospel standards. It was more reflective than the night before and was aimed to reassure the older black American community, but again it reinforced Mayor Lindsay's presence in Harlem. Later that night in Bedford-Stuyvesant, mindful of the value of being seen, he used a city-owned limousine to transport an old man with a leg injury to hospital. It was a tiny gesture among many, but in New York the politics of perception count, and the mayor's Good Samaritan act was widely praised.

As 1969 unfolded, New York's unpredictability engulfed Mayor Lindsay. For much of the late sixties, he was at the peak of his popularity and was being courted as a Republican candidate for the presidency. Standing up to the demands of the sanitation union in the face of a potentially damaging strike had cast him as a firm but friendly character, and his commitment to ghetto neighbourhoods had endeared him to minority communities. But what proved impossible to resolve was taxation. New York had nine per cent of the nation's population but every working day the number swelled disproportionately as commuters flooded into the city from upstate New York, across the bridges from New Jersey and via Amtrak from Delaware and Pennsylvania. Then they returned home again to pay local taxes elsewhere. Lindsay advocated a mandatory 'pass through tax' but it proved impossible to enforce, leaving the city desperately short of funds.

Fractious and racially divisive disputes in the public school system spread like wildfire, including a flawed attempt to desegregate the entirely black and Puerto Rican Harlem Public School 201, a ghetto school mired in teenage crime and scholastic underachievement. According to the city's own data, three out of every four families living in the blighted tenements of the East Harlem

Triangle at 127th and Madison were on welfare. Above the school, the Metro North train lines clamoured away, taking taxpayers home to the 'safety of the suburbs'. To protect the school from noise, it had been built without windows to deaden the sound of the trains passing overhead. The environment and quality of education was bleak, and the world outside was unwelcoming. In the immediate vicinity the unemployment rate stood at seventeen per cent, rising to thirty-six per cent among young black males, and the dilapidated tenements provided a cover for crime and social unrest. This was the landscape in which King Curtis had met his death and which Donny Hathaway had set to music.

Meanwhile, the death of King Curtis had exacerbated Donny Hathaway's fragile mental health. He took breaks from the industry, hid out in Chicago with his mother, and often failed to show up at recording sessions in Midtown Manhattan. He took on residencies at jazz clubs in Greenwich Village but was not always able to fulfil them, and for long periods of time he sat alone, playing the piano as if it held the key to his deep mental anxiety. It is one of soul music's greatest tragedies that the unusually gifted and cerebral Donny Hathaway became paralysed by self-doubt. His influence on the music of the ghetto was already formidable but his life was destined to be a short one, and the genius that King Curtis had recognised was fatally compromised by severe mental illness. His greatest music was still to come but so, too, was his greatest pain.

Miles Davis and his young wife Betty Mabry, 1968.

APRIL

Bitches Brew

Homestead, Pennsylvania, was a place to escape from. Despite its welcoming name it had a history of social strife and ingrained poverty. At its height as a steel town in the late nineteenth century, it had been wholly owned by the Scottish industrialist Andrew Carnegie, a man deceptively known for his generosity who had come to personify benevolent capitalism. The people of Homestead thought otherwise; they regarded him as a ruthless individual who had dragooned the Pinkerton Detective Agency into breaking strikes, intimidating steelworkers and wrecking the homes of those who refused to work for a pittance for the Carnegie Steel Company.

By the time Betty Mabry was at high school, steel manufacturing was in retreat and the past was another country. She gazed out on a Rust Belt town that was perpetually engulfed by smoke and pollution and faced a bleak future. Mabry had actually been born in a rural area of Reidsville, sixty miles from Durham, North Carolina, in 1945, and spent her childhood on her grandmother's farm where she listened to the raw blues of John Lee Hooker, Muddy Waters, Jimmy Reed and Lightnin' Hopkins. Her fascination with the genre – its demanding brutal honesty – remained a constant in her life. It was on the farm that the precociously talented girl began to write lyrics in a school notepad, eventually composing audacious songs that she sang to anyone who would listen.

In 1961 she planned her escape. Aged only sixteen, with the support of an aunt, she headed to Harlem. A tall, elegantly slim teenager, she had an eye for fashion and a youthful reputation for risk-taking. She became one of the first women to bring Black Power into fashion when she grew a voluminous afro. Her stunning hair – natural and stacked – added even more inches to her height, and she was quickly spotted by Manhattan's ultra-cool Wilhelmina Modelling Agency, becoming one of the first black girls to sign for them. For almost a year, she commuted downtown, juggling assignments and studying at an overcrowded nine-storey building at West 27th Street on Seventh Avenue, then the headquarters of the newly established Fashion Institute of Technology. It was a world bright with prospects. Without ever telling lies about her humble past, Mabry began the business of shaping a new persona, one that would challenge every orthodoxy that life presented, and in the process created yet another future for black American music.

In 1964 she released her first single for Columbia, 'Get Ready For Betty', and a year later, still in her teens, opened her own nightclub. The Cellar was a dark dungeon barely visible from the sidewalk, and its experimental playlists attracted her close circle of friends from the worlds of fashion and music. Mabry was smart enough to realise that an invisible demarcation line now separated Harlem from downtown. 'Across 110th Street' was a colloquial term she heard almost daily and Mabry surmised that while there was a vanguard of creative people who would travel north to Harlem for inspiration and authenticity, there was a growing number who were too fearful of the perceived threat of crime and violence to cross the dividing line and so stayed downtown in the relative safety of the Village. Mabry shrewdly chose a venue on 95th and Broadway, sufficiently far from the Village to be seen as uptown but not so deep in the dark heart of Harlem that it would scare away more timid customers. By all accounts it was a remarkable club, a forerunner of New York's disco underground which had a reputation for playing music that stretched the boundaries of pop. Mabry was the hostess, the muse and the DJ, single-decking, playing background tapes, and sometimes handing over the reins to others, including her friend, the singer-producer Lou Courtney. Mabry still carried a torch for the blues, and among the many sounds played there were Little Milton's welfare-line blues classic 'We're Gonna Make It', Slim Harpo's 'Baby Scratch My Back' and tougher mainstream soul records that were chart hits in the mid sixties, notably Sam and Dave's 'Hold On I'm Comin'', Eddie Floyd's 'Knock On Wood', James Brown's 'Cold Sweat', Archie Bell & the Drells' 'Tighten Up' and Johnnie Taylor's 'Who's Making Love'. It was a club that embraced the British Invasion, too, and programmed imported R&B from the Spencer Davis Group, the Animals and Georgie Fame and the Blue Flames.

Mabry led a nomadic social life, visiting bars in Harlem – where she lived with her aunt – and then travelling downtown to counterculture clubs in the Village. She spent week nights at the Bitter End and Café Au Go-Go on Bleecker Street queuing up to see blues legends like Howlin' Wolf and Muddy Waters, but she also came across the emergent stars of new rock. She was attracted to musicians and the feeling was mutual. She had a brief affair with Hugh Masekela, who was on the rebound from his marriage to Miriam Makeba. To pay her way at fashion school, Mabry waited tables by day at Café Figaro, the Greenwich Village coffeehouse at the corner of Bleecker and MacDougal Street, once a haunt of Dylan and Kerouac and a Beat Generation institution. She seemed equally at home in the Harlem of Fat Jack Taylor and the Greenwich Village of Nina Simone.

Sometime in early 1967 Betty Mabry travelled downtown to a new Greenwich Village club called Generation, which had been hastily built into the shell of New York's oldest country and western club, the Village Barn at 52 West 8th Street. Her objective was to see the critically acclaimed family group the Chamber Brothers, who at the time were popular on the festival circuit and at the cutting edge of rock-soul fusion. But she was also keen to check out the opposition and spy on this club which the underground press were heavily promoting. Generation became an important (albeit short-lived) part of the New York live music scene. A year later, it would play host to a remarkable jam session staged as a requiem for the assassinated civil rights leader Martin Luther King, the roll-call including Joni Mitchell, B.B. King, Buddy Guy, Jimi Hendrix, Al Kooper and Ted Nugent. Hendrix had turned up as a surprise guest after his scheduled concert in Newark had been curtailed when rioting swept the area in the aftermath of King's assassination. According to the road crew of Soft Machine, who were supporting, Hendrix played a long heartfelt blues set and then, with head bowed, walked off stage and drove to the Generation. It was the night he decided to buy the venue and soon thereafter Jimi Hendrix and his management converted it into the recording studio Electric Lady, the only artist-owned recording studio in the city.

At the end of the Chamber Brothers' show Mabry approached them about writing a song, an idea of hers that had been simmering for months. 'Uptown (In Harlem)', released by Columbia in 1967, was a soul-food song about partying uptown and the inherent bias that New Yorkers showed Harlem. It was an audacious breakthrough in Mabry's career and a small step towards becoming a respected artist in her own right. To make that happen she had already leant heavily on a regular at the Cellar, a Harlem-based soul singer from Buffalo, New York, whose birth name was Louis Pegues. He had adopted the stage name Lou Courtney, and while hardly an industry veteran, he had racked up enough experience to open doors for Mabry. Courtney was the mighty Lorraine Ellison's musical director and had enjoyed some recent local success in the New York area, mostly with a succession of dance-craze singles on Manhattan indie labels Popside and Riverside, including 'Skate Now', 'Do The Thing', 'Me And You (Doin' The Boogaloo)', 'Psychedelic Shing-A-Ling' and a Verve single called 'Do The Horse'. But Courtney's commercial pursuit of fads and crazes belied a significant talent for songwriting. Among his vast catalogue of songs were Gloria Gaynor's debut 'She'll Be Sorry' (1965), Patti Austin's uptown soul song 'Take Away The Pain Stain' (1966) and an evocative break-up song arranged by Bert de Coteaux called 'I Watched You Slowly Slip Away'. Courtney recorded the song himself in 1965, but it was surpassed in quality the following year by Howard Guyton, the one-time lead singer of the Harlem-based harmony group the Top Notes.

Betty Mabry saw Lou Courtney as a mentor. But more importantly, as a person who could connect her to record labels. In 1966 they hatched a plan together to record a dance-craze record with a difference called 'The Cellar', which focused on a club rather than a dance style. Still only twenty, Mabry was a club owner, a successful model who had appeared on the pages of *Jet*, *Seventeen*, *Ebony* and *Glamour* magazines, and a recording artist in pursuit of a hit single. She was one of the trailblazers for change in the fashion industry. Along with Detroit cover girl Donyale Luna – who became the first African-American model to adorn the cover of *Vogue* in the UK – Mabry stood out as not simply a trendsetter but a force for change. Her next triumph in music proved to be catalytic, shaping not only her own future but changing the direction of soul music and reigniting the reputation of one of the superstars of New York jazz – Miles Davis.

Mabry met Davis at the Village Gate, a basement club on Bleecker Street. One of Davis's entourage invited her to join the jazzman for a drink, and although she had no great knowledge of his music she instinctively understood his mystique and his reputation. The two embarked on a tempestuous but mutually rewarding romance. Betty Mabry and Miles Davis were married on 30 September 1968 in Gary, Indiana. The groom's brother Vernon and his sister Dorothy attended, and Mabry's parents travelled from their home in Pittsburgh. The wedding coincided with the end of Miles Davis's annual residency at the famous Chicago jazz club the Plugged Nickel, and with the benefit of hindsight it marked a fork in the road for soul music. The collision of their attitudes and styles was the lever that redirected both their careers. One road led forward to fusion and jazz-funk, the music of Davis's pianist Herbie Hancock, the Harlem-based guitarist George Benson, Atlantic recording star Roy Ayers and Bobbi Humphrey, whose 'Harlem River Drive' revitalised the flute. The other – represented by Mabry's career – was the journey towards black rock. It led to Vernon Reid's Living Colour, the Black Rock

Coalition, James Blood Ulmer, the former Labelle vocalist turned activist Nona Hendryx and, ultimately, the Minneapolis Sound pioneered at Paisley Park by Prince.

Mabry was intrigued by how the blues had begat rock 'n' roll and could sit for hours exchanging minutiae with old blues legends. Her interests were in many respects a reconnection with her infancy when she'd fallen in love with the hardcore blues played on her grandmother's farm. She felt there was a gap in the market for a bold and sexually alluring black woman to align herself with the gut-bucket R&B sound and the music of seemingly 'dangerous' women like Willie Mae Thornton and her storming original version of 'Hound Dog' or Ruth Brown's '(Mama) He Treats Your Daughter Mean' or Big Maybelle's 'Whole Lotta Shakin' Goin On'. Mabry wanted to be all of them, only sexier. The legacy of strong, opinionated and sexually self-confident female singers came to shape the attitudes of her generation. Nona Hendryx of Labelle was especially proud of the role her group had played in disrupting black music. She told *Vanity Fair*: 'We were a mixture of rock, funk, R&B, gospel. To us, "Lady Marmalade" was dance music, club music. At that time, though, for a girl group to sing about a prostitute and a john . . . well, it wasn't "Baby Love".'

The twenty-year age difference between Mabry and her famous husband invited gossip and speculation, leading inevitably to claims of gold-digging and, more accurately, that Mabry had married Miles Davis to elevate her status in New York's bitterly jealous musical scene. The truth was more subtle. While Mabry was always anxious to progress, she had truly fallen in love with Davis, and was attracted to his unorthodox creativity, his compelling personality and energy, and his at times messianic belief in his own ability. In the spring of 1969 he was appearing at Club Baron on Lenox Avenue with Lou Donaldson. Richard Cook, the venerable jazz critic, writing in the *Guardian*, described Miles Davis as the last grand jazz star. 'His voice is a legendary rasp: words come out in a long guttural cough. When he laughs, it's like a gargle in the throat. When he smiles, which is rarely, he frowns, too. His eyes are mild but unbearably penetrating . . . He is the last, grandest and most imperious figure from a jazz tradition . . . The

Prince of Darkness, the little organizer, the cat everybody knows by one name – Miles.' It was the Prince of Darkness who Mabry married and, ultimately, it was his darkness that would push her away. John Ballon, writing in the crate-digger's bible *Wax Poetics*, has claimed that 'while the marriage only lasted a year Betty's impact on the immortal jazz trumpeter was tremendous . . . Her cutting-edge musical style was too much for Miles to resist.'

Since his infancy listening to jazz on a show called *Harlem Rhythms*, broadcast by the St Louis radio station WWIL, Davis was convinced of the unique place Harlem occupied in the story of black music and he was adamant that the place's relationship with jazz kept him youthful and curious. He moved there for the first time in 1944, in the early days of the bebop revolution, when his new wife was not yet born. He rented a room at 147th and Broadway and, according to his biographer Ian Carr, spent his first month in Harlem on a series of late-night odysseys hunting down his hero Charlie Parker. By the end of the first month, Parker had moved into the same rooming-house as Davis at a time that would be pivotal for Davis and for jazz. 'Miles was extremely fortunate in being able to spend his most formative period in the close company of the fountainhead of the new music,' Carr claims, '. . . and he flung himself into a regime of study that was both exhausting and schizophrenic.' By day he studied musical theory at the Juilliard School and by night he would be in the heartland of Harlem's new jazz scene, bebop citadels such as Minton's Playhouse on 118th or Clark Monroe's Uptown House on West 134th Street.

Harlem's status as the urban home of jazz was captured in the iconic photograph of the front stoop of an apartment block at 17 East 126th Street between Fifth and Madison. It was here in August 1958 that Art Kane, a freelance designer working for *Esquire* magazine, took the black-and-white shot now known as 'A Great Day in Harlem'. Fifty-seven of the great jazz musicians of the era gathered together on the steps of a local brownstone. What was remarkable about the photograph was that Kane was not a photographer, had no equipment of his own and had never taken a professional photograph in his life. He had brainstormed the idea with staff at *Esquire*, and the features editor Harold Hayes contacted the eminent jazz writer Nat Hentoff, who leant on some of the big names to show up. According to an account of the day in the magazine *All About Jazz*, 'notices were put up in all the jazz clubs, and at the Musicians' Union Local 802 office, announcing that the photo shoot was scheduled for ten o'clock on the morning of 12 August 1958'. Whether the timing was foolish or plain ambitious is a moot point, but fifty-seven musicians did indeed turn up, some of them directly from jam sessions or after-hours drinking bouts. The location was chosen for both aesthetic and practical purposes. The stoop allowed the musicians to be banked up in rows and to occupy sloping walls down to the sidewalk, but its real attraction was its closeness to the subway, and to what was then the New York Central Railroad, which had a nearby station at 125th and Park, allowing jazz musicians to travel north from Greenwich Village and the clubs along 52nd Street. One of the musicians answering the call was saxophonist Sonny Rollins, who was twenty-seven years old at the time and already an acclaimed jazz artist. Rollins had grown up in central Harlem and attended P.S. 89 on 135th Street. 'All of the black musicians lived in Harlem, it was the only place you could live,' said Rollins. 'Harlem was the place . . . It was quite a community.' Among the greats who turned up for the photo shoot were Thelonious Monk, Charles Mingus and Lester Young. Onlooker Michael Lipskin was only fifteen when the photograph was taken, and he later joined RCA where he produced Sam Cooke's posthumous album *The Man Who Invented Soul* (1968). He has since told jazz journalist Ian Patterson that the photograph was important in another key respect. 'It cut across jazz idioms, it was sort of like a history of jazz right there . . . That's why there is tremendous significance in the picture – it's not just that it was probably the largest number of jazz musicians ever photographed at once, I think it was also the musical diversity.'

What is rarely noted about the photograph are the absences. Louis Armstrong and Duke Ellington failed to show, Miles Davis was on tour in the Midwest, and Charlie Parker was already dead. Davis's relationship with Parker, at times reckless and addictive, was a harbinger of the creative energies he found in his marriage to Betty Mabry. *NME* editor Neil Spencer, writing for the *Guardian*, has since claimed that in the years before he met Mabry, Davis was running out of gas. 'At forty-one years of age, the crown prince of jazz had unaccountably slipped behind the beat of the times. He and his quintet still held court at New York's Village Gate and were still making albums of poise and invention such as *Miles Smiles* (1966) and *Sorcerer* (1967), but for a new generation weaned on Motown and Black Power, Davis and his music were suddenly *passé*.' Davis had became painfully aware of his own sense of stagnation and in his autobiography admitted that he 'wasn't prepared to be a memory yet'.

Although Davis furiously refuted it, Mabry dragged him out of the trough. She bought up piles of new records, force-feeding him the music of Sly and the Family Stone and insisting that historic jazz be banned from their household to be replaced with Hendrix, Cream and the like. 'Over the next two years, he would pull off a breathtaking act of reinvention,' Spencer wrote, 'disbanding his lauded quintet in favour of electrically charged line-ups using two drummers, two bass players and two, even three, keyboards.' It was an era of exploration that had Mabry's influence stamped on almost everything he did: his stage attitude, his style and, most of all, his albums. In February 1969, as their relationship lurched from all-possessing love to deep and at times abusive disagreements, Davis's Columbia album *Filles De Kilimanjaro* hit the stores. It contained a sixteen-minute track 'Mademoiselle Mabry'. The cover sleeve was a stunning shot of Mabry, with two abstract images of her face blurrily overlaid. It abandoned the familiar tropes of the jazz album – the musician photographed in a chiaroscuro nightclub setting – and screamed of modern catwalk fashion. It held out a generous hand to soul music, which was grasped by Donny Hathaway.

His transformative single 'The Ghetto' was blazing a trail for the new soul jazz and he was by now deeply immersed in recording his solo album *Everything Is Everything*, which included the Christian eulogy 'Thank You Master (For My Soul)', the party-funk song 'Sugar Lee', which features almost every musical trope that hip-hop never invented, the poverty-soul Harlem-inspired song 'Trying Times', and a stunning version of the Nina Simone Black

Power anthem 'Young Gifted And Black'. What was invisible to Hathaway's growing army of fans was a deeply embedded message in the title track, 'Voices Inside (Everything Is Everything)'. On the surface it is a fairly conventional jazz-funk instrumental with rap, but the reference to 'voices inside' was the first worrying sign of auditory hallucinations. Hathaway's mental illness had been diagnosed as paranoid schizophrenia. In 1969 'paranoid schizophrenia' was a relatively new diagnostic term; it had only entered the vocabulary of American psychiatry in the *Diagnostic and Statistical Manual of Mental Disorders* the previous year.

By 1970 Mabry's influence on jazz and funk-rock had reached its peak. *Bitches Brew*, a title she came up with, revealed a new Miles Davis, a man comfortable with electrification and wise to the shifting sounds of Harlem street funk and alternative rock. The era of fusion and jazz-funk had not just arrived, it had swaggered into New York life with all the fabulous arrogance of innovation, hammered down the doors of tradition and opened up a new chapter in the story of uptown music. 'I know the music I played in the house influenced him a lot,' said Mabry in an article in the *San Francisco Chronicle*. 'I was listening to Jimi Hendrix and Sly Stone and Otis Redding.' Her passion for the rough blues of her childhood and the emergent psychedelic sounds of the late sixties electrified Davis but brought him into a conflict with tradition similar to that which had beset Bob Dylan a few years earlier. In July 1965 Dylan played an electric folk set at the Newport Jazz Festival and sections of the audience booed him. Folk traditionalists across Europe were up in arms and turned his concerts into public protests. Among jazz aficionados, Davis's reinvention was similarly unpalatable, but while some tried to turn back the hands of time, others seized the day. The pianist in Davis's 'Second Great Quintet', Herbie Hancock, welcomed change with the same innovative zeal as Betty Mabry. He embarked on his own prodigious career both as a bandleader and soloist, blazing a trail for jazz-funk and electrifying almost every aspect of instrumentation, including the vocoder – the encoder that synthesises the human voice and that gave such distinction to his international jazz-funk classic 'I Thought It Was You' (1978).

Harking back to his childhood in East St Louis, Davis claimed that his most profound influence was his own past. In his autobiography he cites 'roadhouse music, or what some call honky-tonk . . . that shit that they play in black "bucket of blood" clubs . . . the fights that were likely to jump off in those clubs . . . I was trying to play the music I grew up on now, that roadhouse, honky-tonk, funky thing that people used to dance to on Friday and Saturday nights . . . It has to get down inside your body, up into your blood before you can do it correctly.'

Jazz-funk began to enter musical terminology in large part thanks to Davis and Mabry, but it was not only their domain. Among the many in-demand artists performing in jazz clubs in Harlem, who were simultaneously absorbing the street funk out in the ghetto, were Roy Ayers, Lonnie Liston Smith and George Benson (like Mabry, a precociously gifted musician from the steeltown regions of Pennsylvania). Benson was born and raised in Pittsburgh's Hill District, to a mother who was only fifteen years old. It was a jazz stronghold that the Harlem Renaissance poet Claude McKay had once described as 'the crossroads of the world'. Benson began busking at neighbourhood stores with his ukulele and then as an eight-year-old guitar prodigy playing illegally in unlicensed nightclubs. After a period in juvenile detention he graduated from high school and joined one of Brother Jack McDuff's many line-ups, replacing Kenny Burrell as the featured guitarist.

Benson described his move to Harlem in an interview he gave to the *Yorkshire Post*. 'When I put together my first band – I was twenty-two years old – the man we now call Dr Lonnie Smith, he was a new organist from Buffalo, New York, I went and picked him up with the organ with a trailer on the back of my car and we went off to New York City, the Big Apple. We had a manager who promised us that he would find us work and he did, so our career started there.' By 1967 Benson was a solo artist and a bandleader. The eminent jazz label Prestige released his debut album, which they grandly called *The New Boss Guitar Of George Benson*. It was the baptism of a significant new talent. Legend has it that Benson was 'discovered' in 1965 at Harlem's Palm Café by talent scout and Columbia Records producer John Hammond. He certainly played there, but he was also a regular at Showman's Jazz Club on 125th Street at St Nicholas Avenue, and anyone with a pulse in Harlem was tipping him for future stardom. In January 1968 Miles Davis tracked him down to play guitar on a track, 'Paraphernalia', on his album *Miles In The Sky*. Benson was inundated with recording opportunities but spent several hectic years simply trying to survive, hustling shows where he would be paid cash on the night and playing solo where he could to avoid the cost of a band. Many years later, when he was the world's best known jazz guitarist, he admitted, 'I sell more records now in a day than I did in five years.'

By the spring of 1969, over three intensive studio sessions at the Van Gelder Studio in Englewood Cliffs, New Jersey, Benson recorded his *Tell It Like It Is* album, which, like *Bitches Brew*, pointed forward to a soul-jazz fusion that became known as jazz-funk. To hedge his commercial bets, Benson included some cover versions of major soul sounds of the time, including Booker T. and the M.G.'s' 'Soul Limbo', Aaron Neville's 'Tell It Like It Is', Stevie Wonder's 'My Cherie Amour' and Wilson Pickett's 'Land Of 1,000 Dances'. It was a self-conscious meeting of jazz and soul that sought to reach the popular audiences who shopped in the storefronts along 125th Street. A mixture of coincidence and the need for cash brought him into the orbit of some of Harlem's least trustworthy operators. Paul Winley, the owner of the record store Winley Records, had come to the area from Washington DC at the height of the fifties doo-wop boom and broken into the industry by releasing several records by the Jesters, a harmony group from Harlem's Cooper Junior High School. They were a group who lived the doo-wop myth, singing by night beneath the elevated train tracks on the covered corners of 120th Street. Winley formed a writing partnership with organist Dave 'Baby' Cortez, and for most of the mid sixties they hustled songs from the edges of the uptown soul scene. Like Fat Jack Taylor's Rojac Records, success was elusive, but they persevered, often employing deceptive tactics to lure record buyers, for instance, using already half-familiar names such as the Paragons, the Tornados and the Blazers. Sometimes they simply stole the names of existing bands to reel in the naïve; more often than not it was Cortez and a few hired guns working under pseudonyms. By 1965 Cortez had signed a questionable contract with the mob-controlled Roulette Records, but it was a musical reworking of the old saying – thick as thieves. Cortez was moonlighting up in Harlem with Paul Winley, and plans were afoot to record a compilation album for which they needed a guitarist. Cortez made enquiries and approached the cash-strapped George Benson. It was the beginning of a legal nightmare that was to rumble on well into the eighties, by which time Benson would be an international superstar and Winley's daughter Tanya would be driving her father to reissue old funk tracks to feed the burgeoning hip-hop scene and its insatiable appetite for old breaks.

When Benson turned up for the recording session he was paid cash in hand and given instructions by Cortez. The recording sessions were haphazard and rushed, and Benson recalls them as a simple series of jazz-funk and soul grooves he played in inter-play with Cortez's lead keyboards. The saxophonist Willis Jackson, an old comrade from Benson's days in the Jack McDuff Band, was there too, but it is not clear whether he came with Benson or was hired independently by Winley and Cortez. The bassist was another Harlem character, the busker Sterling 'Mister Satan' Magee, who had once had a promising career with the up-tempo R&B song 'Keep On' (1965) on the Harlem-based indie Sylvia Records. However, times were tough, and Magee could make more money as a street artist performing outside Winley's record store on 125th Street than he ever could through royalties. The coins tossed in his guitar case earned him more than any recording contract.

Nothing much came of the sessions and the tapes disappeared into a drawer in Winley's record store – until Benson's career took off. In 1976 Winley went about an outrageous scam. He took the original masters into the studio and dubbed erotic voices over the top of what were instrumental tracks. He rebranded the freelance studio musicians as the Harlem Underground and implied that their leader was George Benson. The deception went deeper. He printed up albums entitled *Erotic Moods* by George Benson and the Harlem Underground Band, with tacky covers variously showing a prominent profile picture of Benson and, in another variation, an image of a limousine driving through Harlem with Benson's name emblazoned on the front. The album was promoted as being an 'XXX Rated New L.P. and Single'. Winley's wife, the soul singer Anne Winley, added much of the sexual moaning, and on one specific track – the underground phenomenon 'Smokin Cheeba Cheeba' – Winley dubbed on drug-deal conversations, street-hustler lingo and references to mojo and marijuana. For George Benson and his management it was flagrant fraud but for others it was a masterclass in soul music manipulation. The song itself was a crude sample of Muddy Waters' 'Hoochie Coochie Man' and begat a whole host of future samplers, including Boogie Down Productions, DMX, Strong Arm Steady and Amy Winehouse, and provided the inspiration for Tone Loc's old-school hip-hop version 'Cheeba Cheeba' (1989).

Benson was enraged when he saw the rip-off album. He felt it undermined his reputation by overtly promoting sex and drugs. More importantly, he argued that a brief freelance studio session under makeshift conditions was now being falsely touted as his work. In the US District Court for the Southern District of New York, Benson's legal team argued that the many misrepresentations on the LP could 'cause irreparable injury to Benson's professional and personal reputation'. They further argued that the scam album was 'much less sophisticated in style than that which has engendered Benson's fame. People induced to buy the album, lured by the expectation of enjoying Benson's unique flavor, may be disappointed in the style and contents, and thus be deterred from purchasing future releases with Benson as star performer.' Benson's injunction was granted and Winley was instructed to withdraw the record from sale and pulp any existing copies. It was in many respects a pyrrhic victory. By 1978, when the injunction was finally in place, Winley had already sold the record to shops across the Five Boroughs and did precious little to retrieve them. And they had already leaked out to the first generation of hip-hop DJs – Afrika Bambaataa, DJ Kool Herc and Grandmaster Flash, who seized the rich promise of the track known as 'Cheeba Cheeba'.

As Benson's fortunes soared and the era of jazz-funk came in earnest, technology was changing music and New York was witnessing an era of disruptive musical change. The city's boundless venues were giving voice to new creative forms. Each weekend became a showcase of reckless diversification and Betty Mabry – focusing on her own career or, more accurately, on her own image – soaked up the influences. Rock music's counterculture was at its height. Janis Joplin, the Mothers of Invention, Ten Years After, Vanilla Fudge and Procol Harum all performed at Bob Graham's Fillmore East, in a converted Yiddish theatre, in the Lower East Side. Jeff Beck and psychedelic soul pioneers Sly and the Family Stone, en route to Woodstock, were performing at the Westbury Music Fair in Jericho, Long Island, in what was once an old abandoned lime pit refashioned as a tented outdoor theatre. Back in Manhattan, the Temptations and Gladys Knight and the Pips were in concert at Madison Square Garden and the venue would play host to the New York leg of the now infamous Rolling Stones tour of America, which the rock critic Robert Christgau described as 'history's first mythic rock and roll tour'. Although the term had yet to be coined, it was the early days of stadium rock and a new grandiosity that would inspire the progressive rock movement. Jazz was being reimagined, too. Art Blakey and Freddie Hubbard were performing at the embattled Columbia University, still a hive of student protest; Herbie Hancock and the as yet unknown George Benson were sharing a stage at the Village Vanguard; and Yusef Lateef, the multi-instrumentalist, was playing in Alphabet City, in a rundown Ukrainian bar called Slugs in the Far East. In his revealing obituary of Lateef, the writer and comedian Peter Keepnews claimed that he 'played world music before world music had a name'.

As Betty Mabry moved daily from Harlem to the Village – from the Cellar soul club to bohemian coffee bars, and from Wilhelmina fashion shoots to backstage parties and decadent opening nights, her path overlapped with a young woman on a very different mission. Jane Alpert had just returned from England where she had jettisoned the chance of a permanent job at Cambridge University Press, preferring to make her mark as a journalist in the new underground. She planned to work for the newspapers that had sprung up with the anti-war movement. Her ambition took her to a loft on East 14th Street and the quixotic offices of *Rat*

Subterranean News, the countercultural newspaper. Just as Mabry had immersed herself in soul music, street style and nightlife, so Alpert had become consumed by radical politics. She met her boyfriend Sam Melville at a Gym Crow protest at Columbia University, and moved downtown to Alphabet City where she became a significant contributor to *Rat Subterranean News* (commonly known as *Rat*), along with cartoonist Robert Crumb and writers William Burroughs and Kurt Vonnegut.

Rat was edited downtown but had a keen eye on the politics of Harlem, giving voice to the rights of minority communities, proselytising on behalf of the twenty-one jailed Panthers, fundraising to support their defence, and commissioning articles from one of the group's leaders, Afeni Shakur. *Rat* was never a soul music paper, but its strident support for sexual liberation and ghetto politics meant that some of the best coverage of black music and the rock-soul fusion was found in its pages, including a daring cover story called 'Shout It Loud I'm Black And Proud' – ostensibly a review of a James Brown show at the Apollo but in fact an essay in support of the politics of Black Power. *Rat* was passionate about causing trouble and was the source of the virulent 'Paul Is Dead' rumour that swept Manhattan in 1969. The rumour claimed that Paul McCartney had been replaced in the Beatles by a cloned lookalike after a fatal car crash, a calumny that played to widespread paranoia about scheming corporations and media distortion.

By the spring of 1969 Alpert had become a regular contributor, drawn in part because *Rat* had enraged her old university when it ran with a provocative cover story criticising the academic land grab on Harlem. The front cover showed a Nazi helmet sitting arrogantly atop the Columbia University Library under the headline 'Heil Columbia'. Journalism was her day job, but by night she had become embroiled in an underground plot to plant bombs in the offices of companies that supported the war effort in Vietnam. In early 1969 she had made reservations under the name of 'Peter Dufay', for two passengers to travel from La Guardia Airport to Miami on an Atlantic Airlines flight. The reservation was part of an escape plan Alpert and Melville had hatched to assist two wanted Québécois terrorists on the run from the Canadian authorities.

Once on board, the nationalists hijacked the flight. It was diverted to Cuba where the men claimed political asylum.

This would prove to be a life-defining year for Alpert. She shared Mabry's lust for the new and took risks that even the most adventurous young women of her generation would have shied away from. Although the term was yet to be in widespread use, they were different threads of what would soon become known as the feminist movement: Mabry developing a bold musical career, and Alpert pursuing radical journalism and street politics. At *Rat* she became one of its most accomplished writers, with a flair for classic investigative journalism as well as angry polemic. One article she wrote was a close-up critique of conditions at the Women's House of Detention, where the Black Panthers Afeni Shakur and Joan Bird were incarcerated. The male Black Panthers had been deliberately kept apart and scattered across facilities in New York State. Michael Tabor had been taken from the Tombs Detention Centre to Rikers Island, where he stayed in a crowded cell, counting the jets overhead and devouring law books in order to understand the charges against him and plan his defence.

Alpert's feature proved to be a prescient piece of journalism. Within a matter of months she, too, would be in the Women's House of Detention, accused of aiding and abetting her partner's bombing campaign in Midtown Manhattan. In her autobiography, *Growing Up Underground*, Alpert described her imprisonment in all its bleak detail. 'A few minutes later,' she wrote, 'my own breakfast was pushed through a slot in my cell. A matron yelled through the opening: I was to clean my cell and get dressed before she returned for the empty tray . . . I looked at the food: gluey oatmeal and a liquid that I supposed was meant to be coffee. I scraped the food into the toilet. Then, after rinsing my lenses under the tap, I inserted them. The cell leaped into focus fouler than I had imagined. By squeezing myself in a corner, I could see the shops of Greenwich Avenue through the barred windows. In the corner of the cell someone had left a pencil stub. I picked it up and inscribed on the wall one of the Panthers' slogans: "Put the pigs in the pokey and the people on the streets." It reassured me to see the militant phrase there, reminding me who I was.'

Meanwhile Mabry's career was gathering its own furious pace. She was writing songs that were provocative and sexually confident, and often from a woman's perspective. Her failing marriage to Miles Davis ended in 1969 by mutual discontent. Davis claimed in his biography that he suspected she was having an affair with Jimi Hendrix, an accusation she has consistently denied. Mabry has since claimed that it was Davis's possessiveness that drove them apart. 'He was afraid that I would leave him if I became famous,' she alleged. 'He had that kind of fear about me . . . It fell apart because of his temper. He would get physical sometimes and I didn't want to be caught in an abusive relationship. That just wasn't my style.'

Hendrix's relationship with Mabry has always been a double-edged sword, lending her life sexual intrigue but also engulfing her in the gossipy and at time malicious world of the groupie, a term that across time has been debased to the point of misogyny. Mabry was a close personal friend of one of Hendrix's many girlfriends, the glamorous and tragic model Devon Wilson, a girl from Milwaukee who had been a teenage prostitute and a sex worker at the Playboy Club. She died in suspicious circumstances at the notorious Chelsea Hotel, with a syringe in her arm. Wilson's love life was crowded, complicated and almost certainly obscured by her own exaggerations; she claimed to have slept with Brian Jones of the Rolling Stones and then Mick Jagger, and by 1969 she was living intermittently with Hendrix, whose many biographers claim that she was the subject of the Hendrix track 'Dolly Dagger'. Wilson was reputedly in the control room when it was recorded. The song depicts her all-consuming sexuality and paints a portrait of a woman who was both magnetic and menacing. It was Wilson – beautiful and always sporting a eye-catching afro – who many, then and since, have mistaken for Mabry. The last photograph to be taken of Davis and Mabry together was hurriedly snapped by a news photographer on Seattle's Rainier Avenue as they entered Dunlap Baptist Church for the funeral service of Jimi Hendrix. Mabry was wearing sunglasses and a widow's veil, clutching Davis's arm, while Wilson was dressed casually in a mini-skirt and striped top. It is not entirely clear who was the closest to Hendrix.

By 1969 it was possible to see yet another strand of new music emerging. The husband-and-wife team Ike and Tina Turner had been chosen as the opening act for the Rolling Stones tour of America, which included two nights at Madison Square Garden. The tour gave new and distinct prominence to Tina, who made the cover of *Rolling Stone* but had yet to escape from her own nightmare of domestic violence and carve out a solo career. Like Mabry, and the R&B-fixated Janis Joplin, Tina Turner had a powerful throaty voice and a primal appeal to rock audiences – assertive, taboo-busting and unashamedly sexual, she gave life to a style of flint-hard R&B which rock critics droolingly described as 'raunchy'.

Funk, rock and jazz were colliding. Jimi Hendrix had been sporadically part of all their lives since returning to Harlem in the spring of 1969. He shared an apartment with the Allen twins in Manhattan's Park West Village near Columbia University, premises that had almost certainly been bought by Fat Jack Taylor from the proceeds of his heroin business. A photograph shows Hendrix with the Allen boys and another of his girlfriends, Faye Pridgon, eating waffles at a famous Harlem hotspot – Wells Chickens and Waffles. Pridgon was one of Fat Jack's circle at Rojac and knew him through a mutual friendship with Etta James. In the now hyped-up biography of the 'groupie', she claims to have lost her virginity to Sam Cooke and has since told the *Guardian* newspaper that she was 'probably among the first liberated, modern-day black females'. Hendrix saw Faye as his Harlem girl. He kept a snapshot of them together outside the Apollo Theater and wrote the song 'Foxy Lady' in her honour.

Mabry knew Hendrix fairly well, too, but she has always bristled at any suggestion that they were romantically linked and refused to be stereotyped as one of his groupies, claiming it was all in the mind of her former husband. 'Well, Miles got older,' she told the *Telegraph* newspaper, 'and you know when you get older, you start hallucinating and imagining things.' That said, she did rack up several lovers in the music industry, including Eric Clapton and Santana's Puerto Rican conga player Michael Carabello, but neither relationship lasted long, and by the end of 1969 the relationship with Davis ended in a Mexican-style divorce. Mabry has claimed that a deal was struck with Columbia Records to record her as a solo artist. Studios were booked, a band was hired which included Wayne Shorter, Billy Cox and Mitch Mitchell (then Hendrix's drummer) and tracks were laid, but the divorce put paid to her debut album. Davis stopped its progress and Columbia seized the tapes.

Undeterred, Mabry continued to write and hunt down publishing deals, helped by Marc Bolan then of psychedelic rock band Tyrannosaurus Rex, whom she met at Café Au Go-Go during their disastrous tour of America in August 1969. Bolan was not yet the glam-rock star of T. Rex fame but he had useful publishing contacts with Essex Publishing in the UK and Richmond House in the USA, and with the producer Tony Visconti. Mabry was simultaneously working on her own material and an album of demos for the Commodores, the graduate band from Tuskegee Institute, who had relocated to New York and had a single-only deal with Atlantic. Mabry's demo album helped them to secure a deal with Motown, although she herself lost out, declining an offer to have her songs managed by Jobete, the all-powerful Motown publishing arm, arguing that she wanted control over her own songs. The *San Francisco Chronicle* saw it as a statement of her fierce independence. 'She walked away from a contract with Motown (and took her songs back from the Commodores) when the company demanded she give up her publishing rights. Although she had been linked to male stars, she wanted to be recognized for her own talents and to retain control of her music. "I didn't want it to be commercialized, really," she says. "I wanted to have a certain kind of purity."'

Paradoxically, for all Mabry's visibility in New York, San Francisco proved to be easier to crack. She signed a deal with Woodstock promoter Michael Lang's Just Sunshine Records, who simultaneously signed the Voices of East Harlem choir. A two-album deal was struck for the eponymous *Betty Davis* (1973) and *They Say I'm Different* (1974). It was agreed in a typically counter-cultural way – at a vegetarian Thanksgiving dinner in 1972. Mabry of course delivered on her promise. Through her boyfriend Michael Carabello, she hired the drummer of Sly and the Family Stone, Greg Errico, as her producer and their master bassist, Larry Graham.

Carabello assembled what he called 'a who's-who list of great musicians in the Bay Area at that time', including the Pointer Sisters and the rhythm section of Tower of Power.

Mabry's style was so far ahead of its time, she probably suffered. Ricky Vincent, the DJ at Radio Station KPFA and author of *Party Music: The Inside Story of the Black Panthers' Band*, looked back on Mabry's career: 'She looked like Beyoncé, she sang like Macy Gray on steroids, and she crafted her own brand of liberated black womanhood.' Her devotees in the world of underground music have frequently used the term 'liberated funk' to describe these sexually ambiguous and challenging songs that predated Madonna by two decades. 'Anti-Love Song' (1973) certainly challenged the pop certainties. It was soul, but then again it wasn't. She was disrupting the genre with hard-boiled rock and provocative lyrics. Another track, 'Stepping In Her I. Miller Shoes', was a requiem to her dead friend Devon Wilson. Wilson was known for her taste in expensive and flamboyant shoes, always designed by Israel Miller. The Jewish shoe designer claimed that he had built his business I. Miller & Sons into an $8,000,000 company from a single dollar he found on a street corner on Manhattan's Union Square. Miller was the forerunner of Jimmy Choo and Christian Louboutin in that he designed shoes for the glamorous urban elite, and in 1969, when Mabry and Wilson were the most talked-about black women in New York, his shoes were their first choice. On the album track 'He Was A Big Freak', Mabry sang about a man who enjoyed being whipped with a turquoise chain, an unintentional evocation of the musical imagination of funk superstar Prince, who Mabry resembled in many ways. Her album covers were truly astonishing, combining her fashion education and provocative sexuality with images of her in denim shorts and silver thigh-high boots, soft-porn suspenders and satin knickers, and, in one prescient photo shoot, in a zebra-skin bathing suit sitting astride a gleaming Harley-Davidson. It was a strident look, one that appears eerily like the album cover for Prince's *Purple Rain*, not released until ten years later. Without question, the Mabry song that caused the greatest controversy at the time was 'Don't Call Her No Tramp' (1974), a fearless defence of sexually liberated black women.

The culturally conservative National Association for the Advancement of Colored Peoples (NAACP) agitated for a radio ban, arguing that the song demeaned black women and glamourised prostitution. Mabry refused to back down and told her critics, 'The song is advancing my life and I'm colored.'

By the end of the seventies, and a decade of pursuing her right to record soul and blistering hardcore rock-funk, Mabry made the decision to disappear. She told one journalist that she 'just lost interest'. It was almost certainly more complex than that, but without bothering to throw a going-away party, she quietly returned to the Rust Belt area of her childhood and spent much of her later adult life nursing her ailing parents. According to Sly and the Family Stone's Greg Errico: 'She disappeared for years and years . . . First time I talked to her, she had really seemed like she had come out of some deep, serious seclusion. Very soft-spoken. She wasn't the same person.'

Mabry's low-key departure from the music scene was in marked contrast to her arrival. She had moved to Harlem as an imposing teenager – beautiful enough to become a top model, tall enough to tower over her many boyfriends, and self-confident enough to blaze a trail in the recording industry – and within a year was being talked about as a pioneer in the crossfire of funk, rock and psychedelic soul. While many of her fellow-models at the Wilhelmina Agency insisted on lipstick, make-up and hairspray, Mabry was confident about her looks and relaxed about her heritage, appearing entirely 'natural' in an industry obsessed with artifice.

This attitude echoed changes in the ghetto streets, not just on the pages of glamour magazines. From the mid sixties onwards, the afro style was visible on street corners, in nightclubs and backstage at soul concerts. Even the Supremes eventually ditched their lacquered beehives and embraced the afro. The cover of their 1968 album *Love Child* hinted for the first time that the Motown Corporation was loosening its once vice-like grip over appearance. Berry Gordy in particular was reluctant to allow Diana Ross to abandon her glittering Las Vegas ball gowns for street style. But *Love Child* shows Ross skulking in a Detroit doorway, sporting a fringed denim mini-skirt, canary-yellow sweatshirt and afro. Soul music became a publicity machine for the hairstyle, as both the famous and the unknown embraced the new look. One of the most talented singers on the Los Angeles indie soul circuit, the mercurial Ty Karim, was an early adopter of the afro. She frequently appeared on stage and in photo shoots with a full-blown natural afro, and paid tribute to the new street look in 'Wear Your Natural, Baby', recorded under the pseudonym of Towana and the Total Destruction. The afro – or what was also known as natural style – was a hairstyle groomed without the need for coconut pomade, processing or artificial gels. It ceased to be just a fashion statement and became a sign of liberation. It was a look that broke out of urban neighbourhoods, first through street style, but was unquestionably helped on its way by the rise of the Black Panthers and the coverage they generated in the press and network news programmes. By 1969 the afro had become a metaphor for black pride, a gesture of unabashed self-awareness, and, for many, a refusal to conform to the demands of white American fashions. Betty Mabry had pioneered the style on the pages of *Ebony* and *Jet* magazine years before and it would hang around during the seventies as the culture of ghetto-fabulous came to influence the last bastion of white control – Hollywood.

Comedian Godfrey Cambridge on the set of *Cotton Comes to Harlem*. The 1969 comedy action movie, shot on location in Harlem, was a forerunner of *Super Fly* and the blaxploitation film genre.

MAY

Freddie's Dead

He had the voice of a baritone and the grace of a gifted cabaret singer, but Ossie Davis never sang for his supper. By the late spring of 1969, he was one of the most respected and recognisable actors in Harlem and about to embark on his first project as a film director. Davis's reputation had soared since 27 February 1965, the day he delivered a powerful eulogy at the funeral of Malcolm X, held in the Childs Memorial Temple Church of God in Christ. He took to the stage of the converted old cinema still known locally as the Bluebird, framed by an old theatrical proscenium arch, and barely glanced at his handwritten notes on the pulpit. He had confided with his wife, Ruby Dee, that he would not look down at the congregation and he would partly memorise key sequences of his eulogy as if he was on stage at the Ambassador.

Light poured through the upper windows, and he could see below him a protective row of police officers guarding the main route through the congregation to the stage. In the front row, a man in a brilliant-white Arabic headdress stood erect. Next to him was an anonymous character in a sharp black suit wearing gloomy dark shades, and behind him were row upon row of men in overcoats, women in mink bucket hats, and men in starched collars. Gangsters, Muslim preachers and the ordinary folks of Harlem had come together to pay their last respects. Outside, wooden police barricades hemmed in the overspill crowds which snaked past the beauty salon and launderette next door all the way along Amsterdam Avenue. A camera crew were perched on the roof, hoping that something would spark which they could then rush back to the news desks for the evening editions. Despite the tense atmosphere and tin-can screeches of the external speaker system, Ossie Davis's voice flowed effortlessly over the heads of the crowd. He spoke with an actor's training and a preacher's self-confidence, as if everyone within miles of the church could bear witness to the body of Malcolm X. 'Here – at this final hour, in this quiet place – Harlem has bid farewell to one of its brightest hopes – extinguished now, and gone from us forever.' It was a eulogy rich in defiance as he addressed not only the crowds but the killers, too.

Malcolm X had been shot while speaking at a rally at the Audubon Ballroom in Washington Heights, and in the terrifying days before his death his home had been firebombed. As hundreds gathered to mourn his passing, there were fears of another bomb blast or revenge killings. The assembled mourners sat soothed and enraptured by Davis's mellifluous voice as he brought calm to the occasion. This, by his own reckoning, was his greatest ever performance, a Shakespearean panegyric to black activism. 'Consigning these mortal remains to earth, the common mother of all, secure in the knowledge that what we place in the ground is no more now a man – but a seed – which, after the winter of our discontent, will come forth again to meet us. And we will know him then for what he was and is – a Prince – our own black shining Prince! – who didn't hesitate to die, because he loved us so.'

By 1968 Davis was a towering Harlem personality. Throughout his life, people claimed to have heard his 'Black Prince' speech, even those who weren't there. Those who were there spoke of Davis not so much as an actor, but as the true voice of Harlem – his rich local baritone like Ben E. King with a poet's verse.

In an industry known for craven stereotypes and poorly realised characters, Davis was demanding change. He was meticulous about the roles he accepted and never agreed to anything until he had returned home to Harlem to discuss draft scripts with his equally talented wife Ruby Dee. The couple would argue into the night, balancing job offers, mindful of the money that the role would make for their family, careful of the impact it would have on their careers, and importantly, of how their decisions might help advance the cause of African-American talent. They had both agreed that Davis should take a pioneering role in *Bonanza*, a top-rating weekly series on network television, which offered him the opportunity to play the role of Sam Davis, the first black cowboy character on the show.

Ruby Dee came with her own authority. She had noticed a new trend emerging in low-budget cinema to which she had been a recent contributor. Troubled by rising costs, spectacular misfires and declining audiences, the film majors were desperate for new income streams and had identified 'urban' audiences as a potential new source of revenue. This was, in part, due to the spectacular success of their friend, the actor and activist Sidney Poitier, who had starred in the 1967 trilogy *To Sir with Love*, *In the Heat of the Night* and *Guess Who's Coming to Dinner*, but also the commercial success of ultra low-budget independent film *Uptight* (1968), which was soon followed by Melvin Van Peebles's short films in the late sixties and then by his breakthrough, *Sweet Sweetback's Baadasssss Song*, which came with a musical soundtrack released by Stax Records.

Uptight was a story of inner-city militancy directed by the blacklisted communist director Jules Dassin. Ruby Dee was his advisor, a scriptwriter and a leading actress. At her insistence, the film was set in the Cleveland ghettos of her childhood and took the unprecedented step of hiring soul musician Booker T. Jones of the Memphis studio group Booker T. and the M.G.'s to score the film. It was undoubtedly the Stax sound that gave the film its tense and driving urban mood. For the first time in its largely conservative history, the Hollywood studio system was showing interest in black subject matter. Films set in inner-city ghettos briefly became fashionable. The production had alerted the Davises to the emergence of a new subgenre of cinema, which the Motown executive and NAACP leader Junius Griffin dubbed 'blaxploitation'.

In the early days of 1969 Davis was flown to Hollywood by Formosa Productions, a new independent set up by Sam Goldwyn Jr, the son of the infamous Hollywood mogul. Goldwyn plied Davis with cocktails and tried to convince him to star in a film adaptation of the Chester Himes novel *Cotton Comes to Harlem*, suggesting he play the role of the detective, Coffin Ed Johnson. Davis prevaricated but agreed he would read the script and ensure that it passed the 'smell test' – that it sounded like a script authentic to contemporary Harlem. In the exchange that followed, it became clear that Davis was the ideal director, but he and his wife dragged their heels and made further stipulations: that the film be shot entirely in Harlem and that a visionary training programme be put in place to encourage local youngsters to learn a trade on set.

Harlem was an unlikely location for a new feature film but Davis was confident that his directorial debut could signal a new era in self-confidence. He turned down the offer to star in the film and cast the emerging Shakespearean actor Raymond St Jacques in the role of Coffin Ed alongside an already well-loved comedian, Godfrey Cambridge, as his sidekick Gravedigger Jones. The interiors were to be shot at Harlem's only film studio – Filmways, Inc. on 127th Street – and exterior crowd scenes were earmarked for an abandoned gas station at 128th and Lexington. Filming did not get off to a good start. Early in the shooting schedule, a group of teenagers fooling around on the rooftops at 153rd and Eighth Avenue threw a bottle down onto the set, which clattered on a script assistant, a young white girl fresh out of college. It was precisely the kind of rash incident that was likely to attract frenzied press coverage and allow the New York dailies to question the wisdom of shooting a film in Harlem. No one was seriously hurt, but to ensure that local teenagers were kept in line the production company signed an agreement with John Shabazz, a local activist and former bodyguard of Malcolm X, who had worked alongside undercover agent Eugene Roberts. He ran a community organisation, the Black Citizens Patrol, who wore black paramilitary-style outfits and had a reputation for confronting drug dealers and making citizens' arrests on young hoodlums caught breaking into cars. They would act as the security force. It was a rite of passage that subsequent film-makers would have to endure. The Harlem hustler Clarence 'Mookie' Jackson became a local collaborator for the film *Across 110th Street* and provided Harlem junkies as extras, as well as sourcing locations that would otherwise be out of bounds to film crews. Although the Black Citizens Patrol delivered on their promise of security, it was not an agreement that Davis was entirely comfortable with; their presence did little to alter the perception that Harlem was dangerous and only to be visited under guard.

Cotton Comes to Harlem was described by *The New York Times* as a knowingly humorous action picture – 'A James Bond with Soul'. More accurately, *The New Yorker* described it as a 'a slam-bang rip-roaring caper, a hilarious comedy about a con-man preacher'. Viewed more analytically, it was a satire on the history and myths of Harlem, with a cast of characters who were exaggerated versions of real people and historical figures. The main storyline concerned a dubious local minister, the Reverend Deke O'Malley, who is raising money for a ship called *The Black Beauty*. During a fundraising rally, masked gunmen alight from a meat truck and steal $87,000 in cash. Coffin Ed and Gravedigger Jones, the bungling detectives, are sent to investigate the crime. The key theme was obvious. Generations of rogues and self-appointed gurus had used religion, spiritual cures or glimpses of the Promised Land to con the gullible. The story satirises Marcus Garvey's Back to Africa movement aboard the ocean ship *Black Star Liner* and O'Malley's name points back to another massive character in Harlem street life: a charismatic Christian leader known simply as 'Father Divine'. Brazenly, the preacher – whose real (albeit self-appointed) name was Major Jealous Divine – claimed to be God but, despite much evidence to the contrary, his International Peace Mission Movement was in fact one of the most successful politico-religious organisations in Harlem throughout the thirties and forties.

When *Cotton Comes to Harlem* hit the screens it divided opinion. It was too close to light comedy for those who liked their social realism grittier and thought it wasn't 'angry enough' and too cheerful for those who considered Harlem the capital city of Black Power. Davis was never fully convinced of his directorial debut but he remained faithful to his own justification of the film in the summer of 1969: 'It's an entertainment,' he told one journalist. 'Black people outwit the establishment and stay one step ahead of the wolf's teeth.' In preparation for his role as Gravedigger Jones, Cambridge did tours of duty with the 28th Precinct Detective Squad in Harlem but refused to believe that a 'message film' would have been the right approach. 'They operate on a basic fallacy that you are going to get a bigot into the theater and convince him,' he remarked to journalists. Vincent Canby, the film critic of *The New York Times*, savaged the film – 'It's strictly for people who don't care much about movies – or who persist in regarding movies as sociology' – but audiences warmed to its feelgood drama.

To much surprise, despite its small production budget, the film was a phenomenal commercial success. United Artists released it as a mid budget multi-cast comedy, and against expectation it became the highest-grossing 'black' film ever, generating revenues of $115.4m within a year. Suddenly the chase was on. Hollywood had woken up to the potential of films set in the ghetto, new titles were green-lit, and films already in production were crudely adapted for black audiences. What Hollywood did not predict was that it was unlocking the conditions for a highly creative and socially persuasive form of soul music – soundtracks. Among the soundtracks that came to dominate soul culture in the years to come was Isaac Hayes's 'Theme From *Shaft*' from the album *Shaft*. It was an Oscar-winner in 1972 and an era-defining club record that helped to popularise funk. And Curtis Mayfield's soundtrack to the film *Super Fly* was that rare commodity – music that was more famous and critically respected than the film that gave it life.

In the summer of 1969 Davis had neither the budget nor the inclination to commission a fully fledged soundtrack. Ruby Dee had been instrumental in hiring Booker T. and the M.G.'s to score *Uptight* a year earlier, but the idea of combining soul music and films was still in its infancy. At the time, the only black artist who was in any way trained to lay back and synchronise film soundtracks was Quincy Jones, who in 1969 was working on the comedy-drama *Bob and Carol and Ted and Alice*. Even then it was a compilation of tunes set to images rather than a soundtrack. Jones and the film's director Paul Mazursky had included Jackie DeShannon's 'What

The World Needs Now' and a song from Jones's own vast jazz collection, Sarah Vaughan's 'I Know That My Redeemer Liveth'. Davis decided that, given his limited resources, he would pursue another strategy: he would build music into the storyline itself and create a live theatre show within the film. For Harlem, there was only one credible option – a concert at the Apollo. To play the role of an unnamed singer at the theatre, Davis cast the Harlem-born actress Melba Moore. She was gaining a reputation in large part due to her performance in the Broadway version of the counter-culture rock musical *Hair*, where she shared the stage with another soul singer, Ronnie Dyson, and was on the brink of major success. She had signed to the New York label Musicor in 1966 but her releases had vanished from sight, overshadowed by the success of the label's major star, Gene Pitney. Two of her recordings survived obscurity. The first was an up-tempo pop record in the familiar Motown style called 'Don't Cry Sing-A-Long With The Music'. While it languished in bargain bins in her native Harlem, it was bootlegged in Europe. Another, 'Magic Touch', had never been released and lay buried as a studio tape until many years later, when it was unearthed and became a cult record on the rare soul scene in the UK. Although both are decent enough, feelgood records, they were overshadowed by the brooding, racially subtle track 'Black Enough (Ain't Now But It's Gonna Be)', a song written for *Cotton Comes to Harlem* and one that stands out as exemplary soul.

The most elusive and amateur among the rush of new urban films that followed *Cotton Comes to Harlem* was one called *The Rip-Off*. It had been hatched in the Manhattan nightclub the Turntable, which was owned by veteran R&B star Lloyd Price. In 1959 Price's national hit 'Stagger Lee' did much to mythologise the ghetto pimp in pop culture and brought juke-joint music into the charts. Then semi-retired, Price had the notion to make a film and quickly called in favours from friends, some of whom were from the well-heeled gangster elite who frequented his venue. 'The idea was to get real, practicing gangsters to play themselves,' Price has since commented. 'We needed the villain romantic lead, the guy with the sable coat and the hat, so I thought, why not get Frank Lucas?' Lucas was one of Harlem's notorious characters, infamous for cutting out the Italian mafia and importing heroin directly from Thailand. According to Lucas, 'It was like *Shaft* before *Shaft*. All the cars in the picture were mine. We did a scene with me chasing Lloyd, shooting out the window of a Mercedes on the West Side Highway. I put seventy, eighty grand into the movie. It was real fun.' Despite the fun, the film was never completed, the rushes vanished, and it is now one of the great lost films of the urban genre, its gangster notoriety doubtless outweighing its quality.

However, one man from the Harlem netherworld had a lasting impact. The story of how Charles McGregor turned around his life to become the unlikely star of one of soul music's most influential records – 'Freddie's Dead (The Theme From Super Fly)' – is truly astonishing.

Charles McGregor was born to Jamaican immigrant parents in Harlem Hospital in 1922. He grew up against the backdrop of the Jazz Age and was already an unruly young boy when the Harlem Renaissance graced his neighbourhood. But neither music nor the arts had much influence on his deprived upbringing and McGregor's life was a tapestry of failure. He was excluded from a series of schools, taken into the care of youth services, and then drifted into a life of crime, running numbers games and selling heroin. His disciplinarian mother ruled the McGregor household like an Old Testament tyrant – using a clothes pin on his nose to make it look more 'white' – and did little to nurture his basic good nature and boisterous wit. By the time he enrolled at Harlem's P.S. 37 he was already a hardened street kid, lawless and difficult to manage. As a teenager, he became a member of the Buccaneers, a Harlem street gang who haunted the areas around 130th and Lenox, and with his gangster friends graduated to armed robbery. By sixteen he was a full-blown heroin addict. In his first court appearance he was dragged as part of a chain gang into the courthouse next to the Tombs Detention Complex in Manhattan and sentenced to five-to-ten, to be served in the maximum security prison of Sing Sing. In 1948, not long after his release, McGregor was charged with the armed robbery of a stationery store at 683 Lenox and was then accused of murdering a fruitseller opposite an all-night R&B club called the King and Queen on 135th Street.

Stripped of any real identity, he became Prisoner 108535, the title he used to correspond with the outside world, and his life was defined by three lengthy prison sentences. Within twelve months in 1958, his brother Roy was shot dead in a Harlem gang killing and his brother-in-law had succumbed to a heroin overdose. Much of his adult life was wasted in America's worst penitentiaries, including Green Haven Correctional Facility, the dark host to the electric chair known as 'Old Sparky', and Clinton Prison, which was nicknamed the 'Ice Box' and located in the snowbound village of Dannemora near the Canadian border. McGregor's raw autobiography *Up from the Walking Dead* lays bare a brutal prison system on the point of eruption and describes a man existing like one of the walking dead. Overcrowding, unsanitary conditions and internal feuds between rival gangs were commonplace. The system was overloaded by discriminatory penal policies which jailed young black and Puerto Rican men in disproportionate numbers, and McGregor described the absurdity of it all: 'Killers, rapists, bank robbers, swindlers, forgers, and muggers all hopping around the prison yard doing the "jerk", the "swim", the "mashed potato" . . . and the "monkey".' With the help of a Legal Aid lawyer, McGregor became a thorn in the side of the prison authorities, bombarding prominent politicians and newspaper editors with letters of complaint in which he railed against prison conditions and the circumstances of his own arrest and incarceration. He was one among many who predicted a dire future for the prisons of New York State. But by the time the worst riots erupted – at Attica State Prison in 1971, where ten staff and twenty-nine inmates died – McGregor had changed his life in the most dramatic way and was about to play an important role in the evolution of soul music.

Paroled in 1967, he was rejected by his mother and barred from her home until he was directed to a social services centre at 145th and Eighth Avenue. The sign on the window read 'Reality House – A Rehabilitation Project for Drug Addicts, Alcoholics and Emotionally Disturbed People'. It was an experimental programme which prepared inmates for life after prison, and it was McGregor's last hope. After twenty-seven years in prison he trained as a therapist and began to take on work as a jobbing actor.

One day in May 1969, documentary film-maker Robert Kaylor arrived at Reality House. He was looking to make a social action film about prison reform and wanted to focus on the innovative work the unit was doing in Harlem. McGregor became a key figure in the documentary and, despite a tiny budget, Kaylor completed a film, *Max-Out*, a fictionalised account of Harlem life. *Max-Out* followed the life of an ex-convict, Melvin River, who is conned in a craps game by a bar-room hustler, played by McGregor. The script was improvised as they shot, and in a crude version of method acting Kaylor coached the balding and burly McGregor to reach back to his young days as a numbers racketeer and bring a version of his criminal self to life. The experience ignited in McGregor a passion for the buzz of filmmaking, and he soon pursued work as an extra and a stuntman, eventually becoming a character actor in the burgeoning subgenre of urban films.

Curiously, it was McGregor, more than any musician, whose life paralleled the development of soul music and cinema. In 1971 he played a bar patron in *The French Connection*; a year later he played Fatback in *Come Back, Charleston Blue* (the sequel to *Cotton Comes to Harlem* which had a score by Donny Hathaway); and then a character called Chink in *Across 110th Street* (1972). Within a few years McGregor was living the life of a professional actor – busy with auditions, rehearsals and script readings. He then played a thinly veiled version of himself in *Hell Up in Harlem* (1973) and, in a memorable comic role, Charlie the cowboy in *Blazing Saddles* (1974). But by far the most important role he managed to secure, and one which became a landmark in soul music, was his portrayal of the drug dealer Fat Freddie in *Super Fly*, a role that was the catalyst for Curtis Mayfield's powerful tragi-soul song 'Freddie's Dead'. The song was released prior to the film and came to define Mayfield's influence on the fortunes of routine, if gritty, exploitation films. As he composed in his basement home in Chicago, Mayfield tried to find some humanity and common decency in a story of drugs and debauchery. He kept at the forefront of his mind a simple tragedy. 'You might not know a lot of pimps and drug dealers,' he told the journalist Michael Gonzalez, 'but we do meet quite a lot of Freddies.' Mayfield had seen in the character a flawed and intrinsically tragic everyman trapped by circumstances beyond his control, trying to make ends meet while hurtling towards personal failure.

Mayfield's *Super Fly* is the stuff of soul legend. It would not be too big an exaggeration to say that the Chicago maven invented a new purpose for soul music – the art of meta-commentary, music that passed critical comment on the scenes it witnessed. 'I don't see why people are complaining about the subject of these films,' he told *Jet* magazine. 'The way you clean up the films is by cleaning up the streets. The music and movies of today are the conditions that exist. You change music and movies by changing the conditions.' By the power of his music, Mayfield took a film that was struggling for narrative coherence, with no clear moral core, and gave it a purpose. According to Mayfield's son, he claimed that the music 'became the film's conscience'.

Super Fly was shot entirely on location in Harlem at the turn of the decade and was financed in an unusual way, through an early version of crowd-funding. The producers approached several Harlem businesses and raised small contributions from around eighteen small investors. In the film's press release, the consortium was described tongue-in-cheek as a group of 'pimps, madams and drug dealers'. There was an element of truth in the assertion but the investors were in fact drawn from a much broader base. In *Variety* magazine, the director Gordon Parks Jr specifically thanked his father, the famous photographer Gordon Parks Sr, and two black dentists, Ed Allen and Cornelius 'Connie' Jenkins, who helped with financing.

Super Fly's storyline was scripted by first-time screenplay writer Phillip Fenty, and his long-time friend, the actor Ron O'Neal, played the central character, the fictitious Harlem hustler Youngblood Priest. The film's success provoked an obvious question: who was the character of Youngblood actually based on? There were several candidates. It could have been Fat Jack Taylor of Rojac Records, but Priest was thin and athletic and Fat Jack was most certainly not. There were two more likely choices, men who became newsworthy in the early seventies as the War on Drugs became a national media obsession – Frank Lucas, who was played by the actor Denzel Washington in *American Gangster*, and Leroy 'Nicky' Barnes, leader of the drug syndicate the Council. They were Harlem's most prominent heroin kingpins, but they were less well-known in 1969 when the drafts of the script were being imagined. The consensus seems to be that *Super Fly* was based on a dealer whose high-profile presence on the streets of Harlem from 1965 to 1969 made him supremely visible and in an indirect way associated with the silver screen. His name was William Terrell and he was known on the streets as 'Goldfinger'. He was a regular at Small's Paradise Club and a close friend of the soul singer Luther Ingram, who was in residency there. Goldfinger had an empire that stretched through Harlem nightclubs, tenement yards and local record shops, fanning out from the blighted area around 116th Street and Eighth Avenue, down into Midtown Manhattan and up into the South Bronx. His nickname was due to a street-savvy marketing campaign: all the heroin wraps from his source were tied up with sparkling gold thread, his ghetto trademark. His customised Cadillac was equipped with a bar and much-needed safe-deposit box, but its showpiece was a stereo tape-deck which automatically played the *Goldfinger* Bond theme when the door opened.

In his autobiography, *Panther Baby*, Jamal Joseph described how the Panthers targeted Goldfinger's patch to block the flow of heroin and redirect drug money to community projects and how 'gold tape meant the drugs were coming from "Goldfinger", a black gangster who adopted the name of the James Bond movie . . . Tens of thousands of poison envelopes on the street; thousands of junkies who would beg, hustle and steal for a fix; millions of dollars to fund the fine clothes, flashy cars, and luxurious homes of the drug dealers. They were, of course, the well-dressed puppets of the white mobs, corrupt police, military and governments, those who truly profited from the drug trade.'

It was fine clothes, flashy cars and luxurious homes that would eventually snag Terrell. He became a casualty of a major investigation by the editorial staff of *Newsday*, headed by campaigning African-American journalist Les Payne. It was described by the *Independent*: 'Though ostensibly shy and gentle, Les Payne had a daring streak that landed him in a team of three reporters following the journey heroin was making from Turkey to the streets of New York City . . . [They produced] a 33-part report, *The Heroin Trail*, which won a Pulitzer prize in 1974.' Terrell's business empire was exposed to the tax man. While the screenplay of *Super Fly* was going through its final draft stages, the Internal Revenue Service (IRS) launched an inquiry into Terrell's conspicuous wealth. It revealed that Goldfinger – a 'bearded bear of a man' from Williamston, North Carolina – was in fact William Sherman Terrell. He was twenty-seven years old, had moved to Harlem as a young boy with his mother Zula Mae, and sold heroin through a network of lieutenants, some of whom included his own family.

As Terrell's wealth grew, he tried to hide his profits in legitimate businesses. For a time he owned a taxi firm called Teasla Taxis and a recording company called Terrell Productions, which he allowed people to believe was somehow connected to the Motown star Tammi Terrell. But bricks and mortar were to become his undoing. The IRS inquiry established that Goldfinger's 'largest income from narcotics activities was in the year 1969, when he made as much as $60,000 a day for about a four-month period'. He also acknowledged that he was good for more than $100,000 a week from a narcotics partnership operation in Detroit, Michigan, which was possibly part of the chain of connections that had linked Fat Jack Taylor to his co-producer, the Detroit guitarist Dave Hamilton.

The evidence at his trial for wilful tax evasion at the District Court for the Southern District of New York in February 1975 proved even more conclusive. It established that 'the last time the defendant filed a personal income tax return was in the year 1960, when he obtained a refund of $84.30; that for the years 1961 through 1966 he filed no personal income tax returns with the Manhattan District of the Internal Revenue Service; and that for the years 1967 through 1970 he did not file any personal income tax return anywhere, and that the Social Security records show no earnings of the defendant beyond the first quarter of 1963'. Yet, despite no discernible income, he had purchased several houses in Englewood, New Jersey, a new enclave for the ghetto-rich across the Harlem River. Terrell had moved there around the same time as Joe Robinson and his wife Sylvia, who established three of the great independent record labels of the era – All Platinum, Stang and Turbo Records. They established a New Jersey base that was hardwired back to Harlem, and in time became home to the pioneering rap label Sugar Hill Records.

Back in 1969, at the height of his wealth and power, Goldfinger had bought a home on Englewood's North Woodland Street and, astonishingly, paid cash for ten Cadillacs, which he gifted to his network of dealers. Harlem was by then a hive of dealer networks – internecine, overlapping and brutally competitive. Investing in front-businesses and property had become the preferred way to conceal cash. One of Goldfinger's contemporaries, the infamous Frank Lucas, had cultivated the myth that his heroin was imported from South East Asia in the coffins of the dead being shipped back from Vietnam. When drugs enforcement officers raided Lucas's home in Teaneck, New Jersey, his wife threw three suitcases containing $584,000 in crumpled bills out of the window. Inside the house, keys to safe-deposit boxes in the Cayman Islands and multiple property deeds were discovered, along with, according to press reports, 'a ticket to a United Nations ball, compliments of the ambassador of Honduras'.

As the *Super Fly* soundtrack climbed the pop charts the term spread like a virus through nightclubs and record stores. Originally, 'super fly' was Harlem street argot for pure cocaine, but as soul mutated into street funk and eventually hip-hop it became a catch-all term for being cool or fashionable, and then commercial companies seized on it as a brand name for vividly coloured basketball shoes.

The stereotypical scenes of hookers, pimps and junkies amidst the ghetto streets in *Super Fly* are rescued from exploitation by the percussive wordplay, commanding lyrics and carefully weighted commentary of the soundtrack. It acts almost as a choral commentary on the film itself, dragging it up a level and bringing its many suppressed messages to creative life. 'Freddie's Dead' – a warning about the fatal inevitability of heroin – was nominated for a Grammy but lost out narrowly to the Temptations' epic street symphony, 'Papa Was A Rolling Stone'.

Black music didn't simply creep up on cinema, it blasted through the doors. Isaac Hayes scored the Oscar-winning title track for *Shaft* (1971); Quincy Jones weighed in with the jazzy soundtrack for the interracial love film *Honky* (1971); and Willie Hutch wrote the soundtrack for *The Mack* (1973), which starred Max Julien and Richard Pryor, and began its life as an idea handwritten on prison toilet paper. Marvin Gaye's only film score and soundtrack was for *Trouble Man* (1972); it broke with the vogue for social commentary and became a multifaceted psychoanalysis of the film's central character Mr T, a pool shark and private eye who operates on the fringes of the law in South Central Los Angeles. Soul soundtracks were in vogue. Most reflected the ghetto underworld and its now stereotypical cast of characters: for instance Don Julian and the Larks in *Shorty the Pimp* (1972), who wrote the soundtrack and starred in the film; Joe Simon's 'Theme From Cleopatra Jones' (1973), the everyday story of a funk goddess and undercover agent. Many were set in a fictionalised and exaggerated Harlem: the remake of the classic gangster film *Little Caesar*, *Black Caesar* (1973) featured a soundtrack by James Brown and Fred Wesley; and the sequel, *Hell Up in Harlem* (1973), included music by vocalist Edwin Starr. To the average cinema-goer, it was more of the same, but some soundtracks brought with them their own subtleties. Roy Ayers' soundtrack for Pam Grier's vigilante film *Coffy* (1973) was early jazz-funk; Osibisa's soundtrack for *Super Fly T.N.T.* (1973) was closer to pan-African dance music; and Bill Harris and Van McCoy's 'Uptown Saturday Night' for the action-comedy film of the same name starring Sidney Poitier, Harry Belafonte, Bill Cosby and Richard Pryor, looked forward to metropolitan disco.

Although the urban cinema genre was burdened with the term 'blaxploitation', there was an unprecedented opportunity for black musicians to work in a new medium. Curtis Mayfield had spent more than a decade in the music industry but had never been schooled in cinema soundtracks. It was only when his final album with the Impressions, *The Young Mods' Forgotten Story*, was released in 1969 that his name came into the mind of the *Super Fly* film-makers. Two particular tracks from that album, the soul charts number one single 'Choice Of Colors' (arranged by Johnny Pate and Donny Hathaway) and the racially charged 'Mighty, Mighty (Spade And Whitey)', showed Mayfield in a new light – less wistful and keenly attuned to the racial fault lines of late sixties America. His solo career would pursue those ideas even more aggressively.

The producer of *Super Fly*, Sig Shore, and his screenwriter Phillip Fenty, hustled their way backstage at an Impressions concert at Madison Square Garden and handed Mayfield a raw draft script of an as yet untitled film. They exaggerated nearly everything: the state of the script, the funding they had in place, and the guaranteed date of principal photography. They pleaded with Mayfield to give their film a fair hearing while they wrote revisions and scouted for locations. It was a crucial moment in Mayfield's career. The Impressions were already destined to split, and Mayfield had told them he planned to go solo. *Billboard* had announced that he was planning to open a 16-track recording studio in his native Chicago, and he was working exhaustively on two solo albums – *Curtis* and *Roots*. He was determined that his independent career would not get off to a false start, and so in a rush of hectic creativity stretching from the summer of 1969 onwards he wrote the anti-racist ballad 'We The People Who Are Darker Than Blue', the plaintive critique of ghetto deprivation 'The Other Side Of Town' and the anti-spiritual '(Don't Worry) If There's A Hell Below, We're All Going To Go'. Soaring above those was one of the great civil rights records of the era, the masterful 'Move On Up', a modernised update on the old Impressions classic 'People Get Ready', which had been recorded back in 1965 in the white heat of the civil rights movement.

Mayfield bore all the characteristics of a workaholic – holing up by day in his basement where he'd whisper and write lyrics to himself and sketch out new songs. The pressure he heaped on himself was driven by an underlying anxiety. He had already failed with two previous labels – Mayfield Records and Windy C – and he knew that it was a case of third strike and he was out. His third attempt was Curtom Records, a funk-infused factory on North Lincoln Avenue in Chicago's South Side. Ignoring everything else in his life, he launched headfirst into management issues and studio politics. His strained home life was already buckling under the pressure of touring, his casual love affairs and the need to write a bank of songs that would feed his solo career. He briefly considered moving to New York when Curtom secured a distribution deal with Buddha Records, but outside Chicago Mayfield would have been a fish out of water. So he complicated his life still further by commuting by plane for weekly management meetings, scribbling notes in the departure lounge and writing songs as he went. The first fragments of 'Freddie's Dead' were written onboard a plane descending into Chicago's O'Hare Airport, hurriedly scrawled on yellow notepaper and saved for another day. For his wellbeing alone, he probably should have turned down the highly speculative *Super Fly* commission, but since his deprived upbringing on Chicago's Cabrini-Green Projects, Mayfield had become fearful of poverty and paranoid about missing out on money and opportunity.

Mayfield is ostensibly one of the self-assured monumental greats of soul music, but his character was much more complex than his quiet thoughtfulness indicated. Like Marvin Gaye, he was a bundle of tangled contradictions. He was a gentle man yet he admitted to spousal abuse; outspoken about drugs, he was a serial abuser of cocaine; and though publicly committed to community politics, he was protective and selfish about his own personal wealth. He described his own voice as 'soft' and 'little' but his determination to succeed was boundless. In a world of bellowing vocals and unrestrained egos, he was a man with a quiet if selective sincerity; his whispered soulful delivery frequently needed a dedicated microphone so that his voice would carry to the back of a theatre. But his opinions – fortified by the march of civil rights – were strident and unshakable. Mayfield's compositions were suffused with a lyrical texture, and in a world of prosaic and predictable emotions, he stood out as distinctive: a poet among the throng.

Many have eulogised Curtis Mayfield; few have drawn attention to the nastier side of his character. Only his son, Todd, in his determinedly fair biography, *Travelling Soul: The Life of Curtis Mayfield*, has come close. 'You saw good and evil,' he wrote. 'The vile part came out when it was business . . . He becomes something that you don't want to be around. When it came to business, he was about business. If he's making money he wants all of it.'

As Mayfield's career soared, it obscured a catalogue of behind-the-scenes disputes, ruined friendships and wrecked creative partnerships. When he set up Curtom Records and split with the Impressions, it was with scant regard for the group who had provided most of his success. When it came to sharing ownership, he was akin to Motown's Berry Gordy, and winced at the thought of diluting stock or cutting a collaborator in on the royalties. It was a mindset not uncommon among those who had fought their way out of childhood poverty and one that was often driven by a fear of losing out, rather than avarice alone. Black musicians had been frequently cheated of royalties in the past and Mayfield's more politically conscious generation were unwilling to be casual victims of the music industry's many ruses.

It was Mayfield's self-preservationist attitude that had led to raging creative arguments with Donny Hathaway and, even more acrimoniously, a fall-out with one of soul music's quiet men, the great Chicago arranger Johnny Pate. Between bouts of mental illness that left him hospitalised, Hathaway had also been commissioned to compose a Harlem soundtrack. *Come Back, Charleston Blue* is a flawed but fascinating film which drew on Chester Himes novels for its inspiration. In part a sequel to *Cotton Comes to Harlem*, it tells the story of a mythical Jazz Age gangster called Charleston Blue, who in the afterlife returns to earth to settle old scores. It is a madcap romp featuring nuns on the run, drag queens and hip fashion photographers. Again, drug crime is at the core of the film and the central character razors his victims with a blue steel blade, made for him in his native Charleston – the Charleston Blue of the title. Film critic Roger Ebert identified one of its key successes as its depiction of Harlem as a place of complexity rather than just a backdrop to crime. 'The movie has been photographed lovingly on location in Harlem,' he wrote, 'and shows this as a place of beauty and ugliness, pride and corruption, community building and drug pushing, all side by side.' What he did not mention was Hathaway and his soundtrack, which was a virtuoso journey from past to present, a fuller realisation of his old university party piece, when his piano shifted from ragtime to funk. The film is elevated by a soundtrack that shows Harlem's history through musical vignettes:

ragtime, big band, bebop and soul. It is a reminder of how deep and diverse Hathaway's creativity was at its height.

By the spring of 1969 Johnny Pate had left Chicago and joined Hathaway in Harlem to pursue his first love – jazz music. It was there that Pate – the one-time Chicago soul producer – composed the phenomenally underrated jazz-funk album *Outrageous*, a series of moody and evocative tracks that closely resembled and prefaced the layered soundtrack of *Super Fly*. It was the forerunner to an orchestral style of soul music yet to come. What is less well known is that Pate's friendship with Mayfield faltered on the back of the *Super Fly* soundtrack. It was a disagreement that drove a wedge into their relationship and spread out like a contagion within the close-knit Chicago soul community. Pate had been Mayfield's closest collaborator throughout much of the sixties since they had worked together at the legendary OKeh label, partnering on songs by Mayfield's schoolfriend Major Lance. Back in 1963 they had collaborated on the dance-craze hit 'The Monkey Time', and prior to his move to Harlem, Pate had been a musical director at Chicago's Universal Studios where he had worked on nearly every Impressions record, including the album *Keep On Pushing*. When Mayfield launched Curtom, Pate continued to collaborate, often acting as the label's diplomat when creative war broke out between Mayfield and Hathaway. It is no great secret that when Mayfield was given the commission to score *Super Fly* he leant heavily on his old friend. Pate held his hand through the art of film composition and provided the elegant soundscape that weaves through the album. It was a time when the role of the 'arranger' – often highly trained and multi-talented musicians like Johnny Pate, Bert de Coteaux and Van McCoy – was asserting its presence on uptown soul. As the film's publicity kicked off, a combustible article in the black celebrity magazine *Jet* threw gasoline on the embers. *Jet* reported Pate as saying, 'I orchestrated and arranged the score to *Super Fly* but Curtis Mayfield got all the credit.' He then added, unhelpfully: 'Everybody is ego-tripping and taking credit for things they didn't do.' The resentment was worsened by a more benign interview for *Billboard* magazine, in which Pate thanked Mayfield for the chance to work on *Super Fly* but then went on to question the fairest way to reward an artist who collaborated on a soundtrack, arguing rightly that it was a different creative beast to a hit single.

It was the final straw for Mayfield. In December 1972 he filed a suit in the US District Court which asked the court to declare him as the sole author to the compositions 'Think' and 'Junkie Chase' (both tracks from the *Super Fly* album). The stakes were raised. A *Daily Variety* report estimated that Mayfield was receiving 'about $5,000,000 from performance and royalties' from the more than two million albums and singles sold to date. Mayfield's income from live performance had also escalated on the back of the film's success. In a review of a performance at the Philharmonic Hall in *The New York Times*, where Mayfield shared the Lincoln Theater stage with blues musician Taj Mahal, reviewer Ian Dove spoke warmly of the way he had brought Harlem street conversation to life. 'He has a sensitive and accurate ear for sidewalk semantics . . . He rails against the pusher man, portrays the stoned junkie and extols that his life is a natural high.'

Pate became enraged with Mayfield's lack of generosity and defended himself, claiming that he had written the 'melodic lines' and so was entitled to half the royalties. In a *Los Angeles Times* article, Pate further claimed that Mayfield had 'merely dictated ideas', while he did the 'arranging, scoring, voicing, or orchestrating'. Mayfield's team countered aggressively, stating that Pate was nothing more than a freelance gun for hire who had worked for a day rate. It was a harsh difference of opinion, and for Pate a wounding diminution of their creative partnership. The court exchanges wrecked their fifteen-year friendship and forced fellow musicians to take sides. Craig McMullen, a former jazz student from the renowned Berklee College of Music in Boston, joined Mayfield's band as a guitarist when the Impressions split but felt that Pate had right on his side. 'Curtis couldn't write music down,' he said many years later. 'So he wasn't going to orally translate those harmonies or those hits. You can listen to it and tell this is some big-band arranger putting this down. So really after all those two had done like brothers in the past, it shouldn't have been a problem. That was just a poor way of doing something as far as I'm concerned'.

It was a view shared by Donny Hathaway, who was admittedly close to Pate and had fallen out with Mayfield two years earlier. Hathaway's mentor, the fastidious King Curtis, who always sided with instrumentalists and was a stickler for musical notation and fully composed scores, had been murdered while *Super Fly* was being shot, but was firmly in Pate's camp. As a way of undermining Mayfield's rigid stance, Hathaway and Pate were known to ask fellow musicians to answer a conundrum: who had written the words to the track 'Think'? Was it Johnny Pate or the master lyricist Curtis Mayfield? The answer was that there were no lyrics; it was an instrumental mood track almost certainly composed by the more musically literate Pate.

Despite all the wrangling, the court case did not hold either man back. In 1973 Pate went on to score two more urban films: the much-sampled *Brother on the Run* and *Shaft in Africa*, the sequel to *Shaft*. The ugly dispute between Mayfield and Pate was nothing compared to the deluge of opprobrium that greeted *Super Fly* on its release. The film not only divided opinion, it shattered it into jagged pieces. Junius Griffin, then president of the Hollywood branch of the venerable NAACP, demanded that Warner Brothers recall prints of the film from distribution and reshoot the ending so that there was a moral consequence. He argued that the Goldfinger character, drug dealer Youngblood Priest, was being treated heroically and should either be killed or punished as a consequence of drug dealing. In an interview with *Newsweek*, Griffin protested that 'we must insist that our children are not exposed to a diet of so-called black movies that glorify black males as pimps, dope pushers, gangsters and super males with vast physical prowess but no cognitive skills'.

The case against *Super Fly* seemed to build with every new headline. A leading Catholic society who moralised about cinema gave the film a 'C' – for 'Condemned' – rating, briefing the press that 'this kind of black liberation serves only to deceive the brothers and play upon the fears of black audiences'. Black Christian leaders saw an opportunity to picket theatres and demonstrators toted placards denouncing *Super Fly* – 'Black Shame for White Profits' and 'We Are Not All Pimps and Whores'. Criticism of the film was at its most focused in a letter written to the *Amsterdam News* by Loyle Hairston, founder of the Harlem Writers Guild. He preempted the criticism that gangsta rap would face in years to come, when he wrote that films like *Super Fly* 'exult in coarseness, violence and all the degrading vulgarities of the hustler's lifestyle. The characters are studies in the grotesque; life in the ghetto is depicted as a menagerie of crude, foul mouthed, mod-dressed, buffooning denizens of crime and corruption.' As the correspondent rose to his task, he denounced the film's characters as a betrayal of black culture: 'Black women are portrayed as "bitches": brutal sex play passes for tenderness; sheer viciousness is the measure of manhood; and cunning the sole example of intelligence.' He concluded with the ultimate put-down: 'The head-scratching, eye-rolling stereotypes of the '30s and '40s were almost appealing by comparison. In some respects their modern-day counterparts are even more objectionable.'

An article in the *Los Angeles Times* mooted a different argument, pointing to the sheer scale of interest in making films within the context of ghetto life. 'Since mid 1970, at least 51 films about blacks have been released,' it claimed. 'Those released in the previous decade could probably be counted on one hand.' It was a breakthrough, but with a whole host of caveats.

Predictably, the furore brought even more attention to *Super Fly* and curious audiences flocked to cinemas to see what all the fuss was about. The film edged further up the rankings and moved into third position behind *The Godfather* and *Play It Again, Sam* in the list of top-grossing films of 1972. It had grossed $20 million in seven months alone. However, success did nothing to calm the storm; in fact it invited even fiercer attacks. Vernon F. Jordan of the National Urban League raged that 'Hollywood is back to its old game of creating stereotypes of Black people for popular consumption . . .'. Tony Brown, the first Dean of Communications at Howard University and the host of a regular PBS talk show, *Tony Brown's Journal*, dismissed the film melodramatically as 'genocide'. Marion Barry, later to become the mayor of Washington DC but then the president of the Washington DC school board, picked up on Brown's headline-grabbing denunciation and formed an organisation called BANG – Blacks Against Narcotics and Genocide. It was an organisation whose name was used to humiliate Barry when in 1990 he was arrested in an FBI sting operation for smoking crack cocaine. He was jailed in a correctional facility where he was further accused of allowing a woman to perform oral sex on him. Barry denied the accusation but the harm done to his career was immeasurable.

Super Fly crystallised a dispute that had existed within the African-American community for decades, at least since the advent of R&B: that popular culture was spiritually corrosive, and music and films were detrimental to young people, especially those who were exposed to social deprivation and vulnerable to drugs and crime. It was a dispute with no easy solution and would recur over the decades to come as urban films came to influence the language of hip-hop and the self-injurious extremes of gangsta rap. But Junius Griffin's deepest failing was his omission in spotting the underlying positive aspect of the film – the great surge of soul music creativity that came in the slipstream of blaxploitation and opened doors in the film world that had hitherto been firmly closed to black musicians.

As for the man whose life supposedly influenced the film, the future was bleaker. William 'Goldfinger' Terrell's outlandish and ill-fated reign ended with a crash. In the vengeful world of narcotics, he had made enemies, and his grip on the highly coveted street-corner trade in Harlem weakened. In the week before Christmas in 1978 his body was dumped near a shopping mall in Yonkers. The thirty-six-year-old had suffered nine gunshot wounds. Police officers reported at the time that they believed Terrell was the victim of a 'hit' and that his 'bullet-riddled' body was 'still warm' when it was found at 4.30 a.m. Super Fly died as he had lived, fatally compromised by the violent drug wars that had engulfed New York and taken an especially fearful grip on Harlem. The clothes that had once been his pride and joy lay bloodstained and dishevelled in the morgue, in a cold basement on First Avenue near 32nd Street. Police had neither the manpower nor the motivation to find his killers: death would no doubt find them first. In the morgue's lobby hung the Latin motto: 'Let conversation cease, let laughter flee. This is the place where death delights in helping the living.'

The arrest photographs of the transvestite Harlem drug dealer known by various pseudonyms including Fannie Hill.

JUNE

Sophisticated Cissy

On 14 May, on the corner of 132nd and Seventh Avenue in Harlem, a police patrol spotted a brand new 1969 Rambler American, presumed stolen from a car rental firm. In the vehicle were three passengers and thirty-four glassine envelopes of heroin. The police interrogated the two males and took down the details of the woman. She gave her name as Shirlene Dixon and provided an address in the St Nicholas housing complex, a fourteen-storey public housing project in central Harlem, just three blocks from the Apollo. She told the arresting officers she was thirty years old, but she looked much younger, and the men were younger still, possibly teenagers. What seemed like a routine drugs bust would turn out to be an element of one of the most compelling mysteries to beset Harlem in 1969, a story that took dogged investigative journalism and nearly fifty years to finally solve.

Some months later, a rabbit hunter from Queens was out in the woods near the town of Chester in Orange County, New York State, when he stumbled upon the decomposing remains of a body.

It had been lying in a shallow grave for some time, and it was not clear to the naked eye the gender of the victim. The corpse was wearing a distinctive T-shirt and socks, and there was a yellow towel around the head – probably used to muffle the sound of gunfire. The hands had been tied behind the back with an electrical cord, in the style of a gangland assassination. While the face appeared to be that of a young, well-proportioned man, the autopsy confirmed it was the body of a woman.

No one came forward to claim the body, and so it was buried in a potter's field plot, number 537, in Middletown, and recorded as 'Unknown'. In the parlance of crime fiction, the dead woman became known as Jane Doe 537. With no one demanding answers, and no evidence as to her identity, the case went stone cold. It was only decades later, in 2015, that a *New York Times* investigation into the unidentified bodies buried at the site unearthed the story of the mysterious woman. By a remarkable combination of luck and forensic detective work, the newspaper's investigation team, working alongside the police, pieced together a life that defies belief. Quite apart from being wrapped up like a crime thriller with murder and intrigue, it also unfolded as an astonishing story of cross-dressing and shifting sexual identity. According to *The New York Times*, 'the investigation yielded a remarkable life story in reverse, from the woods where the woman died to the streets of Harlem, which were newly flooded in the sixties with narcotics – streets she walked on her own terms, dressed like a man and ready with quick lies for the police'.

At the time of the May drugs bust, door-to-door enquiries had thrown up another mystery. Far from being dead, Shirlene Dixon was very much alive and still residing in the St Nicholas Projects. She was not the woman who had been arrested and her name had been used to disguise the real identity of the criminal.

Yan Salomon, a New York State Police investigator, helped with the first piece of the jigsaw: fingerprints. He described how the woman had fallen backwards and that had protected her hands from the elements. The police were able to get fingerprints from the right thumb and two fingers but there were no outstanding matches with law enforcement agencies. However, there was a clue in the clothing. The only notable item on the corpse was a Har-You T-shirt, the emblem of the Harlem Youth Opportunities charity, whose house band were among the most popular of the community soul groups. Youth leader 'Montego Joe' Sanders had put together the Latin jazz orchestra from what was in effect a group of delinquent youths. The band's debut album, a frenetic collection of street funk and afro-Cuban jazz, was in the stores, and at the time Sanders described them as 'emotionally unstable young men with no inspiration and no place to go'.

The garment was a potential lead and raised the prospect that the victim might be a band member, charity worker or someone from the projects who had managed to bag a free T-shirt. They quizzed numerous people at the Har-You offices, interrogated band members and combed through the details of charity workers based in Harlem. But again they drew a blank.

In late 2015, using new state-of-the-art software, police matched the fingerprints to a woman who had been arrested in Harlem several times in 1969 and used different names, including Shirlene Dixon, Fannie Hill and Evelyn Moore.

The New York Times assigned an experienced crime writer, Michael Wilson, to review the case and, unlike previous investigators, he had a stroke of luck. A detective in the 32nd Precinct in Harlem had found an old desk blotter in the basement of the station house. Listed in it were the two male suspects interviewed on 14 May. One was dead, and Wilson tracked down the other, a man who chose to call himself only 'Doug'. He related a story of an enterprising gang of young Harlem criminals who switched gender, used false names and ran intercity drug errands for big-time dealers. He knew the dead girl by the initials 'A. C.' but had no idea what the initials stood for. He told the journalist that she dressed like a man – 'very fashionable . . . knit sweaters, sharkskin slacks'. Chillingly, he also remembered the night she was abducted. Two 'butch' women had arrived at their apartment and dragged his friend away.

It became clear that the name Shirlene Dixon was a red herring. She was neither the girl the police had arrested nor the murder victim. Shirlene Dixon was, as mentioned, a real woman, but sometime in the seventies she and her mother were murdered in

Harlem in an act of domestic violence by her mother's boyfriend. Dixon had lived in the St Nicholas Projects and become involved with a group of lesbian and bisexual women who worked in the local heroin trade, one of whom had cohabited with a girl known only as A.C.

In 2015 *The New York Times* eventually determined that the dead body was that of a thirty-year-old woman called Evelyn Moore. She had lived as both a man and a woman, and disguised her petty criminality with a shifting sexual identity and many pseudonyms, including A.C. She had been born into extreme poverty on a dirt farm in Orangeburg, South Carolina, and as a teenager made her way to New York City completely alone. As the *NYT* reported, she found 'a new identity along the way' and embraced 'a bisexuality that, in that day, was more likely to be kept hidden'.

In June 1969 freedom of sexual expression came to a head downtown when gay rights activists clashed with the police outside the Stonewall Inn in Greenwich Village. After nine policemen had entered the bar, arrested staff members for selling unlicensed alcohol and roughed up the customers, people started to gather outside. Fed up with police harassment, they began shouting at the police and throwing bottles. Over time hundreds of people arrived, and the protest went on sporadically for five days.

Stonewall became a watershed moment in the rise of gay liberation. One of the leading figures was black drag queen Marsha P. Johnson, an unrestrained force of nature who became a gay and transvestite activist. Marsha Johnson was born Malcolm Michaels Jr in Elizabeth, New Jersey, and was brought up in the Catholic faith, a religious belief system she clung to throughout her life, despite becoming one of North America's most public and vociferous drag queens. She moved to Greenwich Village in the sixties, travelling uptown to Harlem where she built a reputation as Queen Marsha, an outrageous singer, dancer and lifestyle activist. A regular at the Stonewall Inn, she arrived at the bar in the early hours of 28 June to find it on fire, and then forced her way through the police barricades. Standing defiantly in the bar, she reputedly threw a shot glass at a mirror thus signalling her refusal to be arrested quietly. On the second night of rioting, it was alleged that she climbed a lamppost and dropped a brick onto a police-car windshield and vociferously resisted arrest. Johnson's stance gave her a reputation across Manhattan as New York's most famous drag queen, and although she was a decent solo singer, she became more renowned as a performer in the New York drag troupe Hot Peaches. They eventually found a degree of fame in the emergent cabaret disco scene but Johnson herself enshrined her New York status when she modelled for Andy Warhol.

What was unknown at the time was her link to sixties soul. As Malcolm Michaels Jr, she had been a local hopeful in Elizabeth, New Jersey, an area rich in soul music talent. She was a contemporary of the neighbourhood's major soul star, the late great Linda Jones, and was in her early years a friend of Jones's twin brother J.J., himself a gifted vocalist. When J.J. was incarcerated in New Jersey's Rahway State Prison, Linda visited him with her producer George Kerr. Kerr was introduced to an aspiring prison group called the Escorts, who, despite being behind bars, became one of the best harmony and sweet soul bands of the seventies. In 1972, the Escorts were making history by recording their debut album *All We Need Is Another Chance* inside Rahway. (Kerr tided up the tracks outside.)

By 1969, the paths of Marsha P. Johnson and Linda Jones had diverged. Jones was by then a regular at the Apollo, driving daily to exhausting shows from her home in New Jersey while she struggled with diabetes, and Johnson was a full-blown gay icon performing with Hot Peaches.

With less furore and fewer headlines, Channel 13's new public service broadcasting show *Soul!* was still searching for an identity, mixing soul music and social issues and recording live performances in front of highly charged studio audiences. From September 1968, the show was created and hosted by the openly gay intellectual Ellis Haizlip, and King Curtis, its musical director, provided the theme song 'Soulful 13' with his band the Kingpins. *Wax Poetics* described the 'sweet mix of smells' that greeted artists at the door of the studio – 'marijuana, potato salad and hair products'.

Among the show's guests in 1969 were B.B. King, the public face of blues revivalism, a then unknown group from Canton, Ohio, called the O'Jays, the Last Poets, who performed 'Die Nigger' in their first-ever TV appearance, Joe Tex, Roberta Flack and Percy Sledge. In one episode Harlem's most celebrated literary figure, the author James Baldwin, spoke frankly of his upbringing in Harlem, his days in exile in Paris, his deep friendship with Marlon Brando, and his life as a black gay man. Controversially for the times, he had accused the Christian churches of providing moral support for slavery. Baldwin's novel *Giovanni's Room*, published in 1956 by Dial Press, was a courageous, pioneering book that divided opinion in his native Harlem. His publisher and agent told him to burn the manuscript because its themes of homosexuality and illicit sex would alienate him from his black readers. But Baldwin always wrote what he wanted to.

Gradually, through appearances such as those by Betty Shabazz (the widow of Malcolm X), Muhammad Ali, Ossie Davis and Ruby Dee, Nation of Islam leader Louis Farrakhan and Maya Angelou, *Soul!* found a voice. It attracted fierce loyalty from black music fans and from Harlem radicals, but its unapologetic promotion of politicised music and such controversial figures worried television bosses and sponsors. Abiodun Oyewole of the Last Poets told *Wax Poetics* that the show 'brought different types of black people together when nothing else did'. The final episode aired on 7 March 1973.

By the summer of 1969 Arthur Conley was one of soul music's most unlikely stars. In a genre notorious for mountainous egos and dogged in-fighting, he was a quiet man, shy to the point of diffidence. Born in McIntosh County, Georgia, he briefly fronted an all-girl gospel group, the Evening Smiles. Their name, chosen by Conley, was taken from the first line of Robert Browning's classic poem 'Love Among the Ruins' – 'where the quiet-coloured end of evening smiles'. His voice broke when he was still a schoolboy and he graduated to an all-male high school group called Arthur and the Corvets. In a failed attempt to reconnect with his father, who had left the family home when Arthur was a child, he moved north to Baltimore before eventually striking up a transformational and semi-parental friendship with Otis Redding. Their initial meeting came at a time when Redding, a consummate businessman, had launched his own label, Jotis Records, which was nationally managed by Atlantic's distribution arm ATCO. None of Conley's early releases made much impact until Redding floated the idea of reworking a Sam Cooke party song called 'Yeah Man'. It was either a stroke of genius or unbridled opportunism. Redding and Conley reimagined the song as a roll-call honouring the great soul singers of the mid sixties – Lou Rawls, Sam and Dave, Wilson Pickett and Otis Redding himself – and in a gesture of goodwill they accorded the greatest status to Redding's old Macon, Georgia, rival – James Brown. Playing fast and loose with copyright ownership, Redding and Conley gutted Cooke's original song, creating one of the era-defining soul records of the sixties, the peerless 'Sweet Soul Music'. It became an all-time classic which simultaneously spotlights the famous and refrains some of the great records of the era, too: The Miracles' 'Going To A Go-Go', Sam and Dave's 'Hold On, I'm Coming', and Wilson Pickett's hyper-energetic 'Mustang Sally'. Sam Cooke was dead by the time Redding and Conley went into the Fame Studios in Alabama and recorded the track, but his management agency swiftly sued, accusing the pair of plagiarism and copyright theft. As a compromise, the late Sam Cooke was co-credited with the song, but before his name appeared on the credits it had already become an international hit, rising to number two on both the pop and soul charts in the USA, and becoming an unrivalled anthem of the Mod movement in Europe.

In February 1967 Arthur Conley was on his way to the Apollo in Harlem. He was sharing a bill, albeit as a low-ranking singer, with Otis, Percy Sledge, Bettye Swann, James Carr and the Chicago sibling group who became known as 'The First Family of Soul', the Five Stairsteps. Nervously Conley took to the stage as singers with more formidable reputations looked on. He was more comfortable with gospel-inspired soul, songs deep in emotional meaning, like his moving rendition of 'There's A Place For Us' and the aching 'Let Nothing Separate Us', but fate had dealt him a very different hand – raucous party songs that audiences craved and which he delivered out of a sense of duty rather than desire. It would be unfair to dismiss him as a one-hit wonder – or to underestimate his rich vocal abilities – but something about the song that made him famous also subtly undermined him. 'Sweet Soul Music' was itself a tribute to other more established singers, and because of its similarity to Cooke's original had variously been dismissed as a 'rip-off', 'derivative', or 'pure unadulterated luck'. The implicit criticism, although irrelevant to his young fans who revered the song, meant that Conley often travelled alone on tour, sitting apart from the others or pretending to sleep. Success became a burden. He was frequently placed near the top of running orders as other more deserving singers looked on bitterly.

Conley's professional discomfort was complicated by a deep and unresolved sexual confusion. He was ill at ease around the sexually bombastic women who travelled with the big soul caravans and terrified of the hostility that seemed to surround homosexuality. Introspective and studious backstage, under the limelight he was a one-man party, disguising his insecurities with a volcanic stage show. A follow-up record – the powerhouse 'Funky Street' – strengthened Conley's reputation in Europe in 1968, but his American career was already going nowhere. The song had been co-written with Conley's producer, the Atlantic studio-engineering guru Tom Dowd, a man who for reasons now buried deep in time Conley could not stand being next to. He never recorded with him again and was already burning bridges at Atlantic Records. Then two events had a bearing on his destiny and perhaps his sexuality, too: the Stax tour of Europe and the untimely death of his mentor and close friend Otis Redding.

In the summer of 1967 Conley had been a late addition to the tour that became an awakening in his young life, the now-legendary Stax/Volt tour of Europe. A young black man from the Deep South, his eyes were opened to different cultures and more socially enlightened societies. The Stax artists were staggered to discover that crowds of mostly white teenagers knew their songs by heart and that the golden generation of British beat musicians, including Mick Jagger, Keith Richards, Brian Jones, Eric Burdon, John Mayall, Roger Daltrey, Pete Townshend and the Beatles, were turning up to see them. In an oft-repeated footnote in pop history, the Beatles even sent limousines to pick up the Stax crew each night, and in an unverified show of respect Paul McCartney reputedly kissed the signet ring of Stax guitarist Steve Cropper, considering him to be the greatest guitar player he had ever heard. Conley watched all this in bewilderment. Every city on the itinerary seemed to throw up another surprise. He had a single released in France. Both sides had been recorded at his troubled sessions at Fame Studios back in Alabama: 'Ha! Ha! Ha! Ha!', written by Otis Redding, and a rendition of the up-tempo R&B dancer 'Keep On Talking' by Fame stalwarts Dan Penn and Spooner Oldham (more persuasively recorded by southern soul singer James Barnett in 1965). It seemed wherever Conley went, his real passion for slow, moody and tear-stained ballads – for instance, the emotionally draining 'I'm A Lonely Stranger' – was usurped by raucous hits such as 'Sweet Soul Music' and 'Funky Street'.

By the time the Stax/Volt Revue tour bus reached the Norwegian capital of Oslo and the most unlikely venue of a handball arena called Njårdhallen, it was running late. Delayed by a puncture, there was no time to soundcheck, so the Stax musicians hijacked equipment from the warm-up band, a Norwegian beat group called the Vanguards. Local DJ Barry Matheson had organised the concert. The turnout was disappointingly low and Matheson eventually lost $10,000 on the show. But in the process of losing out, he created history. Matheson sold the media rights to Norwegian public broadcaster NRK and the show was filmed for posterity. The footage remains the most remarkable documentary of Stax at its towering height. Redding would 'slosh through puddles of Sam and Dave's sweat to get out to the stage', claimed Stax trumpeter Wayne Jackson in an on-screen interview, 'and then he would add a gallon of his own sweat to the lake'.

Mesmerised by what he had witnessed and genuinely moved that he was being treated as a superstar, Conley talked to Redding about staying behind in Europe, but he was discouraged and reluctantly returned to America. At the time of his return, one of the most bizarre and sexually ambiguous dance crazes was dominating jukebox plays and sweeping the urban club scene. The 'cissy soul' craze was dance music that somehow managed to highlight and mock homosexuality. It had begun in underground gay bars in New Orleans and made its way north to Harlem courtesy of touring soul groups playing the Apollo and breakout dance records climbing the urban charts. As far back as 1965, instrumental soul groups were releasing records feeding the cissy craze. That year, the talented Washington DC bandleader Roscoe Bowie released the relentlessly up-tempo 'Broadway Cissy', the flipside to his funk classic 'Barnyard Soul'; but foremost among the bands who pioneered the dance craze were the Meters, a New Orleans outfit who released two party funk tunes, 'Sophisticated Cissy' (1968) and 'Cissy Strut' (1969), on the Jubilee-owned subsidiary Josie Records. The Meters were by then the house band at a local indie in New Orleans, Sansu Records, and the undercarriage of the sound that became New Orleans funk. They drew musically on the city's two grandmasters – Art Neville and Allen Toussaint – and on its sexual underground, which in the next decade produced Labelle's lyrically rich 'Lady Marmalade', a soul song dripping in references to sex for sale.

Although there were other cities that had released cissy funk it became synonymous with New Orleans. Local band George Porter's Joyride released their version of 'Cissy Strut' (Deesu, 1969) and in doing so laid down one of the most famous basslines in the history of funk. The Louisiana-based soul singer Willie West, who also recorded on Deesu, gave the clearest insight into the cissy scene (also spelled 'sissy'). He told *Offbeat* magazine that a dance called the Sophisticated Sissy emerged in New Orleans gay clubs and he described it as 'a dance that the gay guys started where you wave your arms around and switch your booty. I never did it, but saw it in the clubs. It caught on with the straight people. I don't think the white people knew anything about it. It was mainly the black community imitating the way the gays switched and sashayed around.' West claimed that the craze probably began in 1965 at the Nite Cap club in downtown New Orleans, when the Deesu label was in its infancy. It was a time of flux. Deesu had yet to find its identity releasing ballads, old-style R&B and the infectious uptown dance record 'Being With You' (1966) by Maurice Williams.

(He had already enjoyed brief success with the beat record 'Stay' – covered in the UK by the Hollies – which at a modest 1.36 minutes was the shortest song ever to make it to the top of the *Billboard* charts.) Gradually, Deesu found its niche in a nascent form of funk music driven by the Nite Cap's house band, the Meters. Their relentless sound attracted huge crowds that spilled out on to the sidewalks, all the way down to St Charles Avenue, a block away, disrupting traffic and attracting police patrols. Rufus Thomas, the madcap dance-craze grandfather of Stax Records, saw an opportunity. Hearing of the New Orleans sound, he worked with Isaac Hayes and David Porter to improvise a gruff, innuendo-laden vocal version of 'Sophisticated Sissy'. It was released in the summer of 1967, two years prior to Thomas's most famous dance-craze record 'The Funky Chicken', and was in part crafted by Sir Mack Rice. R&B star Rice had relocated to Memphis, where he became one of a small number of musicians to successfully straddle the great cities of sixties soul – Memphis and Detroit. He had a taste for sexual nuance and also wrote the boisterous 'Mustang Sally' for Wilson Pickett and 'Santa Claus Wants Some Lovin'' for bluesman Albert King.

By the summer of 1969 the cissy was the pre-eminent fad in a now crowded dance-craze market and had spread northwards to the nightclubs of Harlem. It had even reached Europe, where Davy 'Bang-Bang' Jones and the Voodoo Funk Machine, an exiled ghetto band based at the Lucky Star club in Amsterdam, rush-released a raucous cover version of 'Sophisticated Sissy'. Coincidentally it would be the Lucky Star club and the coffee shops of Amsterdam that, with time, would become the new home of Arthur Conley.

For much of the sixties it was not clear whether the cissy was a dance craze started by gay men as a statement of sexual freedom, or whether it was denigratory and homophobic. The balance finally tipped as a consequence of stand-up routines among the roughhouse comedians who worked the Chitlin' Circuit as warm-up MCs to the big soul groups. The cross-dressing vaudeville star Jackie 'Moms' Mabley, the boisterous Dewey 'Pigmeat' Markham and latterly comedians such as Nipsey Russell, Godfrey Cambridge, Dick Gregory and Bill Cosby often included gay innuendo in their acts – or in some cases blatantly mocked the extravagant street characters of ghetto life and portrayed them as ridiculous misfits. By the time the cissy craze had curdled in the seventies, there was little doubt that it was openly derogatory. The B-side of Joe Tex's international hit 'Ain't Gonna Bump No More' was a crude comic dance record called 'Be Cool (Willie Is Dancing With A Sissy)'.

There is a photograph of Arthur Conley attending Otis Redding's funeral in Macon City Auditorium, Georgia. He stands alone, separated from the rabble of soul stars who have crowded around the coffin. Nearby, James Brown is weeping. Conley looks shell-shocked. The photograph captures him as he waits to join the cortège that will carry Redding's coffin. He is dressed in a slimline suit with a thin Mod-style tie and looks as if he has just left the Twisted Wheel or Brixton's Ram Jam Club, any of the premier Mod European clubs. He has the look of a man who has already left America behind.

By 1969, disheartened by the way gay men were routinely stereotyped on the soul scene, Conley began to live a largely secret and closeted life. He yearned to return to Europe, and the death of Otis Redding deepened that resolve. It seemed that, without his mentor and personal champion, Conley lost impetus and struggled with the emotional demands of the recording industry. He released only a few more records, including a double A-side featuring a personal requiem for Redding, 'Otis Sleep On'. On the flipside was an ill-conceived cover version of the Beatles' 'Ob-La-Di, Ob-La-Da', which features an absurdly intrusive guitar solo by Duane Allman. It is difficult to find two songs so sublime and so ridiculous on one piece of vinyl. 'Otis Sleep On', underpinned by a gospel choir, thanks Redding for his guidance and conveys regret that their future plans were cut so brutally short. It is a sincere love letter to a friend, and profoundly moving. The record was the brainchild of Redding's schoolfriend and manager Phil Walden, who took Conley under his wing.

Eventually Conley headed to Europe, first on vacation, and then to tour again. There he was surrounded by adoring young Mods and fanatical followers. Atlantic were more than conscious of his cult following in the Modernist movement and secured a distribution deal with Italian label Ri-Fi. Slowly but surely, the insecure boy from Georgia who had recorded the archetypal sixties soul record embraced his sexuality. He spent late nights in gay clubs in Soho and shared gondola rides with male friends in Venice, and although he still held back from coming out, he turned his back on the world of the Apollo. (Ironically, he seems to have been largely unaware that the upstairs bar in the world's most feverish soul venue had itself become a gathering place for the Harlem gay scene.)

One of his last records in the sixties was 'Star Review' (1969), an attempt to relive 'Sweet Soul Music'. It attracted some attention in the European Mod scene but nowhere else. He settled finally in the Netherlands, where he changed his name to Lee Rogers and worked unobtrusively as a radio announcer, concealing his real identity. Many years later, in a small town called Ruurlo in the eastern Netherlands, friends and inquisitive neighbours discovered who he really was. In the eighties Conley was encouraged to return to music and he started up a new group called Lee Roberts and the Sweaters; they recorded a successful live album in Amsterdam in 1980, *Soulin'*, which was released in 1987. By then his hair was a distinguished silver-grey, and his close-cropped beard gave him the appearance of an antique dealer rather than an ageing soul star. He never returned to the Apollo, or his native Georgia, and he died in Ruurlo, at last, as an out gay man.

Arthur Conley's troubled life in New York paralleled the remarkable double life of one of Harlem's most famous boxers: the Adonis-like Emile Griffith. In the summer of 1969 Griffith was training for a forthcoming fight against challenger Dick DiVeronica in Syracuse. He had already won, lost and regained the welterweight title, but was best known on the streets for his stylish dress sense and unashamedly gay lifestyle. Griffith was from the Virgin Islands and came to America as part of the great migration from the Caribbean islands in the fifties. He grew up in an overcrowded slum above a Chinese restaurant in central Harlem, where even from a young age he provided the main income for a sprawling family of brothers, sisters and cousins, who as his wealth grew became ever more reliant on his success. As a youngster Griffith was driven by an interest in fashion and would regularly walk the length of 125th Street, gazing at the hat shops, fashion stores and sparkling windows of Busch the jewellers. He managed to secure a job at a milliner's in Midtown Manhattan and there he learned the techniques of hat design. He worked in a largely female environment, surrounded by a riot of colours in a stuffy warehouse with no air-conditioning. When New York broiled in suffocating heat, Griffith would work stripped to the waist, more than happy to show off his well-honed torso. His boss, hatmaker Howard Albert, was an amateur boxing enthusiast, and as a challenge he joked that he could train Griffith to become a Golden Gloves champion. Egged on by the women in the warehouse, Griffith played along, and the workplace joke became a reality. By 1958, with Albert as his co-manager, Griffith was regularly winning fights at the St Nicholas Arena, a training ground for the world-famous Madison Square Garden. Griffith's celebrity in Harlem spread like wildfire. His fastidious fashion sense, soft-spoken style and demonstrative gestures cast him as one of the ghetto's most renowned and sophisticated cissies. But his powerful fists and mechanical punching made him an object of respect rather than one of ridicule – unusually in a sport synonymous with straight-down-the-line machismo.

Then came a fateful night in March 1962. As Griffith's career took off he was matched in a series of fights with Bernardo 'The Kid' Paret, a Cuban immigrant who had moved to Spanish Harlem as a teenager. The eminent magazine *Sports Illustrated* described Paret as a man defined by arrogance. 'In his heyday, Benny (Kid) Paret was a cocky little man who favored bright, heavy jewellery, but he once cut sugar cane for $2 a day in the fields of Santa Clara, Cuba, where he was born,' their correspondent Gilbert Rogin wrote. The two welterweights had been neighbourhood friends, but Paret's mouthy and impudent personality cast him as the polar opposite of the disarmingly elegant Griffith. Sometime in the early sixties, Paret moved south to Miami to cultivate the commercial opportunities of the burgeoning Cuban diaspora, and left Harlem behind. Either instinctively or at the behest of his management, Paret began to work up a rivalry with Griffith, targeting his sexuality and mocking his style. The hyped-up rivalry tipped into open hatred in

March 1962. According to *Sports Illustrated*, 'it was a fight marked with episodes of anger and resentment – butts, surly shoves, low blows and milling after the bell. The bad blood had its origin in an incident during the weigh-in for the second Griffith–Paret fight . . . in which Paret won a highly regrettable split decision. Smiling fatuously as they posed for the photographers at the scales, Paret had blithely cursed Griffith in Spanish. Griffith vowed that if Paret ever taunted him again in this manner he would fight him then and there . . . when they weighed in for the third fight, Paret did. As before, Paret called Griffith *maricón*, gutter Spanish for homosexual.' Griffith retaliated and Paret laid 'a gratuitous, slighting hand on Emile's back'.

Boxing is infamous for its fake theatrics and contrived weigh-in confrontations, but something more bitter and personal was at stake here. The fight was set up as a vengeful contest about the 'meaning of manhood' and was imbued with unprecedented sexual overtones. It became the most horrific and significant night in Emile Griffith's life. In the twelfth round he lost control and ferociously beat Paret to death. A contemporary report described the end of the fight in all its grotesque detail: 'Emile's hand banging against Benny's jaw as remorselessly as the clapper of a great, dark bell. Paret sagged back against the middle turnbuckle. Griffith's punches drove his head out between the top and middle strands. Benny was helpless, bleeding from his nose and a cut on his right cheek; his puffed eyes were closed. Still Griffith punched him, with mounting and maniacal rage, as though determined, literally, to wipe out both Paret and the memory of his taunt. There were, in all, about fifteen uppercuts, followed by several hooks. Then Referee Goldstein was tugging at Griffith from behind, pulling him off. As Emile, berserk, struggling passionately in Goldstein's embrace, was dragged away, Paret, now obviously senseless, crumpled slowly and collapsed.'

Benny Paret slipped into a coma and died ten days later in the Roosevelt Hospital from massive brain haemorrhaging. An inquest pointed the finger not only at Griffith's uncontrolled attack but at the New York Boxing Board, who had allowed the fight to go ahead, despite three previous fights where there were suspicions that Paret had suffered brain damage.

The death of his one-time friend became the defining moment in Griffith's life and would haunt him until his death in 2013. Traumatised by having killed Paret, Griffith suffered recurring nightmares. He described how the young Benny appeared at the bottom of his bed nightly, challenging Griffith to explain himself. In his remarkable book *A Man's World: The Double Life of Emile Griffith*, the South African-born writer Donald McRae follows Griffith's life in all its nuanced and underground detail from the hidden bars of Harlem to the jazz bars of 48th Street, where he frequently hung out, incognito, with his lovers. McRae refrains Griffith's words through his friend, the writer Ron Ross: 'I keep thinking how strange it is. I kill a man and most people understand and forgive me. However, I love a man and many say this makes me an evil person. To so many people this is an unforgivable sin.'

Griffith earned enough money from boxing to move from Harlem to a luxury apartment in Weehawken, New Jersey, across the river from Manhattan. A *Sports Illustrated* reporter, Milton Gross, gave a vivid description of his home: 'The wall-to-wall carpet in poinsettia red is what first strikes you when you enter the living room of Emile Griffith's apartment. Then the cupids decorating the wall and the delicate furniture: the twin French Provincial tufted couches, the spindly-legged end table supporting a pink Princess telephone.' In a bid to bring ordinariness to his controversial life, in 1971 Griffith married a girlfriend, Mercedes 'Sadie' Donastorg, who was then a member of the dance troupe Prince Rupert and the Slave Girls. Griffith had first met Sadie in the old Bambousay Nightclub in St Thomas, where the pair had danced all night. His best man at the ceremony was Smokin' Joe Frazier, by then heavyweight champion of the world and part-time frontman of the soul-funk band Joe Frazier and the Knockouts. Although Griffith adopted Sadie's daughter, the marriage lasted less than two years and he abandoned his double life. He returned to cruising gay bars and nightclubs for casual sex. In 1992 a violent assault took place outside a bar near the Port Authority Bus Terminal. As described by the *Independent*: 'The debate over Griffith's sexuality was at the centre of the news once again . . . when five thugs attacked him after he had left a gay bar in New York. He was 54 and took a severe beating but still made it home on the train with multiple injuries which required him to spend four months in hospital. His attackers were never captured and Griffith never recovered, his ring damage worsened by the blows from the cowards' baseball bats.' He was already showing the early signs of the boxer's curse, dementia pugilistica, also known as punch-drunk syndrome, and died of kidney failure in a New York care facility in 2013.

One of the great ironies of Harlem in 1969, played out in the lives of both Arthur Conley and Emile Griffith, was that it was such an unkind and corrosive place for gay men. This was in marked contrast to the neighbourhood's past. Harlem had once been the unrivalled capital of gay culture and home to the icons of the Harlem Renaissance: writer and activist Langston Hughes, anthropologist Zora Neale Hurston, playwright Countee Cullen, poet Claude McKay, novelist Wallace Thurman, journalist Angelina Weld Grimké, writer and activist Alice Dunbar-Nelson, and painter Richard Bruce Nugent. In an essay written in 1983, 'T'Aint Nobody's Bizness: Homosexuality in 1920's Harlem', Eric Garber (who often wrote under the pseudonym Andrew Holleran) described a pre-soul underground: 'At the beginning of the twentieth century, a homosexual subculture, uniquely Afro-American in substance, began to take shape in New York's Harlem. Throughout the so-called Harlem Renaissance period, roughly 1920 to 1935, black lesbians and gay men were meeting each other [on] street corners, socializing in cabarets and rent parties, and worshipping in church on Sundays, creating a language, a social structure, and a complex network of institutions.'

One of the heartlands of gay life, pre-dating gay disco by more than fifty years, was a notorious haunt called the Clam House on 133rd Street, where the cross-dressing blues singer Gladys Bentley headlined. The gigantic Bentley, similar in stature to Big Maybelle, held court in a white tuxedo and top hat, and was the forerunner of the disco diva. A powerful chanteuse with a blaring soulful voice, she hollered above the music and urged her audience into ever greater paroxysms of delight. Born in Pennsylvania, she left there, aged sixteen, to become part of the Harlem Renaissance. She recalled her childhood in an *Ebony* magazine feature: 'It seems I was born different. At least, I always thought so . . . From the time I can remember anything, even as I was toddling, I never wanted a man to touch me . . . Soon I began to feel more comfortable in boys' clothes than in dresses.' She had a string of glamorous girlfriends and was frank about her sexuality, once telling a gossip columnist that she had married a white woman in Atlantic City.

The Hamilton Lodge Drag Ball (aka the Faggots' Ball) was held annually on 155th Street throughout the twenties and thirties, and attracted thousands. The events outraged the tabloids: FAG BALLS EXPOSED, shrieked a 1932 Broadway tabloid, 6,000 CROWD HUGE HALL AS QUEER MEN AND WOMEN DANCE. An observer at the time described how the ball brought together 'effeminate men, sissies, wolves, fairies, faggots, the third sex, ladies of the night and male prostitutes . . . for a grand jamboree of dancing, love making, display, rivalry, drinking and advertisement'. Harlem was inventing the polysexual future almost a century ago.

Throughout the sixties, as Motown and mainstream soul dominated, Harlem's underground met at the Rockland Palace in competitions to impersonate the kings and queens of soul – from Little Richard to Diana Ross – in the precursor to what became known as 'voguing'. The stylised dance craze re-emerged in seventies Harlem and mutated into one of the major underground movements of the urban R&B scene, inspiring in turn Madonna, Beyoncé, Rihanna and Ariana Grande. Vogue balls were organised around grandiose names like the House of LaBeija, House of Dupree, House of Xtravaganza, Ninja, Ebony and the House of Saint Laurent and Chanel. But in less enlightened times, such gatherings were strictly underground and never universally welcome in a community steeped in religion.

This tension between private sexual lifestyle and religion was to become one the overwhelming moral dilemmas for gay men and women in the black music industry and was already widespread in 1969. Most soul singers who took to the stage at the Apollo had come from a church background and many had deep and immutable spiritual views. While some could live with the contradictions of drugs, promiscuity and the Lord, others were more troubled by the conflicts thrown up by sexuality. It was a conflict exemplified in the chaotic life of Little Richard. One of a family of twelve children raised in Macon, Georgia, he had sung among the pews of New Hope Baptist Church before he met and performed with the gospel giant Sister Rosetta Tharpe in 1947. Then, bizarrely, he made his first significant income attracting crowds for an eccentric local spiritualist. Doctor Nubilio sported a turban and multicoloured cape, and performed juju routines with the desiccated body of a 'baby' with claws for feet and horns on its head. Nubilio told Little Richard that he was going to be famous and encouraged him to 'go where the grass is greener'. From those contrasting beginnings – his family considered R&B to be 'devil music' – his career and sex life catapulted between the Lord and lascivious showmanship. Little Richard's nascent rock 'n' roll hits of 1957, 'Tutti Frutti' and 'Long Tall Sally', came not only with the shock of the new but with a barely disguised sexuality.

Singer-songwriter Patti Smith once claimed him as her major influence, telling the *New Enquiry* that 'Little Richard was a person that was able to focus a certain physical, anarchistic, and spiritual energy into a form which we call rock 'n' roll . . . I understood it as something that had to do with my future. When I was a little girl, Santa Claus didn't turn me on. Easter Bunny didn't turn me on. God turned me on. Little Richard turned me on.'

In June 1969, a local Harlem-based group called Shades of Jade were performing at the Apollo's keenly contested amateur night. It had been a graveyard slot for many promising acts, but it had also been the launch pad for some of black music's most celebrated stars, among them Ella Fitzgerald, Sarah Vaughan, Frankie Lymon, Wilson Pickett, James Brown, Dionne Warwick and Gladys Knight. Shades of Jade had taken their name from a Latin jazz album by Cal Tjader, and had won several other talent contests in the Bronx, Washington Heights and at Harlem's YMCA. In the group were two young teenagers who would become outstanding backing vocalists in the decade ahead: Alfonso 'Fonzi' Thornton and Luther Vandross.

Thornton was from the Johnson Projects on Lexington Avenue in East Harlem, a racially mixed housing development where the splendidly named Puerto Rican boxer Héctor 'Macho' Comacho also grew up. As a thirteen-year-old, Thornton turned down an opportunity to join the community soul group Voices of East Harlem, in part because he had already met his near neighbours Ann and Pat Vandross, the latter a member of the New York doo-wop group the Crests. It was through the two sisters and another local girl from their public school that Thornton was introduced to their young brother Luther. According to Thornton, 'Luther was a visionary, even when we were young. When I first met him, he had a vocal group called the Shades of Jade . . . It was a group he was developing. They would sing at amateur night at the Apollo just trying to get discovered. Luther was very advanced. He was always that same singer, that same interpreter.' However, that June night, the crowd failed to appreciate the latent talent on stage and Shades of Jade lost the competition. 'The experience taught me that show business is really a process of rejection,' Vandross subsequently admitted, 'until you get to someone who might want to champion your cause.'

Curiously, it was another rejection that led the group to a champion and a major opportunity. In 1968 the Apollo had hired publicists Peter Long and Tony Major to pull together a showtime group of emergent Harlem talent, to be called Listen My Brother. Over 150 teenagers entered the competition, and after a brutal selection process it was whittled down to the final sixteen: Fonzi Thornton and Luther Vandross were still standing. Another successful entrant was the Puerto Rican guitarist Carlos Alomar and a female vocalist, Robin Clark, who worked alongside the sixteen-year-old Vandross in the stockroom at Alexander's Department Store on Lexington. (Clark and Alomar would marry in 1970; they still remain together.) The group released two singles and appeared on early episodes of the PBS educational show *Sesame Street* towards the end of 1969. A young Nile Rodgers, who befriended Fonzi Thornton and eventually recruited him to join the legendary disco band Chic, would also tour with the *Sesame Street* band.

Ultimately, Listen My Brother's cuteness and association with pre-school education meant that they were overshadowed by the more streetwise and ghetto-cool community group the Voices of East Harlem. Both groups had emerged from local talent initiatives, but the Voices were grittier and better suited to the culturally charged times. But long after Listen My Brother had disbanded, Luther Vandross's friendship with fellow members Fonzi Thornton, Robin Clark and Carlos Alomar endured. Clark and Alomar travelled with Vandross to a now-historic session in Philadelphia when they were hired to provide backing vocals for David Bowie's *Young Americans* album, released in 1975. After Bowie reputedly overheard them improvising one of his songs during a break in recording, Vandross was promoted to main backing singer and taken on the subsequent stadium tour. It was *Young Americans*' lush, blue-eyed soul that brought him a step closer to stardom.

In June 1969, however, Vandross was a shy, overweight bundle of suppressed anxieties. He was almost phobic about singing in front of his sisters, who he thought were more talented, and he recoiled from joining both his school and church choirs. Even when his talent was identified and he was chosen to join Listen My Brother, Vandross admitted to feeling humiliated by recent rejections. 'Remember, I was a 16-year-old, 300-pound kid, so when it came time for the lead vocals to be handed out, they didn't want me up there,' he told *The Washington Post*. 'I was the one, mind you, who always put all the harmony together; I had the administrative role, I was real good at it. I used to listen to the Shirelles and the Sweet Inspirations and I always had a good sense of who could do what, who sang top, who sang bottom . . . But they didn't want me to front the group. I carried that with me for a long time.'

One of the few endorsements he received in what was an unhappy period in his life was on a regular trip to the Apollo where he watched the Temptations and Patti LaBelle and the Blue Belles. Vandross was so taken by the all-female band from Trenton, New Jersey, that he became the president of the group's fan club, a role that brought him face to face with a woman who would become one of the most creative figures in modern black music – Nona Hendryx. She blazed a trail for new wave and became a zero-cool gay rights activist in an industry still jittery about open declarations of sexuality. Along with her contemporary Betty Mabry, Hendryx repositioned black women slap bang in the middle of the rock mainstream.

Her self-confidence and ebullient nature was the polar opposite of Vandross's personality. He fought and often lost a battle with his weight, claiming once that he was 'an emotional eater' – and he had much to eat about. Even at the height of his success, he was the subject of prurient interviews about his sexuality, and in California in 1986 he was involved in a car crash that resulted in his best friend's death and injuries to four others. He was eventually charged with vehicular manslaughter and reckless driving.

Vandross became adept at shielding himself from scrutiny about his sexuality. He was gay but resolutely private about his personal life, once telling a newspaper that his emotionally charged music 'is not all from life experience. I'd be a solitary confined mental patient if I lived through everything that I sang about.' In an astute interview with *The Washington Post*, Vandross was described as one of soul music's classic romantics and almost old-fashioned in his distaste for sexualisation of music. 'Vandross is something of an anomaly in today's black pop,' journalist Richard Harrington wrote. 'In the age of sexual innuendo, he is very much the romantic, influenced by groups like the Shirelles and such big-hearted, big-voiced soul divas as Dionne Warwick, Aretha Franklin and Diana Ross. His best-known songs are less about sex than love – the finding and losing of it, and all the attendant joy and pain.'

As gay sensibilities and sexual difference bubbled beneath the surface of soul, something else was happening to the Lord's music: a dispersal of styles that can best be described as the great fragmentation. The coherence that had once held sixties soul together – the secularisation of gospel and the joyful voices of the church – was now breaking apart. By June 1969, 'Cissy Strut' had broken into the Harlem retail charts and was number four on the monthly returns, only to be leapfrogged by Marvin Gaye's 'Too Busy Thinking About My Baby'. Legacy soul records like the Supremes and the Temptations' 'I'm Gonna Make You Love Me', Gladys Knight and the Pips' 'Friendship Train' and Jerry Butler's 'Only The Strong Survive' were still dominating the sales charts but it was increasingly clear that the black music charts were diversifying. The Harlem Top Ten that month is instructive. Records were coming into the R&B stratosphere from every conceivable direction. Funk was battering down the door. The Meters' 'Cissy Strut', James Brown's 'Mother Popcorn', Charles Wright & the Watts 103rd Street Rhythm Band's 'Do Your Thing', Eddie Bo's 'Hook And Sling' and a local Rojac release, Kim Tolliver's '(You Trying To) Cop My Stuff', were all fighting for big plays in Harlem nightclubs. A new generation of summer hits were jostling for attention, among them countercultural songs that had been buoyed by the festival circuit and the seemingly endless Summer of Love. Among them were records like the Friends of Distinction's trippy 'Grazing In The Grass' and the Edwin Hawkins Singers' neo-gospel international hit 'Oh Happy Day'. All came steeped in a sense of otherworldliness. So when the summer arrived in earnest, Harlem played host to one of the most remarkable festivals ever. Now almost forgotten or relegated to a sidebar in the history of pop and rock, it took place over five weekends and captured soul music at a moment of seismic change. The free events held in Mount Morris Park were known officially as the Harlem Cultural Festival but history has bequeathed them another name – Black Woodstock. But before the tickets were distributed through schools, community centres and record stores, whitey was on the moon.

A publicity shot of David Frost with the New York skyline behind him. Frost had arrived in America to launch his late-night talk show.

JULY

The Apollo Mission

David Frost had a predilection for pretty black girls. There was nothing predatory about his wandering eye, but the more his career took him to New York, the harder he found it to be faithful. He was on the verge of becoming a household name in America as the host of a new era-defining chat show, *The David Frost Show*, which was being distributed through network affiliates by the Westinghouse Media Group. While studying English at the University of Cambridge (he graduated with a Third), Frost had been a jazz buff and would-be satirist, and he had become passionate about black music and the story of civil rights. It would be a generous understatement to say that he wanted to prove his commitment by integrating with attractive black women, and so he liked to hang out in Harlem, visiting the jazz dives and cocktail bars uptown. He not only juggled a crowded love life, he happily socialised in places that most of the white executives who ruled American broadcasting only knew by their terrifying reputation.

In July 1969, as the Apollo 11 space mission reached its dramatic height, Frost was poised to launch his transatlantic chat show and become a major force in American broadcasting. He was already a household name in the UK – he had been a major figure in the rise of satire on television on the comedy review show *That Was the Week That Was* (known as *TW3*) – and a central figure in the 'Swinging London' scene. With the lure of more money, bigger budgets and less moral constraint, he jumped ship from the BBC to anchor his own show on the commercial station London Weekend Television. Frost attracted interest in America, and by 1969 was flying regularly between London and New York, the first member of what the tabloid press called the 'jet set'. In negotiating his contract for a US chat show with the Westinghouse Electrical Group, Frost bewildered the conglomerate's lawyers by insisting that if he was to sign up then they must fund a television special celebrating the life and times of the Apollo Theater in Harlem. And it was a deal-breaker: either the Apollo was in or he was out. Thus, towards the end of 1969, in recognition of Harlem's place as the capital city of black creativity, Frost fronted a sixty-minute special on the most famous venue in the history of soul, which included virtuoso performances by James Brown and Vicki Anderson.

Due to the constraints of having to deliver a nightly show to a network of affiliates across the country, Westinghouse decided that the show could not be live, a constraint that Frost turned to his advantage. He stockpiled personality interviews in London and New York, and created shows that would make news rather than reflect it. In 1969 that meant interviewing some of the most combustible figures in world affairs. His first show was broadcast on 7 July 1969 and featured what Britain considered to be the opposite sides of the youth revolution – the sheltered and socially awkward Prince Charles and the charismatic lead singer of the Rolling Stones, Mick Jagger, who had already racked up a series of drugs charges. To oversee the music, Frost hired a well-liked bandleader from Harlem, the jazz pianist Billy Taylor, whose famous Jazzmobile toured the streets and public parks of the ghettos uptown, offering free concerts and music tutoring to local kids. Taylor's radio show was an institution on the Harlem airwaves, and through it he had connections in bebop, big band, R&B and soul. According to *The New York Times*, he had the demeanour of 'a genial professor', and from the first day they met, he became Frost's personal Sherpa, taking him to Harlem nightspots and introducing him to the good, the bad and the ravishing. Taylor also helped to fulfil one of Frost's private fantasies, which dated back to his Cambridge student days – he co-ordinated a jazz album fronted by Frost himself. Despite its saccharine festive cover and Frost's rather detached intros, *From David Frost and Billy Taylor – Merry Christmas* is a much admired and very fine piece of sixties jazz, featuring a stirring gospel choir and Frost's friend Gerri Granger on lead vocals.

On his arrival in New York, Frost was described as the 'best-known Englishman since Winston Churchill', and throughout 1968 he was photographed at society events with the journalist Bernadette Carey, a former *Washington Post* reporter who had been head-hunted as editor-in-chief of the black society magazine *Ebony*. Carey was stunningly good-looking. She had the beginnings of a tangled afro and wore the plunging little black dresses that became *de rigueur* in the media in years to come. She modestly said of her time with Frost: 'David had a network show in America by then and was the toast of New York. He'd taken a house in the Hamptons. I didn't look too bad and I had a fairly decent wardrobe, which David liked.' Like Frost, she had an inquisitive mind, a witty turn of phrase and was always on the chic side of political militancy. It was a relationship that came with a certain daring – love across the races was still controversial. Frost thrived on his reputation as an *enfant terrible* in the eyes of the press, and the couple scandalised some of Britain's more conservative diplomatic corps when they attended an Ambassador's Dinner in Washington DC. Carey was photographed looking captivating in a halter-neck dress, sipping cocktails with Frost. She was in many respects the perfect chaperone; she could network in ghetto bars and high society dinners alike, and she had access to a contacts book that took in the Washington elite and the Black Panthers. She charmed John Freeman, the formidable UK ambassador at the time, who was once Frost's rival when he was a presenter of the BBC current affairs programme *Panorama*. In 1971 Freeman returned from diplomatic duty to become chairman of London Weekend

Television (LWT) and so ostensibly became Frost's boss. In board meetings, joshing with *risqué* small talk, Freeman often teased his friend about his 'weakness' for black women and joked that he had a series of secret photographs that would shock *Playboy*. They have never surfaced and probably never existed.

Sometime in late 1969, while Frost was still dating Carey, he met and fell in love with the actress Diahann Carroll, who at the time was rehearsing for the series *Julia*, an NBC sitcom in which she played a widowed single mother. It was a rule-breaking show. Carroll became famous as the first black woman to become a network television star in what was a challenging, non-stereotypical role. They soon became an item, but Frost was slow to explain this to Carey. There may even have been a third woman in Frost's crowded love life. He doted on the New Jersey soul singer Gerri Granger, who appeared on *The David Frost Show* no fewer than eighteen times, mostly singing soul standards. She was still appearing on the show in 1971 when her memorably dramatic song 'I Go To Pieces (Everytime)' was released by Bell Records into obscurity, only to resurface later in the decade as a standard on the UK's northern soul scene. The label issued promotional copies of her record to DJs but, underwhelmed by the feedback, did not authorise a full release. Granger had secured the stalled recording deal in part through Frost's influence. He was negotiating with Bell to release a Christmas album for his American television show, on which she was a featured vocalist.

Frost's tangled affairs rebounded badly on him. Discovering his infidelity through a third party, Carey broke up their relationship and vowed never to speak to the philandering Frost ever again. The tiny Granger drifted out of his life, too, when the television series ended. His life was now fully committed to Diahann Carroll but she exacted her own kind of personal revenge for his untrustworthiness – she practically ditched him at the altar. Despite lavish rings and promises, Carroll backed off from what was about to be a hastily arranged wedding in Las Vegas, although she kindly calls him 'one of the best things that ever happened to me' to this day.

The David Frost Show came to define the era. According to television historians, 'it became a time capsule of one of the most contentious and creative periods of the twentieth century' and often featured guests designed to intrigue and to enrage. It enthusiastically tackled every area of public debate in the late sixties: feminism, the war in Vietnam, racism and national drugs policy among them. Frost's alternative personality attracted big celebrity names as well as those rebels who felt locked out of mainstream television. A young and intense Dennis Hopper, fresh from directing the iconic *Easy Rider*, appeared on the show, eyes like pissholes in the snow, and berated society for the failures of its drugs law and heavy-handed urban policing. John Lennon and Yoko Ono were beamed live into American homes from a studio in Wembley, North London, in what was a truly eccentric glimpse into their love life. The peaceniks mystified network audiences by throwing acorns into the air as a sign of peace and demanding penal reform to reverse the crisis within the American prison system. They also used the opportunity to plug their banned album *Unfinished Music No. 1: The Two Virgins*, which Frost mocked for a strategically placed price sticker over Lennon's naked cock. Charlton Heston attacked the new left and defended the constitutional freedom to bear arms and own guns. Mother Teresa quietly raged against poverty. Jesse Owens explained why he never shook hands with Hitler, and in one of the very first televised interviews about feminism, Gloria Steinem argued passionately for wages for housework. Black Power activists were regular guests, including Huey Newton of the Black Panthers and Stokely Carmichael, then of the All-African People's Revolutionary Party. The show was a crucible of ideas which anthologised the era and examined subjects that stretched the patience of advertisers and network chiefs. Although it was cast in the relaxed format of a mainstream light-entertainment chat show, *The David Frost Show* became a testing ground for new ideas and for relatively unknown soul singers, among them Ronnie Dyson, Eloise Laws, Dee Dee Warwick and Patti LaBelle. Specials featured Aretha Franklin, Nina Simone and Stevie Wonder, and when the series ended Frost invited Ray Charles to sing the show out with his acidic version of 'America The Beautiful' – a performance dripping in contentious patriotism.

Frost's chat show aired at the height of the hype around the moon landings. On the second night Frost played host to the eminent Harlem politician Adam Clayton Powell Jr, who sparked a national controversy by accusing agents of the state in a conspiracy to assassinate President Kennedy, Malcolm X and Dr Martin Luther King. At the time it was seen as a preposterous outburst by a controversial and divisive black politician. But it was this show that first ignited a flicker of suspicion in the minds of many Americans and triggered widespread conspiracy theories about the role of the FBI. In time, House Select Committees on Assassination would investigate Powell's claims.

The next show featured two of the UK's most adored comedians, Ronnie Barker and Ronnie Corbett – the Two Ronnies – along with another familiar Harlem face, the much loved comedian and one-time soul singer George Kirby. Then Frost changed gear again; this time focusing on Israeli politics and the plight of the Palestinians through interviews with the Israeli military leader Moshe Dayan and the recently elected prime minister Golda Meir. This innovative mixture of comedy, cool music and conflagratory political topics came to define Frost's American show, and remarkably, before it was a week old, he flew back to London to anchor the all-night spectacular on the Apollo 11 space mission in the UK. For months, heightened expectations of a manned moon landing had gripped the popular imagination. Nightly news bulletins had stoked the public's interest, and by 16 July most televisions were tuned to the live telecasts from the Kennedy Space Center in Florida.

The televised coverage of the moon landing was at the time the ITV network's longest ever production – stretching from six p.m. on 20 July to nine a.m. the following morning. News and comments on the mission alternated with a gala variety show hosted by Frost. He had none of Harlem's talent base to draw on so instead resorted to mainstream light entertainers such as Cliff Richard, Cilla Black, Lulu and Engelbert Humperdinck. The author Ray Bradbury had also been invited, but he took exception to what he considered the frivolous style of the programme and walked out of LWT before the show. Frost's ITV show was in minute-by-minute contact with the American networks and corporate communications people at NASA and was extended until three a.m. When, finally, the 'Eagle had landed' he handed over to the American satellite feed of the astronauts stepping down onto the lunar surface. It was a monumental night in television history and did much to affirm Frost's status as the broadcaster of his era.

The New York Times devoted a full-page editorial to the Apollo 11 mission, describing it as a new epoch in scientific understanding. 'Not for 300 years has any comparable quantum leap in man's knowledge of the cosmos taken place in so brief a time,' the newspaper thundered, '. . . already revolutionising mankind's understanding of earth's nearest neighbour in space.' It was an event that grabbed the public imagination: six hundred million watched live on television, a new language was shared in the streets and bars of America – 'the Sea of Tranquillity', 'the Eagle has landed', 'a giant step for mankind' – flags were flown on all national buildings and the returning astronauts were cheered in Congress.

Crowds gathered in the usual places. Times Square swarmed with excited onlookers, and photographers could not resist the temptation of travelling uptown to Harlem to capture night shots of the most famous soul venue of them all, the Apollo Theater, its name now imbued with new meaning. The moon landings gave Harlem a new status – a partial patriotism as it were – as tourists and sightseers flocked to 125th Street to be photographed outside the theatre. Market stalls were hurriedly erected on the street outside the venue and astro kitsch such as plastic rockets, goldfish bowl helmets and a cut-out surface of the moon with spaces for heads to pop through were touted. But amidst all the clamour, one irreducible fact refused to lie down: Apollo 11 had cost a staggering $25.4bn – around $150bn in today's money – while the streets around the Apollo were collapsing ever deeper into poverty.

David Frost returned to New York the following week, to host more live shows in the city and begin the daily routine of travelling uptown to Harlem to film at the Apollo. There he would seek out soul veterans who could reminisce about the unique character of the famous landmark. He was deeply distressed by what he found.

Expecting to find a lively place bustling with talent, he found a decrepit playhouse in serious decline, its best days already behind it and now facing a perilous struggle to survive. Its neon signs and eye-catching exterior masked musty corridors, pockmarked walls, rattling pipes, sticky carpets and reeking toilets with stained and cracked porcelain. Visiting acts were shacked up in long-past-their-prime hotels such as the 'Waldorf of Harlem', the Hotel Theresa, home at various times to Muhammad Ali, Fidel Castro and Jimi Hendrix, and the Grampion Hotel on St Nicholas Avenue. In his memoir, *Only the Strong Survive*, the Impressions singer Jerry Butler described the latter as 'a typical old Harlem hotel: plenty of junkies and rats', one where it was advisable to leave any cash you had on the dresser, so that the junkies who came up the fire escapes to stick you up wouldn't wake you with a pistol.

Butler's fellow band member, Curtis Mayfield, had watched the clock turn midnight and come of age as a sixteen-year-old on stage at the Apollo in 1958. Within a few years the Impressions would be back, smashing box-office records and hurriedly arranging extra shows as 5,000 fans snaked around the building daily. They had come to witness the harmony group that had given subtle voice to civil rights with 'Keep On Pushing' (1964) and 'People Get Ready' (1965), the latter a song that Mayfield's son has described as 'a meditation, a hymn, a love letter to the fathomless strength and endless struggles of Negroes in America'.

Smokey Robinson, too, has vivid memories of the Apollo. The Motown star was still a naïve young singer from Detroit when he was first booked to appear there back in 1958. Robinson knew it as a place where careers were built or broken. 'The Apollo was the acid test, the ultimate proving ground of soul singers, dancers and comics,' he wrote in his autobiography, *Smokey: Inside My Life*, but its reputation preyed on his mind, and when confronted with the demands of the house, he simply froze. 'We were pitiful and I was petrified. I memorized the back wall of the Apollo perfectly – every crack and paint blemish. I was too freaked to look at the audience . . . the whole thing was a disaster.'

By 1969, the Apollo's creative range had narrowed. The demands of a vocal and judgemental audience had effectively chased subtlety out onto the streets and, in the main, audiences were intolerant of the radical poets, the gentler forms of soul or the more demanding and experimental. It is no great surprise that the King of the Apollo was the ferociously industrious high-octane headliner James Brown. More than any other R&B artist, his no-nonsense, high-energy, throat-burning performances defined what was required at the Apollo. On a now enshrined night on 24 October 1962, James Brown and his Famous Flames recorded the dynamic *James Brown Live At The Apollo*, an album of unrestrained R&B which to this day pulses with energy. It was self-financed by Brown when his label boss at King Records in Cincinnati, Syd Nathan, argued against the release of a live recording with no new material. Nathan got it spectacularly wrong. The album erupted in the ghettos and spread like wildfire through the radio stations of the rural South before crossing over to the college bedrooms of white rock 'n' roll fans.

Grammy award-winning academic and music writer Rob Bowman praised Brown's acumen and his outstanding showmanship, and described how he 'single-mindedly proceeded anyway, paying for it out of his own pocket . . . He had been out on the road night after night for a while, and he knew that the magic that was part and parcel of a James Brown show was something no record had ever caught. Hit follows hit without a pause – "I'll Go Crazy", "Try Me", "Think", "Please Please Please", "I Don't Mind", "Night Train", and more. The affirmative screams and cries of the audience are something you've never experienced unless you've seen the Brown Revue in a Black theatre.'

Logic would suggest that Motown's biggest names would have thrived at the Apollo, but they rarely did. Marvin Gaye struggled to win over rumbustious audiences with his suave crooning, the Supremes never quite seduced the crowds, and Little Willie John – the pint-sized tenor who was principally a balladeer (albeit one with a volatile temper and, in 1966, a conviction for manslaughter) – was usurped by his own support act: the incorrigible James Brown. Diana Ross remembers watching in disbelief as the Contours, a minor Detroit group, tore up the show with an act that was almost acrobatic in its energy. The Contours' hyperactive versions of 'Do You Love Me' and 'Can You Jerk Like Me' worked perfectly for an audience accustomed to instant gratification and soulful burlesque. Myths surround the Apollo like a sweat-soaked cape: from the long hook used by the management to drag off underwhelming performers, and audience members bombarding them with rotten fruit, to the hustling gangs, led by older women, who waited at the stage door to make their feelings known to substandard acts.

Wilson Pickett – it must be said – trumped almost every Apollo myth with his tale about a white girlfriend handing him his illegitimate infant in the venue. On being told by her parents that she could not keep the baby, it is alleged that the unfortunate mother turned up at the theatre and handed the infant to Pickett. It appears to be true, but it is just as likely that the couple met in his hotel in private. Perhaps Pickett's love of dramatic self-promotion made him shift the scene to the Apollo for added currency.

Yet, by 1969, something unforeseen had happened, and it was beginning to undermine the Apollo's once impregnable place in soul music. Major names were beginning to favour purpose-built concert halls, and it was a trend that grew throughout the seventies and left the Apollo behind. Suddenly, the Apollo's audience – soul music's equivalent of the seventeenth-century groundlings at Shakespeare's Globe Theatre – were out of step with the major changes reshaping black music. As soul music diversified, some of the new acts did not chime with the boisterous Harlem audiences. Several groups from soul's 'new romantic' era struggled at the Apollo. The Unifics from Washington DC, the Delfonics from Philadelphia, and the Manhattans from Jersey City all appeared at the Apollo in 1969, but were arguably too sophisticated and too romantically stylised to carry the crowd. The most telling example was Luther Vandross, one of the most elegant, silky-voiced soul singers of all time, who was booed off stage on four separate occasions before – at last! – winning the amateur night competition. The Chamber Brothers, massive in Greenwich Village clubs, were too folksy and acoustic to make an impression uptown. The urban beat poets Gil Scott-Heron, the Last Poets and Nikki Giovanni – many of whom lived or rehearsed locally in Harlem – were seen as too intellectual, too culturally complex, to appeal to big popular crowds. And the best of the touring psychedelic soul bands – Baby

Huey and the Babysitters, the Undisputed Truth and to a lesser extent Sly and the Family Stone – were experimenting in music that was not the natural diet of the Apollo crowd. They were welcome, but only just. The Apollo's audience craved traditional showmanship, which was often delivered from another new genre of soul – straightforward family entertainment. In 1969, on an otherwise routine night at the Apollo, two family groups went into battle as opening acts: the Burke family of Chicago, better known as the Five Stairsteps, and the Jacksons from Gary, Indiana, already known as the Jackson 5. At the time, the Five Stairsteps were the more famous of the two families, having just recorded their million-selling song 'Oh Child' (released in April of the following year). But the future was destined to reverse their fortunes. By 1980 the Five Stairsteps had disbanded, and the Burkes' most talented son, Keni, had gone solo, triumphing with his great civil rights club anthem 'Rising To The Top'. Simultaneously, the eighth child of the Jackson brood, Michael, had become black music's most controversial superstar. His 1982 album *Thriller* not only dwarfed anything that Keni Burke ever recorded, but it also became the biggest-selling album ever, rewriting the rules of the pop video, cross-over success and what it meant to be black.

Michael Jackson was not unique. The theatre's capacity for unearthing new talent dated back to the thirties. In 1935 the actor and choreographer Ralph Cooper took on what he thought would be a temporary job as a master of ceremonies at the Apollo introducing travelling jazz acts. He convinced the management that there was money to be made on quieter midweek nights by promoting a talent contest for local singers and performers. It was an inspired idea with two outstanding benefits: the unknown acts performed for free and the idea grew rapidly in scale and status to become soul music's equivalent of *The X Factor*. Amateur night was the toughest boot camp of them all. Every week, aspiring talent would expose themselves to humiliation, in the hope that they might be encouraged to come back or win the coveted cash prize and an opening slot on the full bill. Its reputation grew with every new discovery, but it also attracted an audience unforgiving in their condemnation. New acts underwent torrid abuse, and a crazed 'executioner' would chase them from the stage. Initially, the role was played by Howard 'Sandman' Sims, then by the irrepressible C.P. Lacey – a brilliant mimic and tap-dancer – who was a seven-time amateur night winner himself, through his impersonations of Little Richard, James Brown, Jackie Wilson and, later, Prince and Michael Jackson. If the amateurs fell short, Lacey would take over the show, claiming his initials stood for 'Crowd Pleaser'.

However, past success could not stem the inevitable decline in the Apollo's fortunes. The *New York Magazine* poignantly described the theatre as 'the fraying collar of a once fine shirt', and by 1969 it was abundantly clear that financial problems, the rise of television and home entertainment, and the general malaise of Harlem had left the Apollo staring at a bleak future. What remained triumphant and irreducible was the Apollo's famous marquee – a Harlem landmark – which has been described as 'a giant smile' in an area that did not have its worries to seek.

The weekend of the moon landing was fraught at both Apollos. Anxieties about technical faults were testing everyone at NASA. The fatal setbacks of Apollo 1 in 1967, when three astronauts died after fire engulfed the command module, were still fresh in the mind, and the clock was ticking louder on President Kennedy's famous commitment to land a man on the moon by the end of the decade – now only five months away. Back in Harlem the weekend was marked by a change-over: a soul caravan from the southern states was vacating the theatre and the psychedelic soul band Sly and the Family Stone were arriving from San Francisco en route to the Woodstock Festival. Two of the giants of the southern soul scene, the Stax artist Johnnie Taylor and the blind singer-songwriter Clarence Carter, headlined the southern revue. They were supported by Candi Staton, who was breaking the national scene for the first time with her single 'I'd Rather Be An Old Man's Sweetheart', and C and the Shells, a vocal trio who had just escaped the clutches of Calla Records and were now working with super-producer Jerry 'Swamp Dogg' Williams. Opening the show was a local singer with southern roots, the Florida soul singer Clarence Reid. He had found himself in dire straits and was temporarily working in one of Fat Jack Taylor's fast food joints. During his long summer in Harlem, Reid had recorded an album *Nobody But You Babe*, which was quickly turned round by the Tay-Ster label. Inspired by the moon landings, Fat Jack Taylor, ever the huckster, hurriedly redesigned the album cover, and went with a mocked-up image of Reid in an astronaut's suit and space helmet, standing next to a tattered American flag planted on the Sea of Tranquillity. The graphics are so naïve they might have been done by a local schoolkid, and possibly were.

On the night that Neil Armstrong and Buzz Aldrin stepped on the moon, Harlem was keenly cashing in on the excitement. The Apollo's lobby was festooned in intergalactic kitsch and the management resurrected an old Harlem tradition, inviting the Philadelphia DJ Douglas 'Jocko' Henderson to bring his legendary Rocket Ship Show to the theatre for a special Apollo mission residency. Henderson, the ultimate jive-talking DJ, had hosted live stage shows in New York City, first at Loew's State Theatre on Broadway, then uptown in Harlem when soul music went stratospheric. His act was cheap vaudeville laced with hip R&B street talk. He swung down onto the stage on a precarious rocket ship suspended by wires from the theatre's flies as the sound system announced his descent from space with rocket effects and raucous R&B. Henderson would then host a revue show dressed in a silver astronaut's suit and goldfish bowl headset with wobbling antennae.

This fascination with space gave birth to numerous records, including Joe Simon's chart-busting 'Moon Walk Parts 1 & 2' and Jimmy Reed's *Stay Loose* album on Verve, on which the jazz master is implausibly dressed in a space suit and what looks suspiciously like a white scooter helmet. A rash of small indies tried to cash in, too, including Moon Shot Records, a company that was in almost every respect typical of the myriad of small and undercapitalised soul labels that had emerged in the decade. Its key point of difference was powerful graphics and a lunar label design featuring a multicoloured rocket taking off into space. Moon Shot had launched in early 1966 when NASA selected the first Apollo crew and expectations about a manned moon mission intensified. Like many small indies, it was run from homes and rented offices with an official mailing address in a rented suite in the heart of the music publishing industry on 1631 Broadway, near the famous Brill Building. It specialised in resurrecting the careers of soul singers who had failed elsewhere, some of them outstanding vocalists who deserved another throw of the dice. Among Moon Shot's impressive roster were the Chicago harmony group the Vontastics, the Philadelphia group the Delfonics and veteran soul vocalists Tony Fox, Landy McNeal, Gil Blanding, Jimmie Ray and Cliff Nobles. Nobles was a singer mired in professional misfortune. He had previously recorded a potential hit called 'Love Is Alright' only for DJs to flip the record over and play the instrumental B-side 'The Horse'. The instrumental flourished, but Noble's career stiffed and Moon Shot did not favour much better. Hits were few and far between, and the roster of artists struggled to break through, most of them caught in well worn or dated styles – raucous R&B, doo-wop and harmony soul. However, one group bucked the trend. The Delfonics and their producer Thom Bell pointed forward to a new and more subtle form of soul, which in time became known as the Philly sound, one of the pre-eminent soul music genres of the seventies. When Moon Shot predictably crash-landed, the Delfonics returned to Philadelphia and finally broke through with the powerfully romantic 'Didn't I Blow Your Mind This Time' and 'La-La (Means I Love You)'. Their songs had a silky sophistication that was the polar opposite of Harlem's radical street music, and in time this fed into a thriving stream of 'symphonic' soul music, which paved the way for the Philly sound of Harold Melvin and the Bluenotes, Teddy Pendergrass, the O'Jays and Billy Paul. The success of 'La-La (Means I Love You)' in late 1968 paved the way for the Delfonics' Apollo debut in 1969, but they too joined a now growing list of artists whose music didn't quite fit, and their shows never sold out.

The heightened excitement of July 1969, and the sometimes desperate moneymaking schemes invented by management, leant heavily on the Apollo's stagehands, who were in the main freelance shift workers. They were engaged in a long and bitter dispute over poor working conditions. They had abysmal wages, no health insurance and no retirement benefits. As the dispute escalated in the years to come, the thirty-plus members of the Apollo stage crew joined Local No. 1 of the International Alliance of Theatrical Stage Employees, eventually forcing change and new management agreements. On the night of 20 July, as America excitedly watched the moon landings, the theatre's staff were instructed to clear the Southern Soul Revue and turn round a very different show – Sly and the Family Stone's ragged army of acidheads and hardcore funkateers. Sly Stone, the group's charismatic leader, was a passionate technologist, capable of managing lighting rigs, mixing desks, sound systems and fine-tuning every instrument in the band. Whatever happened in the theatre across the weekend, it came close to provoking a strike. A group of stagehands working the 'lobster shift' – New York's term for unplanned overnights – were arguing with management about their working conditions. So many things had exacerbated the dispute: overnight workload, the Southern Revue's delayed exit, Sly Stone's fastidious technical demands and the urgent one-off demands brought about by the space mission – there were constant media requests to film outside, inside and on the stage of the Apollo.

The big weekend proved to be a baptism of fire for a local soul group, Listen My Brother, who had been offered the chance to make their Apollo debut and open for Sly and the Family Stone. Listen My Brother were one of a number of choral soul groups who had emerged from Harlem's many churches. Often compared with their rivals, the Voices of East Harlem, Listen My Brother's only record release, the vaguely Christian 'Only Love Can Make A Better World', was released in 1969 on Van McCoy and Larry Maxwell's indie Maxwell Records. It was a curiously dated record for the times, immediately followed on Maxwell's roster by the New Perspective's pulsating psychedelic soul song 'Stone Outta My Head', and on the basis of their debut, times were changing faster than the likeable members of Listen My Brother could cope with. After a brief series of appearances on *Sesame Street*, one of which included a song about nursery-level arithmetic called 'Count To 20', they disbanded. But what would become of them was remarkable: Carlos Alomar became David Bowie's guitarist, vocalist Fonzi Thornton joined disco supergroup Chic, and lead vocalist Luther Vandross finally fought off early career setbacks, including those multiple humiliations at the Apollo's amateur nights, to become a towering presence in modern soul music.

On the late afternoon of Sunday, 20 July 1969, the science journalist John Noble Wilford, one of the quiet giants of space reporting, sat down to write his most famous front page for Monday's *New York Times*. 'Men have landed and walked on the moon,' he wrote matter-of-factly. 'Two Americans, astronauts of Apollo 11, steered their fragile four-legged lunar module safely and smoothly to the historic landing yesterday at 04:17:40 P.M., Eastern daylight time. Neil A. Armstrong, the 38-year-old civilian commander, radioed to earth and the mission control room here: "Houston, Tranquillity Base here. The Eagle has landed."' For years Wilford had struggled with the gnomic scientists of NASA – the organisation he branded the Never Say Anything association – trying to gain a lead for the *Times*. Now his biggest moment was about to be sent to press. As Wilford re-read his words, with the paper's iconoclastic front-page editor, John Bertram Oates, they knew they were in a losing battle with the live television coverage, and so agreed that sober reflection was more likely to connect with readers than sensational statements.

Newspapers were facing a difficult time. They had been asleep at the wheel as television screened sitcoms, variety shows and prime-time soaps; now, suddenly and emphatically, television was making and breaking live news. The rules had changed. CBS covered the moon landings for thirty-two continuous hours. Special screens were erected in Central Park so that people could join in as a community, and it was estimated that more than ninety per cent of TV-owning households in America tuned in. Back in the UK David Frost was also making history as both the BBC and ITV stayed on air throughout the night. The BBC had sent reporters to Mission Control in Houston. John Goodson, the BBC network director, recalled: 'When Neil Armstrong stepped onto the moon's surface, the whole BBC control room, with the canteen ladies and security guards standing beside the vision control desk, exploded into cheering and clapping. To us it had been a similar type of relief as it must have been to Armstrong, his crew and Ground Control.'

But amidst the excitement and party atmosphere that gripped bars along 125th Street the first words of disenchantment were being muttered. It is now largely forgotten that the moon landings coincided with the emotional high-point of Black Power, but what appeared glaringly obvious to television viewers was that the entire space mission was white through and through: the astronauts, the support staff and the massed banks of scientists and mathematicians at Mission Control. This false impression was not lost on Otis S. Williams, who had been the manager of the lunar module controls systems, and who sent a short but scathing letter to the *Amsterdam News*. He informed the paper that the lunar module had been manufactured by Grumman Aerospace in Bethpage, Long Island, where over fifty per cent of the company's 3,600 employees were black. Williams listed the employees in both Long Island and Mission Control who were black, and named six managers – all black – who had played a key role in the lunar module project. Williams's compelling statistics were buried in the pages of a small-circulation newspaper distributed to black homes in Harlem, the Bronx and Brooklyn, until the publication of Margot Lee Shetterly's book *Hidden Figures* and the subsequent motion picture highlighted the role of African-Americans in the space race. Finally, their contribution became mainstream knowledge. While the book was well received, the film irritated many critics, prominent among them Tim Grierson, writing for *Screen International*, who said that '*Hidden Figures* is almost patronisingly earnest in its depiction of sexism and racism. An air of do-gooder self-satisfaction hovers over the proceedings.' That may be true of the film, but what it does not explain away was the genuine feeling of marginalisation that many black people felt about the moon mission in 1969. Gil Scott-Heron's 1970 rap poem 'Whitey On The Moon' gave urgent voice to these sentiments. From its opening and recurring line – 'A rat done bit my sister Nell' – to the pay-off line – 'was all that money I made last year for (whitey on the moon)' – it was an acidic and strident message typical of Scott-Heron's politically probing mind.

The most creative and truly imaginative reaction was still brewing in the mind of George Clinton, the insanely gifted Detroit-based songwriter who took soul music into a new galaxy. In the summer of 1969, as Motown shifted the locus of its operation to Los Angeles, the vacuum left in Detroit was filled by Hot Wax, a label set up by former Motown songwriters Holland-Dozier-Holland and a rival indie Westbound Records, owned by the Armenian-American distributor Armen Boladian. The label became home to the Detroit Emeralds and two pioneering funk bands, the Ohio Players and George Clinton's Funkadelic. Clinton had the audacious idea of running two bands simultaneously: Funkadelic and sister band Parliament. Under the Funkadelic banner he released the groundbreaking albums *Free Your Mind . . . And Your Ass Will Follow* (1970) and *Maggot Brain* (1971). Meanwhile, under the Parliament banner, he released the psychedelic soul album *Osmium* and the racially provocative concept album about Washington DC, *Chocolate City*. All four were stepping stones towards Parliament's epic intergalactic funk album *Mothership Connection*, which brazenly reworks the teachings of the Nation of Islam and imagines a wholly new interpretation of the space mission: a manned flight of black astronauts discovering a new planet populated by an eccentric and funk-crazed civilisation.

George Clinton's vision was not his alone. A rival band Masterfleet's debut album *High On The Sea* (1973) became a cult underground record set around a planetary voyage. Wryly, within one track the album is given an Academy Award, presented to Masterfleet by actress Nichelle Nichols who played Lieutenant Uhura in *Star Trek*. Later in the seventies, as disco cut a swathe through the pop charts, the Philadelphian keyboard player Dexter Wansel released his magnum opus *Life On Mars* (1976). It was an unashamedly smart album which drew on a central idea: could soul music produce an album like Gustav Holst's orchestral suite *The Planets*? Using Philadelphia's state-of-the-art Sigma Sound Studios, Wansel orchestrated the disco funk album around a series of tracks, some of them thinly veiled interpretations of *The Planets*. The standout tracks were 'Life On Mars', 'Stargazer', 'One Million Miles From The Ground', 'Rings Of Saturn' and 'Theme From The Planets'. These diverse initiatives, which in their different ways challenged the whites-only image of NASA in 1969, were the first real manifestations of what became known as afro-futurism, the catch-all term for the funk/electro hip-hop of bands such as the Jonzun Crew, Funkadelic, Captain Sky, Warp 9 and Deltron 3030.

David Frost's musical tastes were firmly planted in the past, not in the future. His nostalgic love affair with the jazz nightlife of Harlem, and the Apollo in particular, led to an hour-long televised homage that was shot in July 1969 between shows and whenever Frost could take time out of his nightly chat-show schedule. The programme, *A Salute to the Apollo*, was broadcast as a ninety-minute special on Wednesday 27 August and was in part a tribute to the Apollo's long-time co-founder, the Austrian-born impresario Frank Schiffman, who, in 1969, was in his mid seventies and retiring from the Apollo. The show featured comedians 'Moms' Mabley and 'Pigmeat' Markham, funk stars James Brown and Vicki Anderson, jazz great Billy Eckstine, and the Harlem-born soul jazz singer Gloria Lynne, who graduated from the local Mother African Methodist Episcopal Zion Church Choir to win amateur night. Two other hopefuls, who had won amateur night in the previous weeks, were Claudia Moore, who became a backing vocalist for Roy Ayers Ubiquity, and Edward 'Eddie' Foster, a Bay area singer who had travelled to New York to compete with only a rare soul single 'I Never Knew' (1967) to his name.

After years of being ignored, soul culture was being broadcast by television. In the week Frost's Apollo show was aired, the pioneering *Soul!* show broadcast an interview with the then little-known author Maya Angelou. She discussed her recently published autobiography *I Know Why the Caged Bird Sings*, a tour de force on racism, rape and identity. Supporting Angelou in the studio were Archie Bell & the Drells performing their dance hit 'Tighten Up' and the Calla recording artist Jean Wells singing her 1969 single 'With My Love And What You Got (We Could Turn The World Around)'.

Despite Smokey Robinson's more subtle style, he was a popular act at the Apollo throughout the sixties, almost always appearing on the back of major hits – 'You've Really Got A Hold On Me' (1962), 'Going To A Go-Go' (1965) and 'Tracks Of My Tears'

(1967) – but by 1969 Smokey began to have second thoughts about the venue. He was not alone. The years had been deeply unkind to the old playhouse. It was in a desperate state internally and had not been refurbished for decades. The torn and shabby seats were tight and uncomfortable, and the mezzanine hung down low over the orchestra pit, cutting off sightlines from seats at the rear. None of this mattered too much for solo vocalists but it became increasingly problematic for bigger touring shows and for the gargantuan revues such as the Motown spectaculars, the James Brown Caravan and Ike and Tina Turner's late sixties revue show. These bigger and more professional acts were beginning to question the Apollo's internal architecture and its acoustics, and the venue was increasingly seen as an anachronism. For the newer counterculture acts – Richie Havens, the Chamber Brothers, Gil Scott-Heron, the Last Poets, Nina Simone and even Stevie Wonder – there was a shift to more intimate venues. New concert halls sprung up across the North East, prominent among them the Avery Fisher Hall (now known as the David Geffen Hall), an auditorium within the Lincoln Center which held over 2,000 people and had near-perfect acoustics. This was a sophisticated venue and a perfect environment for those musicians who wanted to have a less raucous relationship with their audience. Miles Davis had performed there in 1964 and the Supremes came the following year, opening up the venue to soul and jazz musicians who in the past had headed uptown to Harlem.

By July 1969, Harlem's biggest problem was perception. Repeatedly portrayed in the press and media as a crime-infested neighbourhood caught up in a drugs epidemic and with cadres of militant young rebels surfacing from within the black and Hispanic communities, Harlem became a no-go area, routinely stigmatised in everyday conversations. Although this was an exaggeration, the perception became entrenched, and the Apollo became a victim of the very neighbourhood that had once delivered so much talent. Surely nothing could get worse for the Apollo. But it did.

A local boy called Darryl Scullack, well known in the area for being on the fringes of the drugs scene, had hired a box to watch Smokey Robinson at the Apollo and invited his friends to join him.

Towards the end of the set, when Robinson had just started to sing his final number, 'Quiet Storm', the singer heard gunshots from the mezzanine area. He, his backing singers, orchestra and band members dived for cover as the panicked audience scattered to the exits. Within minutes, the auditorium of 1,700 people had emptied. A gang had hijacked the box at the top right of the stage and eighteen-year-old Scullack was shot dead. His girlfriend Karen Baker, who was celebrating her birthday, was left seriously wounded. 'I couldn't believe what was happening,' Smokey Robinson told a reporter from the *Amsterdam News*. 'I heard the shot but I thought it was firecrackers.'

The dead youth had been brought up in a neighbourhood due north of the Apollo and was still living with his parents in an apartment at 202 148th Street. He was already known to the police and had recently been charged with robbing the Dunbar Bar on Eighth Avenue. As homicide detectives investigated Scullack's death, it led them to another murder, one of the most notorious in the history of the Harlem drug scene. Days before going to see Smokey Robinson, Scullack had been seen arguing with a well-known bar owner, Wesley Diggs, on the premises of his bar, Diggs Den, and then again at a blues club, the Yardbird Suite. Onlookers thought the argument concerned a drug deal, but it took on a more sinister dimension when Diggs and his entire family were executed in a gangland killing in their suburban colonial-style home in Teaneck, New Jersey. It was an incident described by a New Jersey police officer as the worst murder in the town for four decades. The case was never satisfactorily solved.

The Apollo killing was the very last thing the theatre needed. Its once proud reputation was tarnished and it faced a grim future trying to ward off bankruptcy. David Frost's ninety-minute special gave it fond and nostalgic coverage, but the feelgood factor was eclipsed by the negativity that had encroached on Harlem.

Melancholy eyes and smouldering cigarette. One of the greatest performances of Nina Simone's chaotic life was at the Harlem Cultural Festival aka the Black Woodstock, August 1969.

AUGUST

The Black Woodstock

For sixteen pulsating minutes in the blistering afternoon sun of Sunday 17 August, Nina Simone cast a spell on Harlem. After a meandering piano solo, a half-smile in the direction of her keyboard player, and a series of barely audible grunts to her band, she launched into an inspired version of the song that would come to symbolise 1969 and the changing face of civil rights: the declamatory soul song 'To Be Young, Gifted And Black'. It was a moment unprecedented in its defiance. Ten thousand people stood on the parched grass of a public park: some hung from the branches of leafless trees and still more spilled onto the roads that surrounded Harlem's Mount Morris Park. Gradually, they learned the choral hook line of a song that had only recently been released and was in the infancy of its journey to creative success. Some members of the audience struggled with the words, other lip-synched, trying to keep up with Simone's darting and erratic voice until the soaring final chorus brought the crowd together in a mass incantation: young, gifted and black. The song was the culmination of one of the greatest live shows in the history of soul music, a statement of pride, political resistance and sheer enigmatic genius. *The New Yorker* wrote: 'Simone's explosiveness was well known. In concert, she was quick to call out anyone she noticed talking, to stop and glare or hurl a few insults or even leave the stage . . . Yet her performances, richly improvised, were also confidingly intimate – she *needed* the connection with her audience . . .'

Simone bewitched the crowd with a fiercely political set that spoke not only of her own burning activism but the audience's collective journey from ghetto children to angry adulthood. She dominated what was Harlem's fifth consecutive Sunday of live music, the penultimate in a series of six free events that stretched from 29 June to 24 August. Titled the Harlem Cultural Festival, by its triumphant finale it had become known to those who weren't there as the 'Black Woodstock'. Mount Morris Park was the welcome host to every conceivable strand of black music: the now fully grown child genius Stevie Wonder; the gifted vocalist David Ruffin; the super-professional Gladys Knight and the Pips; the smooth and effortless Lou Rawls; the genre-busting soul group the Fifth Dimension; local indie singers the Mantells; gospel legends the Staple Singers; Harlem's raw-silk vocalist Chuck Jackson; ghetto comedians 'Pigmeat' Markham and 'Moms' Mabley; the blues maestro B.B. King; the psychedelic soul group the Chamber Brothers; former James Brown vocalist Yvonne Fair; and the anti-apartheid jazz trumpeter Hugh Masekela. It was a triumph of diversity.

Comedian and Chess Records artist George Kirby was the ubiquitous MC, cajoling and teasing the crowd. At one point he challenged the audience's expectations by abandoning his comic persona, seizing the microphone and launching into his own mid-tempo song 'What Can I Do?' (1965). Never the greatest singer, Kirby was better known as a network television stand-up comic. He was a frequent guest on *The Dean Martin Show* and Perry Como's *Kraft Music Hall* series where his *pièce de résistance* was not as a soul crooner, but as a mimic, doing disarmingly accurate impressions of the right-wing colossus of cowboy films – John Wayne. A black man parodying a white icon was in itself subversive, but Kirby, a chubby yet agile dancer, pushed the shtick to the limit by galloping around the festival stage on an imaginary horse. The crowd erupted with every imaginary jolt of Kirby's imaginary saddle. This was Harlem – bold, unbowed and unashamedly different.

Simone's performance of 'To Be Young, Gifted And Black' is a book in its own right. Composed by Simone, with lyrics by Weldon Irvine, the song had only just been released by RCA Records and had yet to chart. But within a matter of months, it became an international hit, not only for Simone, but a succession of other artists. Aretha Franklin turned it into a gospel torch song, then Donny Hathaway envisaged it as an educational soliloquy, and through the song's success in the Jamaican charts, local reggae duo Bob Andy and Marcia Griffiths made it a colossal rock-steady pop song.

The lyrics were composed in Midtown Manhattan under the strangest of circumstances. Simone's friend and collaborator Weldon Irvine was travelling downtown from Harlem to meet his girlfriend at the Port Authority Bus Terminal. He had been tasked to find lyrics to a song that would inspire young people about their identity and for two weeks had struggled to come up with much. Suddenly while driving he had what amounted to a creative epiphany. 'It was the only time in my life that I wrestled with creating,' Irvine told the African-American publication *Chicken Bones*. 'Usually, I just open the door and it comes. On the fourteenth day, it came . . . I was in my Ford Galaxy on my way to the bus station to pick up a girlfriend from down south. I was stopped at a red light at Forty-First Street and Eighth Avenue when all the words came to me at once. I tied up traffic at that red light for fifteen minutes, as I scribbled on three napkins and a matchbook cover. A whole bunch of irate taxi drivers were leaning on their horns. I wrote it, put it in the glove compartment.' The scribbled notes were retrieved days later, and when Irvine sat down at a piano in Simone's home in Mount Vernon, together they shaped a masterpiece. It was a collaboration that spoke volumes about their special relationship and dug deep into their respective childhoods. Both were virtuoso pianists. Born Eunice Kathleen Wayman in 1933, Simone was a child prodigy. She made it out of rural poverty in North Carolina to the Juilliard School of Music and eventually the stage at Carnegie Hall. Irvine was an abandoned child who was raised by his academic grandfather on the leafy campus of Hampton College. Irvine knew every square inch of the grounds, including the gym hall where Marvin Gaye and Tammi Terrell were performing when she collapsed with a brain tumour. In circumstances unique in the story of soul music, Irvine had been protected by servants and wore antique knickerbockers. He could differentiate between different vintages of fine wine, and was served crumpets and tea by the staff. His grandfather hired a local tutor to give him piano lessons on the Steinway grand which stood in his grandfather's study. 'It was almost like a Victorian upbringing,' Irvine once said, 'and it instilled in me a sense of history that's very, very rare. Most people, regardless of their ethnicity, don't have the extremes of experience I have.'

After graduation he 'escaped' to Harlem where he joined the sixties influx of talent desperate to be noticed in the local jazz and R&B scene. Like Donny Hathaway and Nina Simone, he was a gifted pianist who was ambitious to stretch traditional jazz and R&B in new inventive directions. When he turned up at an audition to join Simone's band, the temperamental musician was taken aback that a pianist had dared to come to see her. Why would she need a pianist when she herself was a virtuoso? Midway through a song, she gestured to him to join in, and after one note she realised Weldon Irvine was a special talent with perfect pitch. She hired him on the spot, forming one of the great, if not quite fully realised, creative partnerships in the story of soul music. Amidst the chaos of her life and the fractious relationships she had with other musicians, Irvine was the closest thing she had to a true collaborator. Predictably, it would not last.

Simone was still grieving the loss of her closest female friend, the great Harlem playwright Lorraine Hansberry, who had died of cancer in 1965, aged only thirty-four. Hansberry had been a true pioneer. She had broken into the fiercely discriminatory Broadway theatre scene and won the New York Drama Circle's Award in 1965 for her internationally successful play *Raisin in the Sun*. The title had been adapted from a Langston Hughes poem, 'Harlem', which contained the rhetorical line: 'What happens to a dream deferred?/Does it dry up like a raisin in the sun?/Or fester like a sore –/and then run?'

Hansberry became Simone's intellectual mentor, revealing that 'we never talked about men or clothes. It was always Marx, Lenin and revolution – real girls' talk.' Hansberry's political radicalism and friendship with the eccentric pianist brought the two women to the attention of the FBI. Hansberry joined the Bureau's 'security index' along with other Harlem street radicals. At her funeral, Hansberry's friend Paul Robeson sang the eulogy and a letter of condolence from Martin Luther King was read out. According to reports, Simone was too upset to sing at the funeral, but she assured Hansberry's husband Robert Nemiroff that she would remember her in song and that she would record a eulogy that would last for ever. The opportunity soon arose. The dead writer's closest friends from the world of politics and theatre organised a tribute night that included scenes from her most famous plays, fragments of personal correspondence and readings from unpublished works, and it was given the title 'Young, Gifted and Black', a term which she herself had coined. It was this tribute that jolted Simone to compose a song of the same title, and the seeds of a modern soul classic were sown.

The unique creative partnership between Simone and Irvine promised to be one of the great collaborations of soul – up there with Isaac Hayes and David Porter at Stax, and with Holland-Dozier-Holland in their period of high creativity at Motown. But it was a short-lived and tempestuous partnership. In the first six months of 1969 they had worked together on the countercultural anthem 'Revolution (Parts 1 And 2)', the anti-love song 'Whatever I Am (You Made Me)' and the mournful 'How Long Must I Wander', a highly personal song about the singer's own weariness in the face of success. Then there was the tribute to Hansberry, which became one of the most famous songs of the decade.

Simone had already burned many bridges – even with her own family. Irvine lasted two and a half years with her and always spoke fondly of her. But her career was lurching from one self-inflicted problem to another – including tax problems and eventual bankruptcy. Unsettled and often rootless, her life was scarred by divorce, reckless and predatory sexual relations, and finally full-blown mental illness. The broken creative partnership between Simone and Irvine was, however, not all down to the singer; Irvine was never the easiest either.

Even at the height of Black Woodstock the tension in her life was palpable. Backstage, in a Winnebago parked behind the hip mosaic stage scenery, she and her husband-manager Andy Stroud, a former Harlem cop who had taken a vice-like grip on her affairs, screamed at each other. Several people who worked with them talked of the 'startling ferocity' of their fights. 'Andy was a leech,' Simone said in one interview. 'Just a week into our marriage and all I'd dream of was to see him walk out the door.' Eventually she walked out, tipping her business affairs into a mess that took decades to rectify. Residencies in Las Vegas, which had been a goldmine for the Supremes and the Temptations, fell apart. Booked to perform at Caesars Palace at the height of the Detroit rebellion in the summer of 1967, she broke her contract, complaining that she was 'playing a city almost segregated and stuffed full of gamblers and whores. I lasted four days and walked out.' In Harlem's local newspaper, the *Amsterdam News*, she was described as 'the stormy petrel of the piano who had walked out on many a concert'. Yet, set against her ferocious temper was a searing and beguiling honesty. The Nobel prize-winning writer Toni Morrison described her as 'indestructible. Incorruptible. She even scared me a little.' Simone, for all her influence on others, had often been her own worst enemy. She refused for years to sing, or even acknowledge, her timeless cocktail soul song 'My Baby Just Cares For Me', dismissing it as trite and superficial. She held out against the song until it was picked up by the perfume giant Chanel for a European advertising campaign, an agreement that delivered her a small fortune at a time of dire financial need.

In part chased away by Simone's temperament, the emotionally complex Irvine struck out on his own. Throughout the seventies he was one of the pioneers of jazz-funk and what later became known as 'acid jazz', producing the seminal album *Liberated Brother* and the rare-groove masterpiece *Jungle Juice*. The singer Jamiroquai once called him 'the greatest fusionist in the business' and rapper Mos Def, respecting his musical diversity, called him an 'artist without borders'. Despite a decent career with RCA – he produced the Fatback Band, Tom Browne and Charles Earland – he drifted away from recording into education where he became yet another figure from Harlem's musical vanguard to give creative voice to hip-hop, acting as a mentor and musical resource for Tribe Called Quest, Ice Cube, KRS-One, and his close friend Mos Def. What was truly remarkable about Weldon Irvine's later life was its sad parallel with Simone's decline. He disappeared from the music industry, struggling with bipolar disorder. On 9 April 2002, by then fifty-nine years old, he killed himself with a rifle on the front lawn of an office complex near the Nassau Coliseum, in Uniondale, New York. He left no suicide note and his death mystified his closest friends in urban music, from whom he had successfully hidden his mental illness over many years.

Simone's performance at the Harlem Cultural Festival was unshrinking in its political advocacy. She sang a blisteringly impassioned version of her controversial feminist quartet 'Four Women', which had been banned by radio stations in New York and Philadelphia. Its story unfolds over time: first, there is a slave woman, Aunt Sarah, then the mixed-race child of a slave owner and his slave, the yellow-skinned Saffronia, then a street prostitute, Sweet Thing, and finally a deceptively sweet lady called Peaches, who speaks the line that so worried radio bosses: 'My skin is brown/ my manner is tough/I'll kill the first mother I see/my life has been too rough.' She then closed her Harlem set with a poem she had been given by David Nelson, one of the original Last Poets, the radical wordsmiths who had formed there in Mount Morris Park the summer before, at a rally. She stood up, walked to the front of the apron stage, and swung around in slow semi-circles, directly addressing the crowd and reading from a sheaf of paper. The paper blew gently in the summer breeze, but the words were far from gentle. It was a poem that refrained Malcolm X's famous phrase – 'by any means necessary' – and advocated Black Power through armed resistance. Claudia Roth Pierpont, a journalist for *The New Yorker*, described the moment: 'She read the words from a sheet of paper, moving across the stage and repeatedly exhorting the crowd to answer the question "Are you ready, black people? . . . Are you ready to do what is necessary?" The crowd responded to this rather vague injunction with a mild cheer, prompted by the bongos behind her and the demand in her voice. And then: "Are you ready to kill, if necessary?" Now a bigger, if somewhat incongruous, cheer rose from the heart of a smiling crowd filled with little kids dancing on a sunny afternoon. "Are you ready to smash white things, to burn buildings, are you ready?" she cried. "Are you ready to build black things?" . . . Despite her best efforts, Simone failed to incite a riot in Harlem that day in 1969. The crowd received the poem as it had received her songs: with noisy affirmation, but merely as part of a performance. People applauded and went on their way. There are many possible reasons: no brutal incident of the kind that frequently set off riots, massive weariness, the knowledge of people elsewhere trapped in riot-devastated cities, maybe even hope.'

It was 'To Be Young, Gifted And Black', rather than the incendiary poem 'Are You Ready?' or the pan-historic 'Four Women', that became the anthem of Harlem in 1969. The tone had been set on the very first day of the month-long festival, when another of Harlem's spirited soul jazz singers took to the stage. Anna Marie Wooldridge – better known by her stage name Abbey Lincoln – had a pedigree background. A club jazz singer who had grown up in Chicago, she had studiously emulated the voice and onstage persona of the great Billie Holiday, and in 1965 became one of the first female pioneers to appear onstage with a full-blown afro. Lincoln's status in Harlem grew when she became the featured vocalist on Max Roach's landmark civil rights album *We Insist!* – a brilliant concept album often known simply as *The Freedom Now Suite*. One of the songs, a meandering jazz track called 'Protest', became infamous for its avant-garde stance, featuring one minute and twenty seconds of Abbey Lincoln screaming. Two further tracks, 'All Africa' and 'Tears For Johannesburg', a critique of the Sharpeville massacre, were among the very first musical acknowledgements of South African apartheid. What is remarkable about 'Tears For Johannesburg' is that it was released a full ten years before Gil Scott-Heron's jazz-funk hit 'Johannesburg' (1975) and more than twenty years before Eddy Grant's international reggae pop hit 'Gimme Hope Jo'anna' (1988). It also featured the Harlem-based drummer Babatunde Olatunji, a performer and creative advisor to the Harlem Cultural Festival. This was the year of the dashiki shirt, and according to reports in the *Amsterdam News*, at least half the crowd of 40,000 people had come dressed in quasi-African clothing.

A year of festivals, stretched out around the world, was bringing live performance to new levels of creativity. It was the year of Altamont, the fatal concert held at the speedway track in northern California headlined by the Rolling Stones. A Hells Angels chapter, ostensibly there to provide concert security, stabbed a young African-American man to death in the crowd. On 5 July 1969 the Stones in the Park free festival was held in London's Hyde Park and at nightfall transformed into a candle-lit wake for Brian Jones. He had drowned in his swimming pool, having overdosed on drugs and alcohol, on 2 July. Later in July, Rhode Island's Newport Jazz Festival tried to hold together the feuding factions of tradition and experiment with the George Benson Quartet and Herbie Hancock's Sextet bookending the festival – both taking a break from Harlem residencies to headline on different nights. In August the festival circuit roared with even greater intensity. Rumours spread that all four of the Beatles would perform at a festival on the Isle of Wight – they didn't – but 150,000 travelled by boat and ferry to see headliner Bob Dylan. Then there was Houston's Soul Bowl '69, a three-day benefit concert at the Houston Astrodome where Aretha Franklin, Ray Charles and Sam and Dave performed to raise money for low-cost ghetto housing and to support micro-businesses in inner-city America. Next came the epic sprawl of Woodstock, held over three days in August 1969 in the farmlands of upstate New York.

Pop music history was being chronicled in ways it had never been before. Rock writer Greil Marcus's article on Woodstock was featured prominently on the cover of the newly born *Rolling Stone*. It not only became the starting pistol for an ornate and tendentious era of rock journalism to come, but more importantly, it set the subcultural template for festivals as yet unimagined. 'It was Sunday afternoon and Joe Cocker and the Grease Band had finished their powerhouse set', Marcus reported, 'and suddenly the sky turned black and everyone knew it was going to rain again. It did. The ground on which two or three thousand kids were sitting was begging to be turned into mud and it got its wish and it couldn't have mattered less to anyone. The wind hit, then too; it seemed to come from a half-forgotten Biblical Apocalypse but no one was ready for the last judgement so we turned calamity into celebration . . . The kids yelled "fuck the rain, fuck the rain" . . . it was really just another chance for a new kind of fun . . . In front of the bandstand a black boy and a white boy took off their clothes and danced in the mud and rain, round and round in a circle that grew larger as more joined in.'

All the potent images of a successful festival were there: powerhouse sets, apocalyptic rain, a frisson of unruliness, tantalising mud, naked writhing dancers and a spirit of unreserved abandon. Compared to the efficiently run Harlem Cultural Festival, which was plotted methodically over a six-month period and part of a much wider policy of opening New York's public parks to local communities, Woodstock was a chaotic mess. Now seen as the most famous rock festival ever, it was the accidental brainchild of four young white graduates, some of whom were fabulously wealthy. John Roberts, heir to a family fortune earned in the pharmaceutical industry, initially placed an advert in *The New York Times* that read: 'Young men with unlimited capital looking for interesting, legitimate investment opportunities and business propositions.' An idea emerged to build a recording studio and creative retreat for rock musicians in Woodstock, where Bob Dylan had a home and where a posse of liberal musicians such as the Band, George Harrison, the Incredible String Band and Van Morrison had made their temporary base. The idea to fund the new studio somehow transmogrified into a hurried and ill-conceived rock concert, driven by the blundering brass neck of self-confident young men with no proven expertise. The organisers found a location in an industrial park in nearby Wallkill, Orange County, but the residents protested, and a local referendum chased them away. Bands were confirmed, then backed out. Security was in place, then it was not. At last, a 600-acre dairy farm in Bethel, New York, was leased and Woodstock was on. As crowds converged on the site, a lack of toilet facilities and food concessions marred their enjoyment, and for all the hype that has since gathered around the event, it was an organisational disaster. The festival actually took place over sixty miles from Woodstock, but somehow the lure of the name stuck. Fencing, ticket booths and parking facilities were not ready, and the queues for fresh water and toilets snaked for miles. By contrast, the Harlem festival was a triumph of public service, mostly pulled together by the staff of the city's Parks Department and unheralded community workers. It was a timely lesson in racial stereotyping: the young wealthy white entrepreneurs made a monumental hash of planning while a black-run public event, running over six Sundays, smoothly came together with no significant trouble, no arrests and no record of public inconvenience.

The so-called Black Woodstock was the creative vision of one-time soul singer and public employee Tony Lawrence, who had run annual musical concerts in Harlem for several years. Among his many calling cards was a role as an uncredited extra in the James Bond film *Dr No*, but it was a festival he organised the year before in Harlem that proved to be the breakthrough. In searing ninety-three-degrees heat Count Basie and His Orchestra entertained a celebratory audience. Among them was the mayor of New York, John Lindsay. He was mesmerised by the crowd of young people dancing to 'The Horse', a galloping dance-craze hit for the Philadelphia-based soul singer Cliff Nobles, who was also on the bill. Impressed with the professionalism of the event, Lindsay encouraged Tony Lawrence to repeat it the following summer, in what was an election year. Mayor Lindsay was seeking re-election and calculated that his popularity in inner-city ghettos like Harlem and Bedford-Stuyvesant would be strengthened by offering free events in the city's parks. He hired Lawrence as a cultural executive, and plans for the Harlem Cultural Festival of 1969 were ramped up. The mayor leant on his supporters in the corporate world, and Maxwell House, the instant coffee company, offered substantial sponsorship. Lawrence reeled in further investment, sold documentary rights to television networks, and gleaned smaller commitments from local businesses, who were allowed to pitch soul food stalls around the park. Those who baulked at the small concession fees were allowed to fill garbage cans full of ice and hawk soda to the crowds. In total Lawrence raised $250,000 – a substantial figure for what was still perceived as a ghetto event – and spent $15,000 on local radio ads. He then hired a backing band composed of freelance musicians living in Harlem and spent the early summer rehearsing them into a tight live band who could back nearly anyone. Lawrence also pursued an audience differentiation strategy that worked well. He spread the festival over six weeks, focusing on distinctive groups: jazz fans, Motown and contemporary soul fans, spiritual and gospel audiences, political activists, the Hispanic communities of East Harlem, and the local fashion and beauty scene. A whole day was dedicated to the music of the East Harlem barrios featuring Mongo Santamaría, Ray Barretto, Cal Tjader and Herbie Mann, and another day focused on the spiritual scene, a massed Christian celebration led by the towering Mahalia Jackson, featuring Herman Stevens and the Voices of Faith. The Reverend Jesse Jackson's Operation Breadbasket Band flew in from Chicago, led by the Memphis saxophonist Ben Branch, who only a year before had been the last person to speak with Martin Luther King before he was killed by an assassin's bullet in Memphis. It was the gospel day that attracted the smallest crowd – only 15,000 people came to watch the performances. The older generation appeared to be less enthusiastic about open-air pop festivals, and that day's torrential rain chased away the half-hearted. The day ended with organiser Tony Lawrence – a very competent soul singer in his own right – taking the stage to thank Mahalia Jackson and as an encore joining with her in a rain-sodden version of the civil rights anthem 'We Shall Overcome'.

The Harlem Cultural Festival was political in three very different senses. First, Nina Simone's stunning performance gave voice to strident radicalism and openly endorsed Black Power. Second, supporters of the jailed Black Panthers swept through the streets, collecting for bail money and distributing campaign leaflets. Third, and more connected to Manhattan, it was a series of concerts that took place against a very different kind of civic politics – a battle for the heart and soul of New York City and its public parks. It was a time when racially polarising politics were being played out across virtually every walk of life. For instance East Harlem's Puerto Rican community were incensed about garbage and poor public cleansing. A series of destabilising school disputes took place across the Five Boroughs, first at Harlem's Intermediate School 201, and then – in what become known as the Ocean-Brownsville dispute in Brooklyn – aspirational black parents were pitted against a predominantly white Jewish teaching union, bringing barely concealed anti-Semitism flaring to the surface. Then there were the parks. Supposedly places of recreation and natural beauty – places of escape immune to politics – they became a battleground for opposing communities and divergent views of how the ungovernable city should be run.

Tony Lawrence's boss and the civic power behind the Harlem Cultural Festival was August Heckscher II, the grandson of a German immigrant and philanthropist who made his millions in zinc mining. Later in life he donated money to public parks through the Heckscher Foundation, which created children's playgrounds in Lower Manhattan and in Central Park. His grandson, driven by a family passion for green spaces, rose to be John F. Kennedy's special consultant in the arts, and in 1967 he left the White House to become Parks Commissioner for New York City. When Tony Lawrence was not hustling radio stations and recording companies to support black artists, he had a desk in Heckscher's office, where they conceived of a grand plan to take soul music to public parks across the Five Boroughs, using Harlem and Bedford-Stuyvesant as their test beds. Heckscher was a skinny white liberal with artfully arranged grey hair, a pointed beard and horn-rimmed glasses. He was an unlikely champion of soul music, a patron of the arts who was always immaculately dressed in crisp white shirts and bow ties, and someone who it seemed unlikely had heard of Sly and the Family Stone. But Heckscher's family background and liberal views made him a passionate champion of public parks for all citizens, including the most socially deprived. Not everyone agreed. The jewel in the crown of outdoor Manhattan, Central Park, was at the time the fulcrum of a dispute about beauty versus utilitarianism: should the park be maintained as natural space or should it be put to greater public use, attracting those who would otherwise not benefit? Heckscher's predecessor had already taken a major step in the latter direction by closing the park to traffic on a Sunday. This opened it up to limitless recreational possibilities. But he had faced criticism from within his own department, where park curators criticised a Barbra Streisand concert sponsored by Rheingold Beer as a commercial invasion and a grotesque travesty. Two other initiatives attracted fierce criticism from protectionists: the building of Lasker Ice Rink and the Shakespeare in the Park events at the open-air Delacorte Theater, at 81st Street and Central Park West, which opened in 1962 with James Earl Jones in *The Merchant of Venice*. Critics resented the erosion of grass and the intrusion of man-made concrete structures into what had been cherished land for the wealthy residents of the Upper West Side.

Despite his sophisticated style, Heckscher was unfazed by noisy crowds and saw them as part of the lifeblood of American democracy. He argued against overbearing protectionism in his biography, *Alive in the City*. 'To put tidiness as the first and only consideration and to be blind to the big things that were happening . . . seemed a betrayal of the city's best hope.' Heckscher became Tony Lawrence and soul music's strongest ally, arguing passionately that the people of Harlem contributed substantially to the city's tax income and so deserved to see the benefits in their own neighbourhood, and in their own local parks. They identified Mount Morris Park as a place perfectly situated to open its gates to concerts, festivals and public demonstrations.

By the high summer of 1969, Lawrence had secured most of the performers who would eventually show up at the Harlem festival. He also managed to get early sight of the acts who were lining up to do Woodstock, too, knowing that the much talked-about upstate festival overlapped with the final days of the Harlem event. He harassed agents and managers to encourage their acts to stop off in Harlem, but some from the more mystical end of the folk scene were wholly unsuited to the predominantly black R&B crowd.

Others, especially from the new psychedelic soul movement, conveniently overlapped. Surprise guests who did show up on their way to Woodstock via the Apollo were the San Francisco freak show Sly and the Family Stone. They had left the West Coast having rehearsed a mind-blowing hallucinogenic funk-rock show aimed at Woodstock's predominantly white hippie crowd. By the time they reached the open-air stage in Harlem, Sly Stone had skilfully recalibrated the show. They eventually delivered two hours of hardcore R&B that shook the speakers which had been harnessed to trees throughout the park. The soulful beatnik Richie Havens, already an established underground star in Greenwich Village, was Woodstock's opening act. He had played a virtuoso set for over three hours on the Friday, to cover for bands who were still stuck on rural roads. Woodstock and its acid troubadours had brought the entire area to a standstill. Havens had returned to his native New York by Sunday and showed up at Harlem, keen not to be left out.

Stevie Wonder was appearing at the Apollo on Saturday 19 July as part of a Motown show, and agreed to stay on to perform in the park the following day. It was a transformative performance that said much about the future direction of the phenomenally talented child prodigy. He had already dropped the 'Little' from his name back in 1964, and now nineteen years old and a fully grown youth, he was on the cusp of what was to become a remarkable adulthood. Stevie Morris had been blind from birth, a victim of retinopathy of prematurity, and throughout his early career at Motown was a ward of the state of Michigan, studying at the Lansing Institute for the Blind. It would be an exaggeration to say that Motown regarded his blindness as a commercial novelty, but it was something that label bosses, and the singer himself, exploited. Little Stevie Wonder's second studio album was a tribute to Ray Charles, the most famous blind artist in modern R&B history. Motown called the album *A Tribute To Uncle Ray*, thus implying a degree of familial bond between the two artists. In 1965 Stevie Wonder was part of a Motortown Revue that travelled to Europe and performed at the Paris Olympia. On his days off, he visited the school where the blind educator Louis Braille studied, and he was photographed sitting at Braille's desk in a museum in the village of Coupvray, east of Paris. He spent time playing with the crude coding machine that Braille had invented. Wonder was already fluent in contracted braille, which he had been taught since childhood, but more importantly the visit fed his curiosity towards machine-aided innovations for the blind. This in turn fed his fascination for musical synthesisers, then in the early stages of development. To be allowed permission to travel abroad on tour, Wonder was required to write an essay in braille about every city he visited, a task that was strictly monitored by his blind tutor Ted Hull. On his return from Europe, Wonder embarked on a lifelong project of connecting with blind artists from across the musical spectrum, especially those he had met as a rising R&B superstar. He had already befriended Ray Charles and the Atlantic recording artist Clarence Carter, who had studied at the Alabama Institute for the Negro Blind, the famous meeting place of the Blind Boys of Alabama gospel group. With every interview and casual conversation Wonder stored information on songs, education for the blind and what later in life he referred to as 'innervisions' – the title of his award-winning album of 1973.

On stage in Harlem, Wonder's set hinted at the changes to come. It was drizzling when he took to the stage, sporting a chocolate-brown Regency-style coat, bright yellow ruff and his trademark dark glasses. Sitting at his electric piano, protected from the damp by a stagehand holding a giant orange parasol, Wonder launched into renditions of his major 1969 songs, among them 'For Once In My Life', 'Yester-Me, Yester-You, Yesterday' and the love song he co-wrote with Motown's Sylvia Moy – 'My Cherie Amour'. But it was the B-side of 'My Cherie Amour' that had come to fascinate him. It was a song that was fast becoming a modern festival classic, and in time it would be covered by a multitude of artists, among them Georgie Fame, Della Reese, Wilson Pickett, Billy Preston, Chuck Jackson, Frank Sinatra, Dusty Springfield and Marvin Gaye. The song was 'Sunny', an evergreen classic that had been recorded in 1966 by the Nashville soul singer Bobby Hebb. Wonder had met Hebb backstage during the Beatles' second American tour in 1966 and a surprise conversation turned the apparently feelgood summer song 'Sunny' on its head. Hebb confided that both his parents, William and Ovalla, and his older brother Harold were blind. Hebb had not only grown up surrounded by blindness in his family, but had performed on the streets of Nashville and onstage at the Grand Ole Opry as part of a blind washboard band known as Hebb's Kitchen Cabinet Orchestra. Hebb's parents had taught him rudimentary musical skills around their kitchen at home, and it transpired that both Hebb and Wonder had used kitchen utensils as instruments (the pair were virtuoso spoons players). But it was the hidden meaning of 'Sunny' that really grabbed Wonder's imagination. On 22 November 1963, President John F. Kennedy was assassinated in Dallas, and a few hours later on the same night Hebb's brother Harold – a member of Nashville soul group the Marigolds – had been stabbed to death outside Club Baron, an R&B haunt on Nashville's Jefferson Street. Harold was far from being an innocent bystander. He had spent time in the Tennessee Penitentiary, where he had met the incarcerated R&B star Johnny Bragg, lead singer of the doo-wop jail group the Prisonaires. Bragg had reconnected with Harold, and had joined him as a singer with the Marigolds. Inside the club, Harold had argued with two men and they all went outside. He was attacked, and while dying of knife wounds, grabbed a gun from the club's security guard and shot dead one of his attackers. Devastated by the two events, Bobby Hebb tried to write a song that might give him some emotional comfort amidst the chaos. What ostensibly sounds like a breezy summer love song was in fact personal therapy. It may have had its genesis in the Deep South but by the early sixties Hebb had moved north to New York and into a Harlem apartment where he got to know King Curtis and Bernard Purdie.

For a year or more Hebb was the featured singer at the Blue Morocco club in the Bronx, an upscale nightspot owned by Bobby and Sylvia Robinson. He hung out after hours with the Harlem jazz set and befriended Thelonious Monk. It was after such a night that he returned home to discover that his brother had been murdered. He sat up through the night staring out at the purple-red sun rising over Harlem. The song lay dormant from 1963 to 1966 when it resurfaced on a demo tape sent to the producer Jerry Ross at Mercury Studios. Within weeks it was an international pop hit.

Wonder's cover version was stirring and emotional, coaxed to a climax by his jazzy harmonica. It was a highlight in a set full of new directions; his version of the hit single 'Yester-Me, Yester-You, Yesterday' seeming to signal a new maturity. Here were the first obvious signs that the young prodigy of Motown's past was blossoming into a true talent.

Many myths have grown up about the Black Woodstock, some so fanciful that they barely deserve repeating. It was widely believed in the racially tainted minds of some journalists that the show was a front for drug dealers when in fact its greatest co-ordinating force was the Parks Department. It was rumoured that the event was so volatile that the police refused to attend and security was provided by the Black Panthers. That is a falsehood that has grown with time, but even on the basis of the few photographs and film reels that have survived, there is a sizeable police presence, and uniformed officers can be seen lining the front of the stage. Police officers can also be seen backstage surrounding Mahalia Jackson's dressing room – a converted caravan – as she hugs the visiting mayor. The myth has another obvious flaw: at the time, most of the Harlem Branch of the Black Panthers were in jail or on the run, in many cases far from Harlem. The organisers did provide additional security. Lawrence hired his colleague John Shabazz, a Harlem community leader with connections both to the Nation of Islam and to the more conservative NAACP. Shabazz mobilised fifty sturdy teenagers from the Harlem projects – what he described as a 'citizens' security force' – who were given basic training in crowd control, first aid and conflict resolution, then presented with paramilitary uniforms and given the flashy name of the Commanders. The youths were paid $3,000, but it was the Parks Department rather than the Black Panthers who footed the bill. Another grumbling criticism was that money intended for local expenditure in Harlem had leaked out to the millionaires of Motown, but Lawrence had already agreed spending targets with his bosses in City Hall, one of which was to maximise local spend. All the refreshments stalls were local businesses. The sound equipment was provided by Ed Bagwell's News Voice International, an electronics company well known in local soul circuits, and almost all of Harlem's record stores – Bobby Robinson's Records, Paul Winley's and Fat Jack Taylor's Rojac Records – had a presence.

Cleverly Tony Lawrence saw another opportunity to act local. He met with the Apollo's management and shaped running orders around the artists he knew either lived nearby or would be visiting Harlem. Motown's traditional summer party at the Apollo provided the backbone of one day. Stevie Wonder, Chuck Jackson, David Ruffin, and Gladys Knight and the Pips all agreed to perform. Unlike many ghetto shows, the Harlem Cultural Festival paid all its musicians, and it could afford to pay sizeable appearance fees to those who could attract the crowds. Simone's manager (her husband Andy) proved to be one of the toughest negotiators, and although the so-called High Priestess of Soul lived locally in upmarket Mount Vernon, she secured a fee the equal of most major concert halls. Tony Lawrence plugged the festivals relentlessly through local radio appearances, and although he was never a soul singer from the top drawer, his name was well enough known for DJs to invite him to talk shows. At a meeting with the rough-edged record company executive Nate McCalla, it was suggested that he cut a record for Calla subsidiary Lo Lo Records. Studio time was booked, and in June 1969 Lawrence rushed out a bizarre record – a so-what soul song called 'Me And You' with an unapologetic B-side called 'Harlem Cultural Festival' – a half-sung, half-spoken plug for the festival that was only weeks away. What was even more remarkable than Tony Lawrence's promotional chutzpah was the talent queuing behind him at Lo Lo Records. The next three releases featured the gifted Harlem soul singer Bobby Hill's 'To The Bitter End', Top Shelf's 'No Second Thoughts', written by the formidable Larry Saunders, and 'Easier To Say Than Do' by Sam Dees, the great southern soul singer from Birmingham, Alabama, who had only just set foot in Manhattan. Within a matter of a couple of short years he would sign for Atlantic Records and produce one of the greatest soul albums of all time, the peerless *The Show Must Go On*.

In July Lawrence invited the press to a downtown press launch. Many journalists had turned up hopeful that the anger surrounding the mass arrest of the Harlem Black Panthers would erupt, but they were soon disarmed by a friendly and welcoming affair. Lawrence had hired the al fresco Promenade Café at the Lincoln Center, normally a quiet place where classical music fans gathered to sip coffee and discuss the latest cello scandals, but for a day in July 1969 it was a riot of colour and unrestrained fun. The African drummer and Columbia recording artist Babatunde Olatunji opened the event with a virtuoso performance of Yoruba-inspired afro-beat drumming. Olatunji was virtually unknown downtown but was a well-connected Harlem character, having recently opened an African jazz centre there. Best known as a musical partner of John Coltrane, Olatunji's background was unusual. He had emigrated from Nigeria to study at Morehouse, Martin Luther King's college, and then won a scholarship to New York University where he mastered in public policy and set up a small Afro-jazz ensemble. In 1969 his album *Drums Of Passion* became America's fastest-selling African album and a landmark in the evolution of what later became known as 'world music'. Supporting Olatunji and singing out to the busy traffic on Fifth Avenue were Clara Walker and the Gospel Redeemers. It was an event that screamed of populism and had the effect of reminding New Yorkers that Harlem was open for business and not the no-go ghetto of their feverish imagination.

The TV network CBS were attracted by the press launch and committed to broadcasting an hour-long show of festival highlights. It was the only significant commitment from a television station. A wrangle over rights has still not been resolved. When the festival got under way only one TV producer showed any real interest – the Ukrainian-American Harold 'Hal' Tulchin. He did not bring an impressive track record. Tulchin had earned a living directing pack shot commercials for Timex watches and had produced the short-lived crossword puzzle show, *Across the Board*. In contrast to the media frenzy that was feeding Woodstock, the Harlem festival was all but ignored. Only Tulchin's second-hand video cameras were there to record the event and capture some defining moments in a year of unrivalled change. The television networks were initially keen but when Tulchin showed them his footage, they all backed off, unsettled in part by Nina Simone's finale.

On the fourth weekend, 40,000 people crushed into Mount Morris Park for what had been advertised as a 'Caribbean Festival'. The gates opened at one thirty, and by two the 'house full' signs were being put up. Unknown to the audience, who had come expecting feelgood Hispanic and West Indian music, a surprise guest had arrived, desperate to play. At the time Sly and the Family Stone were one of the biggest names in black music, and at the height of the afternoon the tiny Sly Stone, resplendent in black leather coat and gold medallion, teased the crowd with barely disguised drug references and ultra-modern psychedelic soul. The band were in New York on their way to perform at Woodstock and played a rollercoaster set of hits – 'Everyday People', 'Dance To The Music', and peaking with the junk-funk anthem 'I Want To Take You Higher'. Stone was finely tuned to the very different audiences, and he delivered the same set in different ways. Harlem was treated to hardcore acid funk and Woodstock to blazing guitars and countercultural rock. The same but different.

In her autobiography *Rage to Survive*, Etta James described him as 'a wizard' and a 'straight-up genius'. 'I've never seen a talent like Sly's,' she wrote. 'When it comes to grooves and flat-out feeling, only Otis and James Brown came close.' Soul music was being shaped by electrification, primitive computer technology and the early days of the synthesiser. A generation of young and tech-savvy musicians were pushing to the fore, mostly keyboard players or multi-instrumentalists. Among their ranks were Stevie Wonder, Donny Hathaway, Herbie Hancock and, of course, Sly Stone. Etta James claimed: 'Sly didn't need an engineer. He could play all the instruments and damn near sing all the tracks. He internationalized R&B, integrated it, slicked it up, and put it out in a way where the whole world loved it. He was futuristic, so advanced that he could hardly keep up with himself.'

Unfortunately for soul music history, only a few musicians signed away their performance rights. Hal Tulchin was broke and could not afford to pay the commercial clearances, and thus the greatest soul festival of all time was never broadcast. It has lain unloved in the vaults for decades, unseen and unedited, only periodically escaping in clipped form for outings on YouTube. Ten years before his death, Tulchin admitted, 'I was the only one filming any of it – mostly on spec. It was a peanuts operation, because nobody really cared about black shows . . . But I knew it was going to be like real estate, and sooner or later someone would [take an] interest in it.' That someone has not yet come forward, but many have shown tentative interest. Film director Morgan Neville, who has watched the days of footage, told the Smithsonian that 'the footage shows seas of some 100,000 blacks whose dress and manner blend a Fourth of July picnic, a Sunday Best church revival, an urban rock concert and a rural civil rights rally . . . You see the generations teetering. As opposed to, say, Wattstax, where you see a kitschy funkifying of seventies America. This is different: the tension between soul and funk, civil disobedience versus Black Power, the tension of Harlem itself at the time.'

By six a.m. on the Sunday morning, amidst scenes of flagging debauchery, The Who took to the stage at Woodstock, playing the major songs from their rock opera *Tommy* and culminating in a trilogy of pop songs that owed their origins to R&B: 'Summertime Blues', 'Shaking All Over' and their international hit 'My Generation'. The Who had been scheduled to be the penultimate act before Jefferson Airplane, on what was supposed to be an epic Saturday night. By the time they left the stage, Harlem was waking up to a gospel Sunday, and the Harlem Festival Jazz Band were already lugging their equipment onstage. Woodstock was now so far behind schedule and so deeply mired in chaos that some were already drifting away, disillusioned.

Two fans who had travelled upstate from New York's Lower East Side – David McCurdy and his girlfriend Judy – had found a lift home. Fed up after a day sheltering under sodden magazines miles from the stage, they made their way to a ramshackle and congested car park, where nothing seemed to move for hours. McCurdy briefly considered making a detour to Harlem to catch Nina Simone, but by the time the car made its way down Harlem River Drive, they decided to head home to their apartment as blues guitarist B.B. King took to the stage. Another capacity crowd had squeezed into Mount Morris Park. The two passengers had much on their mind and spoke only fleetingly on the drive back from Woodstock. They had become accustomed to using pseudonyms when with strangers. McCurdy was not the man's real name – it had been stolen from a dead boy's grave and a fraudulent birth certificate secured. 'David McCurdy' was in fact the hippie insurrectionist 'Mad Bomber' Sam Melville and his companion, 'Judy', was Jane Alpert, the *Rat* journalist. The following day they reignited their bombing campaign against corporate America.

Melville left the safe house that his cell had rented carrying a crudely made bomb with a timer mechanism and planted it at the Marine Midland Building, 140 Broadway, a fifty-two-storey glass skyscraper owned by W.R. Grace, a chemicals conglomerate that was soon to become embroiled in a major asbestos scandal. Melville had no great knowledge of what Grace Chemicals produced, but he guessed with some accuracy that the company were implicated in chemical warfare in Vietnam. The crude bomb exploded at eleven p.m. that night, near an elevator shaft on the eighth floor of the building. *The New York Times* reported that 'the blast knocked out several banks of elevators, shut off electricity to the floor for twelve hours, shattered windows and ripped out sections of the tiled ceilings'. Sixteen late-night clerical workers suffered cuts and bruises, but no one was killed.

It was the morning of Monday 18 August when Melville had begun the meticulous task of preparing the bomb, spreading out the components and the bundled dynamite on a wooden table. At the same time, Woodstock was drawing to a controversial climax. The crowd had dwindled as the sun rose, and few remained to witness one of the most iconic performances in the history of rock – the voodoo child of American R&B Jimi Hendrix's two-hour, uninterrupted set. It ended with a medley that included his desecrating solo performance of 'The Star-Spangled Banner', a moment that would become emblematic not only of Woodstock but of America itself. It was an instrumental, yet it seemed to speak in angry volumes: raging against patriotism, the Vietnam War and Richard Nixon's compromised presidency. Hendrix's dramatic denouement has cultivated its own powerful myths: that he burned the American flag, that he smashed his guitar into the stars and stripes, and that he had made the calculated decision to end with the national anthem, to raise his profile and notoriety. None were true. Professor Joel Brattin, one of the world's foremost experts on Hendrix, claims there was no flag and that '"The Star-Spangled Banner" was not played on its own. It was part of a medley lasting over half an hour, one of the longest such medleys. The medley also included hits like "Voodoo Child" . . . and "Purple Haze", and an unaccompanied improvisation lasting nearly five minutes. Hendrix performed the national anthem as a solo in the midst of this medley. It was not the first time Hendrix had performed "The Star-Spangled Banner" – by a long shot. In fact, there are nearly fifty live recordings of Hendrix playing the national anthem, twenty-eight made before Woodstock.'

Later that day, Hendrix returned to Harlem where he was sharing an apartment with the Allen twins. They had not travelled to Woodstock but instead had manned a stall, hired by Rojac Records, selling vinyl overstocks and God only knows what else to the Sunday crowds at the Harlem festival. Hendrix joined them later that night at their uptown apartment on 96th and Columbus Avenue, a home they had borrowed courtesy of the irrepressible Fat Jack Taylor. Hendrix had much on his mind. He was undecided about where to base himself – London or New York – and was concerned about the constraints being placed on him by his management. Hendrix was at a crossroads in his creative life, too – a rock god loved by predominately white audiences across Europe, he yearned to be accepted by his own community. He had won the Apollo's amateur night earlier in the sixties as a fledgling R&B guitarist, but by the summer of 1969 he was a global superstar in danger of leaving his roots behind. Together Hendrix and the Allens began to imagine a very different type of show, one that would take fuller shape in the days to come. The Allens convinced Hendrix to give something back to Harlem and the wider cause of Black Power. He agreed. They talked about a fundraiser for the jailed Black Panthers, or a show that would support a charity. Hendrix began to talk about news images he had seen when in London, images that he could not shake from his mind, of starving and dying children in Biafra. They had the kernel of an idea but they all agreed – it was time that the voodoo child played Harlem again.

Jimi Hendrix, working as a freelance guitarist, plays behind Wilson Pickett at an Atlantic Records launch in the Prelude Club, Harlem. His friend, Cornell Dupree, a collaborator with Donny Hathaway and King Curtis, is on the left. The album being promoted, Percy Sledge's *When A Man Loves A Woman*, is displayed next to Hendrix.

SEPTEMBER

Return of the Voodoo Child

A purple haze floated like translucent silk across the skyline. Carbon monoxide smouldered in the setting sun and the drifting smoke from the oil and petrochemical plants near Astoria and Newtown Creek caught the sunlight. The strange light show seemed to dance at first, then retreated for several hours, before being subsumed into a brooding darkness. Jimi Hendrix had returned to his adoptive home and vowed he'd light up the Harlem night and entice people out onto the streets with all the disruptive magic that a Fender Stratocaster could impart.

The circumstances that brought Hendrix back to Harlem, to the corner of 139th and Lenox, were far from straightforward. It was a benefit concert, but not of the kind that Harlem had witnessed before. It was a thread that stretched all the way to the White House and back to the tired and fateful days of March 1968 when President Johnson wearily considered his resignation. He was by then a lame-duck president, brought to his knees by the Vietnam War but still working dutifully behind the scenes, trying to resolve the problems of a war abroad while his critics screamed for more funding to be directed to poverty programmes in America's riot-torn ghettos. It was an irresolvable dilemma and, as if that wasn't enough, another body blow was struck. The State Department was being inundated with unprecedented levels of correspondence about the situation in Biafra. It was a place LBJ neither knew nor understood, and what limited knowledge he had was gleaned from scant CIA dossiers. So, with a distracted mind and a pitiful understanding of the problem, he failed to grasp the scale of public outrage. One day, as many as 25,000 letters arrived on the desk of the beleaguered Secretary of State, Dean Rusk, sent in the main by Middle American housewives, Christians and taxpayers who were appalled by America's sluggishness in the face of famine and genocide in the Nigerian Civil War. American news channels aired nightly images from the newly independent Biafra, where war had left emaciated children dying in their hundreds of thousands. Spooked by the sheer volume of complaints and vainly grasping for any strategy that would make even the slightest impact, President Johnson told his closest aides to try to influence the networks, with the infamous comment, 'Just get those nigger babies off my TV set.'

Hendrix had watched the Biafra airlift unfold on television until it reached its horrific height in 1969. The sight of starving children in Africa pricked the conscience of many of his fellow musicians at a time when there was raised political awareness but the idea of doing a benefit concert was still largely untried. Unlike the concerned but dithering world of rock and pop, the churches of Europe and America had risen to the challenge and were engaged in a remarkable intervention. In the face of political vacillation, congregations sent relief aid by land, sea and, most dramatically of all, by airlift. The Swiss Red Cross – one of the most active global charities – were estimating, conservatively, that 3,000 children were dying daily. Television images were tearing at the conscience of First World citizens, but the longer their governments were complicit in the support of a 'One Nigeria' policy, the more they left Biafra to starve. Official inertia was widespread. Governments, reluctant to intervene in a civil war, stood back as private citizens took the initiative and answered the call to supply relief to the needy.

Harlem was a hotspot not only of public debate but also of airlift activity. Churches acted as drop-off centres, accepting gifts, cash donations and food. There were more than 400 or more churches in the Harlem area alone, and they were among the congregations with the most heightened awareness of African independence movements. The pan-African culture that had swept the neighbourhood since the mid sixties, and which had mostly found its expression in fashion, hairstyles and music, had also cultivated a deeper sense of identity politics and closer communion with distant African nations. The Congress of Racial Equality, a civil rights group founded in 1942 in the earliest days of the movement, was among the most vocal organisations, demanding immediate support for Biafra. It was immediately understood on the streets of Harlem that political advocacy alone was not enough, and it took the Herculean effort of the World Council of Churches, and a cross-denominational aid effort, to begin to address the famine. The East Harlem Protestant Parish Church became a nerve centre, spreading the word and collecting money and food packages. A concert party of Harlem church choirs, including some of the singers who had appeared at the Harlem Cultural Festival, performed at a candle-lit vigil outside the UN Secretariat. The American Committee to Keep Biafra Alive was one of many organisations that claimed not to be taking sides, but there was righteous anger at the silence and inaction of the elected political leadership. The black radical magazine *Liberator* – a major voice in Harlem intellectual circles – accused the US government of enabling genocide by not facilitating food shipments into the secessionist rebel areas. By the time the civil war ended in 1970 up to two million people had died of starvation.

In the Mayfair flat he shared with his girlfriend, Kathy Etchingham, Hendrix regularly watched the world unfold on the evening ITN news. One horrific report by the fearless war correspondent Michael Nicholson followed the plight of a young boy who had been captured by a Nigerian government officer. The army officer assured the boy he would come to no harm and then shot him dead, on camera. Night after night, there were images of children already too emaciated to be saved, their bones visible through paper-thin skin and their bellies expanded with hunger. Among all the many social issues that were synonymous with the sixties – civil rights, drugs legislation, Black Power and the war in Vietnam – it was the plight of the Biafran children that emotionally engaged Jimi Hendrix.

As he improvised the idea of a benefit concert with the Allen twins and Fat Jack Taylor, it became clear that he was planning the show without the full knowledge of his management. The initial idea was to approach the Apollo and stage a concert there, but the theatre's policy was that visiting acts take on a week's residency, and Hendrix refused to be tied down, in part because it would then involve his manager, Michael Jeffery. Their relationship was at breaking point, and many within Hendrix's close circle of musicians, among them Eric Burdon of the Animals and later the funk-rock band War, were counselling Hendrix to ditch Jeffery.

Jeffery, born in Peckham, owned several clubs in the North East of England, and was rumoured to have worked for British Intelligence. He met Hendrix after the Animals' bassist Chas Chandler spotted 'Jimmy James' playing at Cafe Wha? in Greenwich Village, towards the end of the Animals' 1966 American tour. Keen to move into management, Chandler befriended Hendrix, but lacking the necessary cash to underwrite a recording career, involved Jeffery in his plans. It was a misguided act of necessity which tied Hendrix to the unlikeable Jeffery until the guitarist's suspicious death in a Notting Hill hotel in September 1970.

The Allen twins already had a base at Fat Jack Taylor's Rojac Records on 116th Street, so they used it as the benefit-show office. It was agreed with Hendrix that the concert would be free to the people of Harlem, but that the charity Biafra Calls would be allowed to collect donations at the event, and that any money raised through sponsorship would go to the charity. According to an interview with Hendrix in *Rolling Stone*, it was a time of creative flux for him, as he dismantled his famous UK band, the Jimi Hendrix Experience, and fashioned a new outfit which he called a 'sky church sort of thing', an opaque term which mystified the journalist but likely meant a fusion of the two big genres in

Hendrix's life: psychedelia and the black American music of the church. He even talked about hiring 'three soul sisters' to join the new church. It might have made more sense had Hendrix simply said he was following in the tracks of Sly and the Family Stone, and Baby Huey and the Babysitters, showcasing psychedelic soul – but he rarely made plain sense, nor was he ever likely to admit to following others.

For a brief few hours the Allens scouted their own backyard, the warren-like St Nicholas apartment blocks that sit immediately behind the Apollo, but there was no obvious place to erect a stage and no venue amongst the community halls that was big enough to accommodate the crowd. They talked to Har-You, the Harlem youth charity, but their rehearsal space was downtown, beyond the boundaries of Harlem itself. Harlem had been a hotbed of community activism for decades, and one of the most successful and enduring community movements had been the block associations whereby neighbours joined forces to improve their housing, combat crime and lobby for better housing legislation. Eventually, through conversations with other community groups, they arrived at the United Block Association, one of the area's biggest and most powerful community groups. They agreed to host the concert and identified a suitable location – a vacant lot on 139th Street at Lenox.

With the encouragement and largesse of Fat Jack Taylor, the Allens began to assemble a supporting cast. They had not yet settled on a name for the show and variously called it 'Biafra Calls' and 'The Mystique of Harlem'. Their first major breakthrough was securing two major female singers, Big Maybelle and Maxine Brown. Big Maybelle was close to Fat Jack's operations and at the time was in residency at the Apollo as a guest star on a bill that included Barbara Acklin, the Chi-Lites and Jackie Wilson. Another piece of luck delivered the great Maxine Brown to the fold. She had recently left Wand Records, in part squeezed out by female rival Dionne Warwick, and was negotiating the next phase of her career. She took the decision that performing with Hendrix would do her no harm and might even put her in the eyeline of new opportunities. Unknown or obscure local talent was easier to secure, and within hours the Allens had signed up the LaRocque Bey Dancers and the 128th and 129th Streets Block Association Steel Band.

Fat Jack Taylor weighed in with another favour. The benefit needed a skilled backing band who could support the vocalists and, if necessary, provide back-up to Hendrix. To attract attention they were referred to as 'The Sam and Dave Band' but in reality they were the Rojac/Tay-Ster act known as Chuck-a-Luck & the Lovemen Ltd. Chuck-a-Luck aka Little Charles Whitworth had provided the backing musicians for the Apollo's 1968 Christmas Extravaganza featuring Sam and Dave, the Unifics and the then little-known family group the Jackson 5. Whitworth's recording career with Taylor had kept him in Harlem, but perhaps his greatest contribution to soul music came with the last part of his band's name, Ltd. Repackaged as Love, Togetherness and Devotion, they became a successful soul band in the seventies, by then featuring singer Jeffrey Osborne.

Flyers were distributed to local record stores and community groups, and a few days before the show they called a press conference, enticing New York's music journalists to congregate at an oyster bar. Frank's Oyster and Chop House was a famous Harlem eatery on 125th Street, near the Baby Grand Club. A photograph of the Allen twins, Hendrix and his girlfriend Faye shows them about to tuck into plates of chicken and waffles. Surrounded by plates of high-end fast food, Jimi told a *New York Times* reporter: 'I want to show that music is universal – that there is no white rock or black rock. Some of these kids haven't got the $6 to go to Madison Square Garden – besides I used to play up here myself at Small's over 135th and Seventh.'

Hendrix's girlfriend Faye Pridgon – who appears in the centrefold of the 1968 album *Electric Ladyland* – was another of Harlem's electric personalities. She was born in Moultrie, Georgia, and had moved to New York with her remarkable mother, an insurance clerk by day and music fan by night. It was through her mother that she first met R&B star Little Willie John, Sam Cooke and then James Brown, Jimi Hendrix and eventually Sly Stone. Hendrix and Pridgon were a couple for much of his time in Harlem. It was a far from simple relationship. Hendrix was at times besotted, then distracted. She was insistent on her right to see other men but remained devoted to Hendrix. She first met him at one of Fat Jack Taylor's notorious parties and then again at the Apollo. 'I liked skinny, raw-boned, over-fucked, underfed-looking guys,' she told the *Observer*, admitting that she was the woman who inspired Hendrix's 'Foxy Lady'. A sometime songwriter, Pridgon was briefly signed to Atlantic Records on a one-year contract but her debut album was never released and remains buried in Atlantic's vaults, unfinished and unloved.

Twelve days after Woodstock, Hendrix stepped onto the low platform stage that was crammed in between two decrepit tenement blocks. The show was to become part of rock music's great hidden history, unknown to most and barely reported by the music press. Hendrix had by now formed Gypsy Sun and Rainbows aka A Band of Gypsies, featuring Hendrix on guitar and vocal, Larry Lee on guitar and vocal, Billy Cox on bass, percussionists Juma Sultan and Jerry Velez, and the solitary survivor from London, Mitch Mitchell, on drums. In an article entitled 'Hendrix in Hip Harlem' by Richard Robinson, *Disc* magazine reported that 5,000 people showed up to see him, adding: 'Maxine Brown and Big Maybelle appeared before Jimi and by the time Hendrix came on, which was after midnight, the crowd had dwindled to about 500 and by the time he had finished playing the estimated crowd figure was 200 with about 50 white hippies among them.' *GO* magazine reported: 'Jimi Hendrix is going back to his roots. He hasn't played a real black club since the old roustabout days when he was Jimmy James, backing up the likes of the Isley Brothers, Little Richard, and Wilson Pickett . . . The stage was a wooden platform four feet above the ground, and members of the Sam & Dave band were there to back up a succession of local talent. I was hoping Jimi would come out in a blue tuxedo and break right into "Midnight Hour" or "Land Of A Thousand Dances". But true to form (call him psychedelic, you may call him "far out", but whatever he's YOURS), he came out in white silk pants, fringes down to the ground, silk shirt and pink scarf wrapped around his head.'

The most illuminating review, by an unnamed contributor, appeared in the monthly rock magazine *Circus*. 'The Harlem concert was the greatest I'd ever seen him do. He had enthusiasm and willingness to boogie. For the finale he played a warped, hi-screech version of "The Star-Spangled Banner", which went dripping and screaming into dissonancy. Coming back from that, he said, "Now we're gonna play the Harlem National Anthem," and stepped on his trusty wah-wah pedal for a dynamite version of "Voodoo Child (Slight Return)". Towards the end he turned and flew into the amplifier, chipping off a corner, but he came bouncing back with a big smile and a peace-sign as if to say, "yeah, but don't forget." He did this again, much to the cheers of the street. He shot everyone a Black Power wrist, which got some reaction, and then a peace sign, which got even more. And then, to top it all off, he flipped everyone another sign, which sort of brought the sky down. He is a master performer when he wants to be one, and this concert gave him the necessary inspiration.'

Hendrix was at the height of his powers. But curiously for a musician famed around the world, the Harlem Benefit Concert posed a dilemma: whether to charge headlong into the empire of progressive rock or return to his R&B roots. According to anecdotal reports, he stood with the Allen twins and Fat Jack Taylor at the side of the makeshift stage watching a largely unknown ghetto soul singer J.D. Bryant play out his set. Bryant was one of a number of singers in the lower reaches of the bill and was brought onto the stage by the effervescent MC Eddie O'Jay, whose radio show *Soul at Sunrise* had a huge audience dedicated to traditional soul and R&B. Hendrix knew Bryant only vaguely from the Chitlin' Circuit clubs he had played in prior to his transformative move to England. Fat Jack Taylor knew him, too, and had tried unsuccessfully to sign him to Rojac.

Bryant's voice was like an emotional siren, blaring out over the urban dereliction and working the crowd into a frenzy. It was a performance that made Hendrix nervous. His guitar pyrotechnics and electric rock theatre had been perfectly modulated to suit the countercultural crowds at Woodstock but he was witnessing a very different performance for a very different crowd. Bryant opened with a frenetic version of Larry Williams' 'Bony Moronie' and then did a crowd-pleasing cover of 'Hold On I'm Coming', supported by Little Charles Whitworth and the 'Sam and Dave Band'. Bryant controlled the crowd effortlessly, and Hendrix and his entourage were visibly impressed – it was a masterclass of old-school R&B, a nostalgic throwback to younger days.

Bryant – often known simply as Jay Dee – was one of soul music's great unsung male vocalists, edged out of the limelight by better funded rivals and recurring bouts of bad luck. He was a close friend of Benny Gordon of the Soul Brothers, and for a time shared his house in Brooklyn, so he, too, may have hailed from South Carolina, but his origins are hazy. He seems to have arrived on the soul scene in 1961, when he signed for Herald Records, a New York indie which spanned doo-wop, blues and early soul. The label occupied offices above the Ed Sullivan Theater in Midtown Manhattan but his Herald release, a routine era-constrained ballad 'I Could Have Cried' and a failed attempt at a summer hit called 'Come Summer' was saved from mediocrity by his powerful gospel voice and the imaginative organ sounds of Dave 'Baby' Cortez. He then moved to a second New York indie, Alfa Records, where he fronted a short-lived group called the Kiddie-Os. By 1965 he had gravitated to Harlem and signed to Bobby Robinson's Enjoy Records, the storefront indie which had launched with recordings by King Curtis, discovered Gladys Knight and the Pips, and released an early recording by another great Harlem-based singer, Jimmy Armstrong. Bryant and Armstrong became friends, hustling to get noticed in a crowded creative marketplace. Then an infamous divorce affected both their careers.

Motown owner Berry Gordy had fallen out with his wife Raynoma, and she had opened a Motown branch office in New York where she attracted a formidable roster of talent, including her lover, the writer-producer Eddie Singleton. Frustrated by being edged out of the wealth generated by Motown in Detroit, Raynoma bootlegged one of the company's biggest mid sixties hits, Mary Wells's infectious 'My Guy'. Motown retaliated and instigated an FBI investigation. Raynoma and her partner were duly arrested, further souring relations and hastening the divorce. With money from the divorce settlement, Raynoma and Singleton moved to Washington DC where they set up a soul indie called Shrine

Records. To launch the label, Singleton drew on his contacts in Harlem and identified Jimmy Armstrong, J.D. Bryant and Ray Pollard as future Shrine artists. It was to be a journey marred by bad management and misfortune.

Shrine is a case study in missed opportunities and horrendous fortunes. It was launched on the back of misplaced revenge, and from the outset was undercapitalised. Before national distribution and sales were in place, it released far too many records. Raynoma has always maintained that her former husband used Motown's formidable clout in the marketplace to undermine Shrine by blocking its distribution and curtailing radio promotion, but either way, by the time Armstrong and Bryant recorded for Shrine the label was running on hot air. Bryant's only Shrine release was a small masterpiece, a storming up-tempo soul record written by Singleton called 'I Won't Be Coming Back'. It attracted precious little attention and was waxed at a time when Shrine were already struggling to pay their bills. Then, in the tense spring of 1968, when downtown Washington DC burned in the riotous aftermath of Martin Luther King's assassination, much of Shrine's remaining stock was lost. Bryant's record vanished into obscurity. It is now one of the most expensive collectors' records in the world.

Bryant was unknown to Hendrix but his origins and style were familiar. This was a show Hendrix had seen many hundreds of times before, dating back to his days in Nashville when he had just left the army and met his friend and collaborator Bill Cox. But Bryant's performance momentarily unsettled Hendrix and threw him into doubt about how he could please what was left of the crowd. Coming so soon after his triumph at Woodstock, Hendrix's 'secret' Harlem benefit gig has frequently been represented as an underground success story: one for the initiated. The opposite was true. As mentioned, 5,000 people had turned up to watch Maxine Brown, Big Maybelle and J.D. Bryant's steam-engine show, with its wailing gospel heights and lurid sexuality. By the time Hendrix reached the stage, the crowd had shrunk to a few hundred. Most of the Harlem teenagers who had come for R&B and a free night out did not have the near-religious respect for Hendrix that his fans in the countercultural world had. The cult that had built around him, which would gather even greater momentum after his untimely death, was always biggest in Europe, and largely narrated through the pages of the alternative press. In Harlem he was word-of-mouth, and his reputation for guitar wizardry had only really connected with the soul vanguard. Most local kids had not even heard of him, but if they were among the hardcore who stayed to watch his entire set they would have gone away struck by two things: his effortless command of R&B and a level of guitar showmanship which was bold, innovative and almost unhinged.

In a review in *Jet*, Billy Cox described Hendrix and his band facing some difficulties. 'The gig in Harlem did not get off to a good start. We were booed,' he told the reporter. 'But then Jimi walked over to me and said, "Let's take 'em home and give them some of the stuff we played at the Del Morocco."' He proposed old-school R&B. 'We then went into Freddie King's "San-Ho-Zay,"' Cox told *Jet*. 'The three of us threw in some steps just like a lot of the Chitlin' Circuit groups would do. We had been initiated back down south on what it took to put on a show. And a show we put on!!! The crowd went crazy. We had them where we wanted them – in our hands. After that, we mixed it up with some Chitlin' Circuit to remind them we could play, so they would listen to Hendrix material and we could take them to the next dimension of music.'

Del Morocco had been one club among many in Hendrix's nomadic life as an R&B session guitarist. At the age of seventeen, he had dropped out of high school and joined the army in order to avoid a jail sentence hanging over him after a spate of car thefts and joyriding. After he completed basic training, he was assigned to the 101st Airborne Division and posted to Fort Campbell, Kentucky. While stationed there, he volunteered as a paratrooper, and it was in the camp barracks, sixty miles from the pulsing heart of Nashville, that Hendrix famously met his friend and guitar partner Billy Cox, who was to work with Hendrix off and on until his death. Geography and instinct took the two of them to Nashville, where they formed a soul band, the King Casuals, and soon became the resident band at Del Morocco.

At the time, Nashville was known globally as the capital city of country music and home of the Grand Ole Opry, but its underground R&B scene was equally vibrant. It was the stage for local blues and soul singers such as Roscoe Shelton, Earl Gaines and Gene Allison, and home to a formidable rack of local independent labels including Excello, Sims and Sound Stage 7. Hendrix flourished there and then toured extensively with Sam Cooke, Jackie Wilson, the Mighty Hannibal, Little Richard and the Isley Brothers. He backed Don Covay and Wilson Pickett, and shared stages with B.B. King and Bobby Womack and the Valentinos. Time and again these tours brought Hendrix to the Apollo in Harlem and he came to see the city within a city as his home. Reflecting on life back in 1964, Hendrix said, 'I went to New York and won first place in the Apollo amateur contest, you know, $25. I stayed up there, starved to death about 2 or 3 weeks, then I got [a job] with the Isley Brothers.' As his reputation soared, he became known as a virtuoso – and a troublemaker. He was keen to be featured prominently on stage but slow to soundcheck or catch the tour bus to the next venue. He was sacked on several occasions, dropped by major touring bands for poor time-keeping. He parted company with Little Richard in the summer of 1965 soon after he had made his first television appearance on the pioneering *Night Train*. On the show, Hendrix features prominently in a cover version of Junior Walker's 'Shotgun', rather intrusive behind vocal duo Buddy and Stacy, the opening act for Little Richard. It was a tour with mixed consequences. As Hendrix's relationship with his famous boss soured, the tour also faced a crisis when, in April 1965, Little Richard was bounced from the Paramount Theatre, only two days into a residency. The management leaked the news to press agencies, providing them with a histrionic account of the disagreements: 'The colourful rock 'n' roll star billed as Little Richard claims he was bounced from the big show at the Paramount after playing only two days of a scheduled ten-day gig. The promoters of the divertissement counter that he was uncooperative, stayed on stage too long, and committed other sins cardinal in the profession.' There is no accurate list of the cardinal sins, or how they may have affected the divertissement, but with Little Richard's residency effectively scrapped, Hendrix drifted uptown again.

Unemployed and penniless, he began to take any work he could find in and around Harlem, befriending the well-connected saxophonist Lonnie Youngblood and the ubiquitous King Curtis. It was through Youngblood that Hendrix met Jimmy Norman, a supremely talented vocalist and arranger who had settled in Harlem after a spell in L.A.'s independent soul scene. Norman wrote the lyrics for 'Time Is On My Side', a hit for both Irma Thomas and the Rolling Stones, but by the spring of 1966 was looking for his next break and had signed for Samar Records, the Rochester indie which had offices in Harlem. In 1966 Samar hit an astonishingly creative vein of releases by employing the proto-disco producers Johnny Brantley, Bert de Coteaux, Bert Keyes and Eddie Drennon. Hendrix was employed on a daily session basis, joining Norman on a string of solo releases including 'You're Only Hurting Yourself', 'That Little Old Groovemaker' and 'Can You Blame Me', and then, with Norman, as a surrogate member of a group called the Icemen who released the singles 'Sugar Baby' and '(My Girl) She's A Fox'. The latter opens with a tantalising and showy guitar solo by Hendrix and then settles into a doo-wop harmony soul sound, as if time itself is being stretched. It has never been conclusively established how many sessions Hendrix worked on, and he may also have been a studio musician on Samar's Motownesque singles 'Dial L For Lonely' by Madeline Wilson and 'Best Thing For You Baby' by Gloria Parker.

By night, Jimmy Norman and Hendrix worked the studios, grabbing downtime and recording under the radar. They recorded alternative versions of their Samar songs and at least two of them, 'Groovemaker' and '(My Girl) She's a Fox', had a life later in Hendrix's career. The latter was a thematic testing ground for 'Foxy Lady', which was the opening track on Hendrix's 1968 debut album *Are You Experienced*. What is also remarkable about the gifted Norman is his string of collaborations. When Hendrix moved to London, Norman moved across the river to the South Bronx, where he shared a home with musicians who had recently arrived from Jamaica, among them the unknown Bob Marley.

The pair became writing partners, and for six months Norman joined Marley in Kingston, where they co-wrote several reggae songs. Norman had the good fortune to be close to two of the genuine superstars of popular music but his own talents remained unrecognised for many years to come.

On the evening of 5 May 1966, between studio sessions for Samar, Hendrix was hired to appear at a Harlem launch party to celebrate a new slate of releases by Atlantic Records. The venue was the Prelude Club, an old jazz haunt on 125th Street. The roster of releases included Percy Sledge's *When A Man Loves A Woman*, Esther Phillips's answer record 'When A Women Loves A Man', Don Covay's 'You Put Something On Me' and Wilson Pickett's 'Ninety-Nine And A Half (Won't Do)'. The guest list was a who's who of the soul scene. All the featured artists were there, along with backing band King Curtis and the Kingpins featuring Jimi Hendrix, and Atlantic bosses Nesuhi Ertegun and Jerry Wexler. New York's celebrity photographer, William 'PoPsie' Randolph, was there to document the night. Benny Goodman bought him his first camera and Miles Davis posed for him in a session that came to define Harlem's bebop era. By 1969 Randolph was accustomed to earning huge fees from the music industry. To get the best shot, he prowled backstage and surveyed the alleyways to the rear of the Prelude, but it was inside, on the main stage, that he took one of his most memorable photographs. Wilson Pickett is in a tuxedo, white shirt and skinny tie, screaming into a vintage Shure stand microphone, and immediately behind him, silhouetted in front of flock wallpaper, is Aretha Franklin's guitarist Cornell Dupree. To the right, laughing along with Dupree, is Hendrix, also in a tuxedo but sporting a Wyatt Earp-style bow tie and playing a white Fender Duo-Sonic.

Sales of R&B singles were at an all-time high, crashing through racial barriers, but the album market was in its infancy and there was still some nervousness about putting black musicians on album covers. Despite the resources lavished on Atlantic's major album release – Percy Sledge's *When A Man Loves A Woman* – there is no visible sign of the artist himself. Instead, a glamorous white woman with pink lipstick and heavy eye-liner stares serenely at a vase of marigolds. Sledge, with his gappy teeth and jowly face, is demoted to the rear of the album cover, a policy that most record labels including Motown frequently pursued.

Four months after Randolph's era-defining photograph was taken, Hendrix flew to Heathrow Airport on his first trip to London. All he carried with him was his guitar, a change of clothes, plastic hair curlers, and a jar of acne cream. It was an inauspicious start to one of the greatest transformations in pop history. Within a matter of months, the jobbing R&B guitarist, who had been reduced to begging for sessions from his Harlem contacts, was poised to become an international superstar and the king of psychedelia.

In one of the few photographs to have survived from Hendrix's benefit show, four rows into the dwindling crowd, staring into the camera amidst a group of young black teenagers, is a solitary white man. He is bearded, has scruffy brown hair, and his piercing eyes are looking up, entranced, at Hendrix. The unknown figure is eerily similar to Sam Melville, who at the time was engaged in a downtown bombing campaign. Melville was a Hendrix fan. He had left Woodstock early, frustrated by the rain and the disorganisation, and so missed Hendrix in concert there. He had grown up near Harlem and frequently visited the area as a teenager. Melville's presence on the uptown streets increased during the Gym Crow demonstrations at nearby Columbia University, and he was a vocal supporter of the Black Panthers, to whom he supplied stolen dynamite. It can never be proven that the lone white man clearly visible at Hendrix's show is the self-styled Mad Bomber Melville. But the resemblance is uncanny.

On 18 September, two weeks after the fundraiser, Melville embarked on the next phase of his bombing mission, this time unequivocally aimed at the Vietnam War. He set out to plant explosives at the Federal Office Building on Federal Plaza, then the biggest single federal building in New York and home to the Department of Commerce and, significantly, the Army Inspector General. The explosion damaged an unoccupied office suite, an elevator shaft and, according to *The New York Times*, 'a six-foot-square hole had been ripped in the wall opposite the shaftway that contained circuit breakers, electric panels, ducts and utility wires', closing the military offices for days. Ominously for Melville, the newspaper wrote: 'Late today, Joseph Ponder, a special agent who is supervising, said simply that an investigation was underway.' Quietly, and with the help of informers in the counterculture, the FBI were already following a number of different leads, and their dogged investigation was tightening the net around Melville and his Lower East Side cell. He had planned the bombing to minimise risk and maximise publicity. The device was primed to explode at two a.m. when the building was largely unoccupied and when security was focused elsewhere in New York. President Nixon had arrived at the height of anti-war sentiment to deliver an address to the General Assembly of the United Nations. His speech was guarded and conciliatory, but offered no great breakthrough in American thinking and disguised more than it revealed. It was, in the words of Melville's co-conspirator Jane Alpert, no more than cynical theatre. 'The continuing involvement of the United States in the Vietnam War remained the essential condition for all our bombings,' she wrote in her autobiography *Growing Up Underground*. 'Nixon, since taking office in January 1969 had reneged on virtually every promise he made in the campaign. He produced no "secret plan" for peace: he had widened rather than called a halt to war; and instead of withdrawing troops, he had instituted the paper-stuffing tactic of lowering troop ceilings. Photographs of children on fire from American napalm and adults shot down in cold blood by American soldiers had become part of the steady diet of the news programs and part of our political assumptions as well. While public opinion polls showed the majority of Americans opposed the war, reports of atrocities multiplied, all of them officially denied by the administration.'

The cumulative impact of the leaked Pentagon Papers, the dramatic image of 'Napalm girl' Phan Thị Kim Phúc, the emerging details of the My Lai massacre, and the expansion of the war into Cambodia had irrevocably turned a substantial majority against the war. It was not only the young and militant; as with Biafra, the spiritually concerned conscience of Harlem's Christian churches had also turned against Nixon.

In the weeks after the concert, Hendrix remained in New York, mostly recording tracks at the Hit Factory and the state-of-the-art Record Plant studios on 44th Street. Coincidentally, engineers at the latter studio were trying to make sense of the chaos of the Woodstock tapes, having taken on the mountainous task of mixing the concert recordings. Throughout September Hendrix recorded or worked on at least fourteen tracks: 'Jam Back At The House', 'Burning Desire', 'Valleys Of Neptune', 'Lord I Sing The Blues For Me And You', 'Lover Man', 'Message To Love', 'Drinking Wine (Key To The Highway', 'Izabella', 'Power Of Soul', 'Stepping Stone', 'Keep On Groovin'', 'Sky Blues Today', 'Room Full Of Mirrors' and 'Night Bird Flying'. It was a time of extraordinary creativity and upheaval. Two of Hendrix's closest musical allies left: guitarist Larry Lee returned to his native Memphis to work with Al Green, and drummer Mitch Mitchell returned to the UK to work with Jack Bruce, the former Cream star. The Allen twins, who provided backing vocals and extra instrumentation on several tracks, had begun to conceive of an entirely new band project called the Ghetto Fighters, the core of which would be the twins, Hendrix and a posse of guest musicians. The name had come about through a strange turn of events. One day on 125th Street, while the twins were out flyposting the neighbourhood, they found themselves embroiled in a dispute with Claude 'Mookie' Jackson, the businessman-gangster who headed up the Harlem Fair Play Committee. It appears that Jackson provoked a fight and the Allens stood their ground. Impressed with their stance, Jackson supposedly walked away, claiming that he was beyond street brawls and that he was not interested in 'ghetto fighters'. On hearing the story, the term stuck in Hendrix's mind and he later said it would be a great band name. He briefly thought of using it for himself but then committed to producing an album with the twins.

Hendrix informally called them his 'Harlem plans', but they were tragically cut short when he died under suspicious circumstances during a trip to London. The death was a body blow to the Allen twins. The benefit concert had been a success, despite the crowds dispersing before Hendrix's set. At its height, 5,000 people had come to a late night charity show in the heart of Harlem, and the event had raised Hendrix's profile as well as money for a worthy cause. However, the Ghetto Fighters went on to partially record background vocals on three of Hendrix's posthumous studio albums, *The Cry Of Love*, *Rainbow Bridge* and *War Heroes*.

Soon after Hendrix's death, the Allen twins converted to Islam, changed their names to Tunde' Ra Aleem and TaharQa Aleem, and rebranded themselves as the Fantastic Aleems. Although their partnership with Hendrix was cut short, they battled on to become a creative force for two subsequent generations of Harlem musicians. First, they leant heavily on their old mentor Fat Jack Taylor and opened Harlem World, at 116th Street and Lenox Avenue; it was one of the first dedicated rap ballrooms and a pioneering home of hip-hop. It was there that they discovered Dr Jeckyll & Mr Hyde. Then they worked with Luther Vandross and their old friend from the St Nicholas Projects, Leroy Burgess, to create disco boogie records. 'Hooked On Your Love' showcased Vandross and 'Release Yourself' featured Burgess. Always fiercely innovative, the Fantastic Aleems returned to their vaults. Rather than try to resurrect old Hendrix tracks, they created an album called *Urban Street Tales*, describing it as 'a unique brand of storytelling – episodes of raw street adventures that replicate the beat of Harlem'. One heroic tale told of a remarkable night in Harlem when Lonnie Youngblood drove recklessly through the streets with Hendrix's Flying V guitar in the trunk. As police sirens blared and tyres screeched, jive-talking Harlem gangsters hustled through the night, and the guitar was eventually delivered to Hendrix – 'the musically eccentric showman given to playing guitar with his teeth'. . . a 'certifiable genius-in-the-making'.

The certifiable genius was buried in his native Seattle on 29 October 1970. A small private funeral service was held at Dunlap Baptist Church. Manager Michael Jeffery chartered a private jet to take Hendrix's closest collaborators to Seattle. Noel Redding and Mitch Mitchell were there, so too was the albino rock guitarist Johnny Winter, and several R&B buddies from the past.

Miles Davis travelled in the jet with his wife Betty and Hendrix's girlfriend, Devon Wilson, who was shrouded in a black headscarf.

Hendrix's management banned the Harlem contingent from travelling and anyone associated with the Block Party concert was considered persona non grata. The Aleems and Fat Jack Taylor were left grumpily behind.

Two of the most prominent members of the Harlem Panthers, Alice Faye Williams (aka Afeni Shakur) and Michael Tabor, were released on bail awaiting trial. During the period, Shakur had a brief affair that led to the birth of her son, the rapper Tupac Shakur. Tabor chose to abscond and sought political asylum in Africa.

OCTOBER

Prisoners of War

Paranoia was in the air. Hundreds of journalists swarmed in and around the New York City Criminal Courts Building on Center Street as American justice was laid bare. Curiously, a number of the commentators came not to judge the legal merits of the trial but to check out the hair. In almost every written report of the arraignment of the Black Panthers, there was a baffling fixation on their style, and a pitiful silence about what the Panthers actually stood for. Never before had black leather jackets, berets, sunglasses and afro hairstyles so enraptured a press corps. They were aghast when Alice Faye Williams, known as Afeni Shakur, dismissed her legal representatives and vowed to defend herself. They marvelled as her husband Lumumba Shakur took notes of the proceedings and then buried his pencil deep in his hair. They gathered around the lines of protesting Panthers outside the court, hoping for militant quotes and desperate to be seen in their company. Then he came among them. Michael Tabor was transported to the court from his cell on Rikers Island and thrilled the journalists with his new look. Tabor had followed in the footsteps of the great Memphis musician Isaac Hayes and shaved off all his hair. He wore a sawn-off denim jacket like an extra from *The Warriors*, and when he turned provocatively to the cameras, observers could see, scrawled across the back, three uncompromising letters – POW. It was graffiti and propaganda of the most sensational kind. Tabor, the Harlem street kid turned intellectual, had declared himself a prisoner of war and demanded all the rights extended to captured prisoners in military confrontations, as enshrined in the Geneva Convention. He was at war with the American system and had come to court to confront its racism. They hung on his every word in the hope that he would provide them with headlines and the belligerent, and now bald, Tabor was up to the task.

When the charges were laid before the court in the case of *The People of the State of New York* v. *Lumumba Shakur et al*, twenty-one members of the Black Panther Party were indicted on twelve counts of 'conspiring to bomb various sites in New York – police stations, department stores and other public buildings – and to kill police officers'. State Supreme Court Justice John M. Murtagh presided over the court. He became a key character in what was a face-off between two radically different legal interpretations. Murtagh insisted that this was 'just a criminal indictment', but the Panthers and their supporters were adamant that it was a political trial, that evidence had been fabricated, and that the very notion of political dissent was on trial. America was struggling to cope with an era that had become a battleground for the soul of democracy.

Meanwhile, as Michael Tabor waited to face trial, his acquaintance Sam Melville reached the reckless heights of his bombing campaign against corporate capitalism and the war in Vietnam. The two had known each other since 1968 and the Gym Crow protests that had beset Columbia University. Both made their living from the small concessions they could earn selling radical newspapers. Tabor sold *The Panther* and Melville *The Guardian*. They struck a deal. Melville would sell a batch of Tabor's Black Panther papers on campus, in the Village and downtown, while Tabor would shift copies of the new-left *Guardian* in the ghettos of Harlem and the South Bronx. While white journalists stood back from the Panthers, uneasy at the frisson of danger they had come to represent, Melville tried to build deeper relationships and was genuinely unfazed by their street-tough advocacy. He was already committed to revolutionary violence and saw the Panthers as allies.

Melville had begun his bombing campaign in earnest in the July of 1969. Using dynamite stolen from the Explo Industrial Plant in the Bronx, he offered to gift a box of it to the remnants of the Black Panthers in Harlem, and then stored the rest in a refrigerator at an apartment he rented under the name of 'David McCurdy'. His small band of radicals tested the explosives by blowing up a munitions plant in Washington, New Jersey, which was owned by Pyronics Inc., a manufacturer of military grenades. Melville's next target was the premises of the United Fruit Company, which sat on a pier that jutted out into the Hudson River and was the corporation's major port of entry into New York. United Fruit was loathed by the new left for its colonising role in Latin America. It owned 3.5 million acres of arable land in Central America and the Caribbean, had grown to become the single largest landowner in Guatemala, and controlled up to 9,000 miles of railroad through Colombia and Ecuador. Melville had chosen to blast the pier on Cuban Independence day, 26 July.

Melville had taken to scrawling the slogan GEORGE METESKY WAS HERE wherever he struck, as well as on buildings across Manhattan. In 1957 George Metesky had been diagnosed as a paranoid schizophrenic and incarcerated in Matteawan State Hospital for the Criminally Insane after a series of pipe bombings from 1940 to 1956, which were aimed at discrediting his former employee, Consolidated Edison. He blamed the company for the debilitating tuberculosis which had developed after a workplace injury. By 1969 he had become a bizarre folk hero to the radical left. Melville had read about Metesky's case in a radical political pamphlet and come to believe that his vengeful bombing campaign was inspired by hatred of uncaring capitalism rather than insanity. The authorities disagreed; Metesky's propensity for bombing public places like cinemas did not help his defence.

In the late summer of 1969, graffiti began to appear across the Five Boroughs. The hieroglyphics took several years to decode and nothing about their obscure semiotics helped the authorities with their enquiries.

Taki 183 was a Greek-born teenager from Washington Heights, who used cheap marker pens to write his name as he travelled as a delivery boy across Manhattan. Taki was a diminutive nickname, derived from the Greek name Demetrius, and it appeared everywhere on the No. 2 IRT line in the Bronx, at Forest Parkway on the J line, on the walls at Flushing Avenue and on the BMT-RR line at Prospect Avenue in Brooklyn. Far from home and nervous about the turf he was crossing, Taki 183 even left his mark on the subway stations from Nostrand to New Lots Avenue in Brooklyn. The great American travel writer Paul Theroux, in his essay 'Subway Odyssey', described the New York subway as a series of dungeons which in their darkness attracted new forms of identity. He wrote: 'the 'vandalized station signs, the crazy semiliterate messages, the monkey scratches on the walls, the dampness, the neglect, the visible evidence of destruction and violence – they combine to produce a sense of disgust and horror'.

Demetrius's daily workload took him from his home just north of Harlem, in turf controlled by local gang the Savage Nomads, to the garment districts of 34th Street and then on to his next drop-off. Over the stifling summer of 1969, his 'tag' – TAKI 183 – became ubiquitous across the city, and was soon joined by others: JULIO 204, JOE 136, BARBARA 62, EEL 159, YANK 135 and LEO 136. It was simple code for their teenage nicknames and the streets where they lived. But the streetwise virus spread across New York and made them seem like an urban sudoku which not only baffled older residents but left the authorities at a loss as to how to curtail the craze. The vast majority of taggers were motivated by low-level boredom and a thoughtless desire to leave their mark. Technology had been their friend. Taki had taken advantage of the availability of cheap marker pens, on sale at most convenience stores, and a job that took him across the Five Boroughs by subway. Taki 183 unintentionally ignited the spark that became the boom in graffiti which in later years engulfed New York, an uncomfortable craze that sat somewhere between art and crime. As graffiti became more showy, with the advent of easily available aerosol cans, and ever present on the sides of subway trains, deep fears of urban decay gripped New York and fed the gestation of an entirely new form of music – hip-hop.

By October 1969 Metesky was ancient history and the graffiti that Sam Melville left behind was a mystery that teased the police and added insult to the seemingly random bombings that were now causing concern across Manhattan. The media heaped suspicion on the Black Panthers, presuming that it was the realisation of the bomb plot that the Panther 21 had been arrested for. It seemed that in the newsrooms of New York the Black Panthers had become an obsession. According to one journalist, writing retrospectively for *The New York Times*, 'an ironic tension emerged in the way the press treated the Black Panthers: journalists were at once fascinated and frightened by them.' The Black Panther trial began in earnest in October 1969 and dominated newspaper front pages for months, as the Panthers challenged the court's authority and eventually exposed New York's secret police squad BOSS and the FBI to be the main conspirators.

Melville knew most of the prominent Black Panthers, including Tabor and Lumumba Shakur. He had also befriended Black Power activist H. Rap Brown, and together they trained an underground cell at a secret training camp on a farm hidden in the arable fields of upstate New York. On 7 October Melville planted another bomb, this time at an army induction centre on Whitehall Street, near Battery Park. The blast broke through several load-bearing walls, ruptured water pipes and disrupted the power supply. Debris hurtled into neighbouring buildings and shattered windows all along the tight narrow street.

Although Melville and the Harlem Panthers shared many beliefs, they were from very different communities. Melville was a product of the new left and the sixties counterculture of drugs, festivals and anti-war demonstrations; the Panthers took their radicalisation from the mobilisation of the civil rights movement and its inevitable hardening into Black Power. But there was one issue they shared: a passionate objection to the war in Vietnam. For Melville it was a war of profit and American imperialism; for the Panthers it was a war that was recruiting young black teenagers as cannon fodder.

The war in Vietnam had reached a point of national crisis by late 1969. The media, who had been broadly patriotic about the war, were visibly turning and a new mood of dark scepticism was in the air. The Pentagon Papers, which proved that the Johnson administration had systematically lied about the progress of the war to the American people, had yet to be leaked to *The New York Times* (and then more dramatically to the *Washington Post*), but they were known of in informed circles, and keeping a lid on the scandal was now virtually impossible.

A moving and controversial issue of *Life* magazine carried a detailed audit of the 242 deaths announced by the Pentagon between 28 May and 3 June 1969. Bearing the headline 'The Faces of the American Dead in Vietnam: One Week's Toll', this was powerful journalism. It gave the dead a name, an identity – a life. The feature opened a floodgate of reports of the dead and the dying across the national, regional and local press.

On 15 October the Vietnam Moratorium Committee called for a national work stoppage and a series of coordinated local protests, but the day of demonstrations snowballed into a national movement culminating in two million people besieging Washington DC to protest against the war. Back in New York, Mayor John Lindsay had risked opprobrium by ordering that the US flag be flown at half-mast on the day, as a mark of respect for the dead in Vietnam. Opposition to the war had reached its tipping point, and *The New York Times* described the event as 'that of a great and peaceful army of dissent moving through the city'. Folk singer and activist Pete Seeger led the demonstrations with a rendition of John Lennon's anthemic 'Give Peace A Chance', but inside the White House, resentful that he was being blamed for what he believed was his predecessor Johnson's war, President Nixon let it be known that he was too busy watching Ohio State play Purdue in a televised football game to care about the demonstration. Nixon's snub was aimed at those in mainstream American society who still patriotically backed the war and resented the Moratorium. In Harlem, police cars and fire engines drove with their headlights blaring as a gesture of support for the military, but in the main they were jeered at from the crowded sidewalks.

And then things got worse. Throughout October 1969, freelance reporter Seymour M. Hersh was busy chasing down an exclusive that would traumatise mainstream America. Hersh had gained access to a military tribunal at Fort Benning, Georgia, where his curiosity was piqued by the word 'Pinkville'. It transpired that it was a military code word for the Viet Cong stronghold of My Lai.

According to *The Washington Post*, in the early morning of 16 March 1968 'helicopters carrying US soldiers flew into a tiny village on the eastern side of South Vietnam, bordering the South China Sea. They'd arrived by a series of hamlets, known as My Lai, expecting to find a booby-trapped stronghold of their enemy, the Viet Cong. Instead, all they saw were noncombatants: women, children, elderly men. Many of them were preparing for breakfast. The Americans, about 100 soldiers . . . proceeded to massacre them. Over the next several hours, the civilians . . . were shot and thrown in ditches. The body count: 504 people from more than 240 families. Some women were raped. Huts and homes were burned. Even the livestock was destroyed.

'Right after the attack, the soldiers – who had been told by their superiors the night before that everyone they'd see would be a Viet Cong guerrilla or sympathizer – kept quiet about what they'd done. For more than a year and a half, the public wouldn't know about the atrocity. Top military officials initially tried to keep a lid on the killings and commanders even touted the mission to the press as a tactical feat.'

At the heart of the military tribunal at Fort Benning was a twenty-six-year-old soldier called William L. Calley Jr, whom Hersh described as 'a mild-mannered, boyish-looking Vietnam combat veteran with the nickname Rusty'. It was Calley who had given the explicit orders to kill and then participated in the execution of unarmed villagers. He was charged with the premeditated murder of 109 Vietnamese civilians. Hersh's exposé of his actions won him the Pulitzer Prize in 1970. Even in the earliest days of the Vietnam War, there was always a national consensus that war was ugly, but Calley's admissions and Hersh's forensic analysis of the events tipped public sympathy against the beleaguered military. Investigative journalism was proving to be America's Achilles heel.

*

Soul music inevitably paralleled the journey from patriotism to disgust. In the early to mid sixties Vietnam-related soul songs were broadly patriotic, in many cases taking the form of love letters to soldiers overseas: typical among them Marvin Gaye's 'A Soldier's Plea' (1962), The Velvelettes' 'Your Heart Belongs To Me' (1962) and William Bell's 'A Soldier's Goodbye' (1966), a song Bell wrote for Stax when he was drafted. They all focused on distant love rather than the vicissitudes of the war. By the late sixties and early seventies the tone had hardened. The Dells' 'Does Anybody Know I'm Here' (1968) was an emotional ballad sung by a lonely forgotten soldier in a faraway land; Roy C's 'Open Letter To The President' (1971), a soulful plea to Nixon to end the war; and Freda Payne's 'Bring The Boys Home' (1971) argued for disengagement and troop withdrawal. But by some distance, the most stunning record of the entire Vietnam War was Jerry 'Swamp Dogg' Williams's 'Sam Stone' (1971). Originally written and performed by the country folk singer John Prine and a song of fierce social realism, the soul version is raised to a new level of pathos by Williams's gospel-inspired voice. A drug-addicted and traumatised Vietnam vet, Sam Stone's life disintegrates as his disbelieving children look on. This is the real and brutal aftermath of the Vietnam War.

In October 1969 another war was looming within soul music, and it was about to take place between the sexes in the bedrooms of black America. The ultra-talented and visionary Jerry Williams was a driver of that change, too. An unknown soul singer called Doris Curry was living a hand-to-mouth existence in a tenement block in Harlem, having moved there from Sandersville, Georgia. She had been born into a dirt-poor sharecropping family who eked out an existence on the banks of the Savannah River. As a teenager, Curry had toured the south with local gospel groups, and at the age of eighteen she made the decision to head north to Harlem, chasing fame in the fiercely competitive soul scene. On her arrival in 1963, she shacked up with other migrants from Georgia and joined a long queue of hopefuls looking for hired work as a backing singer at the Apollo.

Curry had been inventive with her CV, claiming that she was a singer with the famous gospel group Albertina Walker and the Caravans; in fact she had appeared only on the same bill with her local church choir. But she did have one bit of luck. At the time, her native Georgia was a dominant force in soul music. Little Richard, James Brown and Otis Redding were all from the small town of Macon, Georgia, and partly through her connections with their backing singers, she began to secure intermittent work. Sometime in 1967 Curry married and changed her name to Willingham, then she landed a couple of temporary jobs as the featured singer with the Lost Souls. Still unable to find regular work, in 1968 she secured a more credible one-off deal with the US label Jay Boy and released 'You Can't Do That', which despite its gritty appeal and international distribution faded from view. Ready to call it a day, and take any job she could, Doris Willingham had a chance meeting with Jerry Williams. Their careers thus far had been parallel failures. Williams had been signed briefly to Calla Records, where he fronted the great uptown soul song 'If You Ask Me (Because I Love You'), but it nose-dived, so he took work as a producer with Gene Pitney, losing out on a production credit on the hit 'She's A Heartbreaker'. Feeling cheated and undermined, Williams took occasional work at Atlantic Records, producing for the fledgling student band the Commodores. By the time he met Willingham, who was battered by a string of missed opportunities, failed relationships and life in dank Harlem apartments, he had had an idea – one that would point to yet another different future for soul music. He wanted to make a concept album.

The idea of a concept album was still relatively new. In the aftermath of the Mothers of Invention's *Freak Out!* (1966) and the Beatles' *Sgt. Pepper's Lonely Hearts Club Band* (1967), they were mainly associated with progressive rock bands. But that was about to change. The Temptations had released the groundbreaking ghetto album *Puzzle People* (1969), which broke with Motown's bubble-gum soul and addressed wider social themes. It incorporated the race-conscious records 'Message From A Blackman' and 'Slave', the heroin song 'Don't Let The Joneses Get You Down', and the teenage runaway message song 'Running Away (Ain't Gonna

Help You)'. Williams's idea was different again. He wanted to turn love on its head, to tell some home truths about relationships through a set of painfully honest songs about the deeper realities of romance: loneliness, failure, infidelity, break-ups and divorce. It was a radical idea. And Doris Willingham's own traumas were not few; she had just split from her husband after a disastrous marriage. Williams and Willingham decided that before the album was even recorded she would adopt a new name. Rather than use her birth name of Curry, they hunted for a new one, and it came from a very different world to that of the nightclubs and low-rent apartments of Harlem.

Doris Duke was a New York socialite, multi-millionaire and celebrity whose unconventional lifestyle and numerous lovers – Errol Flynn, General George Patton and bebop pianist Joe Castro to name but three – kept her in the gossip columns. Both Williams and Willingham liked the name Doris Duke and so it stuck. Williams hunted around for cheap studio deals, but the prices in New York forced him to look south. The pair ended up in Macon where Otis Redding's former manager Phil Walden and his brother Alan had opened Capricorn Studios. So circumstances dictated that Doris head back to Georgia for the first time since she had left home. There, over a matter of a few intense weeks, they recorded one of the greatest underground deep soul albums – *I'm A Loser* – a painful and emotionally charged album that reflects on lost opportunities ('Ghost Of Myself)', failed relationships ('We're More Than Strangers') and, most powerfully of all, infidelity in 'To The Other Woman (I'm The Other Woman)'. It was this final soul-destroying track that took black music in another new direction.

Doris Duke had created a personality and tone of voice that was nothing less than revolutionary. Here was a song that was frank about infidelity and, by the sheer shift of its axis, took women as its audience. It was feminism in an intimate confessional sense – women speaking to women. The album opened the floodgates to some of the great female soul records of the seventies: Sandra Phillips's *Too Many People In One Bed* (1970), Millie Jackson's *It Hurts So Good* (1973) and *Caught Up* (1974), Bettye Crutcher's 'Call Me When All Else Fails' (1974) and Shirley Brown's phone conversation classic 'Woman To Woman' (1974).

One single from the era, inspired by adulterous love, has since become an all-time soul music standard. '(If Loving You Is Wrong) I Don't Want To Be Right' came out of the Stax studios and was first sung by Luther Ingram, then Millie Jackson, Isaac Hayes, Bobby Bland, Percy Sledge and David Ruffin, and in the wider pop world by Rod Stewart and Tom Jones among others.

Unexpectedly, infidelity became a dramatic factor in the Panther 21 trial. Since the Panthers' arrest in the dawn-raids of April, their legal representatives had been fighting a campaign to set reasonable bail conditions. They were all rejected. When bail conditions were eventually set by the court they were draconian – between $50,000 and $150,000 – and unprecedented in the New York legal system. Although the bail was beyond the meagre means of the Black Panther Party, a fundraising campaign got under way. At first it was local to Harlem, but it soon gathered momentum downtown through the alternative newspapers promoting their cause, and celebrities began to lend their weight. Fundraising took on a new and controversial dynamic when a group of well-heeled socialites from New York's liberal elite offered support. The American composer and conductor Leonard Bernstein and his wife, the Chilean actress Felicia Montealegre, decided to host a party at their Park Avenue duplex. It was a gathering that bitterly divided New York society. The Bernsteins' party was savaged by Tom Wolfe, who wrote an essay for the *New York* magazine called 'Radical Chic: That Party at Lenny's'. The essay mocked the very idea of privileged artists hosting a party on behalf of Black Power and derided those in attendance for assuaging their white liberal guilt by rubbing shoulders with the Panthers. Like so much of Wolfe's writing it was clever (it was he who first coined the phrase 'radical chic'), brutally observed, satirical, but it was profoundly cynical.

Felicia Montealegre fought back, saying: 'As a civil libertarian, I asked a number of people to my house . . . in order to hear the lawyer and others involved with the Panther 21 discuss the problem of civil liberties as applicable to the men now awaiting trial, and to help raise funds for their legal expenses . . . It was for this deeply serious purpose that our meeting was called. The frivolous way in which it was reported as a “fashionable” event is unworthy of the times, and offensive to all people who are committed to humanitarian principles of justice.’ Predictably, her well-intentioned defence did nothing to offset the sneering and, according to a report in the rival *New York Post*, Wolfe’s piece ‘devastated the white intellectual community, and Panther defence contributions . . . abruptly dropped off to nearly nothing’. The impact really was toxic. The Panthers struggled to raise much financial support. Basking in his cleverness, Wolfe never seemed to find the time to coin a smartass phrase for the squalid conditions in which they were being held. It was his elite privilege to ignore them.

One, perhaps unexpected, strand of society that did raise funds in support of bail was that of the radicalised Christian churches across Harlem. They were prominent in their opposition to the war in Vietnam, supported the campaign to raise funds for Biafra, and helped to fund outreach projects for the hungry and poor, aiding breakfast clubs in Harlem that were organised by the Black Panthers. The church money, raised over three months of intensive campaigning and topped up by white women’s groups, was tiny compared to the two million dollars that was needed. Just enough was raised to provide bail for one individual. As the Panthers were being held in different detention centres across New York State, they were only allowed to communicate with each other in pre-trial legal meetings. At one meeting, they collectively decided that the first person to be freed from prison should be Alice Williams.

By then using her married name of Afeni Shakur, she had been held in the Women’s House of Detention since April 1969. Her husband, Lumumba, the de facto leader of the Harlem Panthers, had conducted their brief Muslim wedding ceremony in an apartment near the Apollo. It was a marriage bound as much by ideology as love, and they split when Afeni fell pregnant with another man’s child while out on bail. The couple, brought together in struggle, studiously ignored each other during the lengthy court proceedings to come, and never spoke to each other again. Afeni’s as-yet unborn child was her son Tupac, the rap superstar and doomed king of ‘thug life’.

The Shakurs' story was one of love, infidelity and reaffirmation that not even the most troubled deep-soul singer could have imagined. At the time, many suspected the child's father was Sam Napier, a quietly authoritative man who was the distribution manager of the Panthers' newspaper. A victim of the internal feuding, he was brutally killed in April 1971. Seventeen-year-old Mark Holder taped up his eyes and mouth, forced him to lie on a cot and then shot him in the head before setting fire to the office. It was a punishment killing for his loyalty to the Huey Newton faction of the self-imploding Panthers. Tupac Shakur's father was in fact a member of the Jersey City branch of the Black Panther Party called Bill Garland. He had met Afeni at a meeting while she was out on bail. When it came to registering the birth, Afeni stated that the father was dead, thus seeming to endorse Sam Napier's being the father. However, Garland contested the registration in a paternity suit and DNA tests confirmed that he was indeed the father of Tupac. By then, though, the rapper had been killed in a drive-by shooting in Las Vegas. He was twenty-five.

During the Panthers' trial Afeni Shakur and Michael Tabor waived their rights to legal counsel and defended themselves. Each time one of them took to their feet, a palpable surge of expectation swept through the courtroom. The eloquent Shakur and Tabor were the unexpected stars of the proceedings – bringing to mind Nina Simone and Marvin Gaye in full impassioned flow.

Each day, the next generation of young Panthers, drawn from across the Five Boroughs, would descend on the court, sometimes marching in paramilitary style, sometimes clustering around the entrance with banners and forcing the press, legal secretaries and witnesses to run the gauntlet outside the court. There was a permanent police presence, countless stand-offs and at times a festival-like atmosphere with the hot-dog stalls, the pungent smell of sugar-scented nuts and the occasional gospel singer testifying for the Panthers. Famous faces showed up. Jane Fonda, never one to steer clear of a political cause, attended, as did Harry Belafonte, effortlessly elegant in suit and overcoat. The writer Jean Genet deliberately dressed as a tramp and argued loudly in French with journalists. Donny Hathaway, dark eyes hidden beneath his ghetto cap, walked impatiently past the throng outside. He was a member of Jesse Jackson's civil rights movement PUSH, and when a Cook County tactical unit shot and killed Chicago's leading Black Panther Fred Hampton in December 1969, Hathaway joined the committee to support a civil prosecution and aid Hampton's family.

Unlike the great civil rights cases of the fifties and early sixties, the Panther 21 trial had neither the swelling gospel choirs and moral authority of the church behind it nor the clear-cut biblical morality of right and wrong. This was a trial that divided and, in some respects, frightened the moderate black community. Each day there was another dispute, and another, and another. The pre-trial deliberations and jury selection stretched out over months, and almost two years passed from the first arrests to the verdict.

Judge John Murtagh was a story in his own right. He was of Irish ancestry and had a habit of pausing like a punctuation mark at the end of sentences, and when his next words were significant or dramatic the pause grew even longer. His swept-back silver hair was split by a centre parting as deep as an axe mark. In March 1964 he had grabbed headlines as the judge in the notorious Lenny Bruce case. The hipster comedian Bruce had been appearing at Café Au Go-Go in Greenwich Village. Unfortunately, one of the people in the audience was a former CIA agent, Herbert Ruhe, who had been appointed as a licensing inspector. According to the prosecution, Ruhe had a 'phenomenally well-developed memory' and as Bruce improvised his way through the show, he scribbled down terms including 'jack me off', 'nice tits', and 'go come in a chicken'. A few nights later, acting on Ruhe's evidence, a squad of four police officers went to the venue and recorded Bruce's routine. Bruce was promptly arrested, taken to the offices of the Sixth Precinct on West 10th Street and charged with indecency. Despite a petition supporting his right to be 'allowed to perform free from censorship or harassment', signed by entertainers and authors including Bob Dylan, Norman Mailer and Elizabeth Taylor, Judge Murtagh concluded that Bruce's act 'appealed to prurient interest', was 'patently offensive to the average person in the community', and lacked 'redeeming social importance'. He sentenced the comedian to four months in the workhouse but Bruce didn't live long enough to see through his appeal. He died of acute morphine poisoning in his Hollywood home in 1966.

Life magazine described the Panther 21 trial as 'a bedlam of insults, threats and contemptuous behaviour'. There were near daily exchanges between the judge who demanded respect and the Panthers who demanded justice; neither listened to the other. In his book *The Savage City*, social scientist T.J. English claimed that 'the defendants used the judge as a foil, referring to him in court variously as a "pig", a "faggot", a "liar", a "hanging racist", a "fascist lackey", a "grandee vulture", and most theatrically of all, "a dried-up cracker in female robes".' Murtagh bore it all with a barely disguised contempt and, irrespective of the insults thrown at him, pushed the trial forwards to its inevitable conclusion. He came to both loathe and admire Michael Tabor, whose booming voice filled the courtroom and whose studious and colourful language revealed him as having an acute legal mind that had not had the privileges of university education. Murtagh once confessed to a journalist that if circumstances were different Tabor would be working for him, not calling him a tub-faced bigot. A police officer who had been called as a witness also told reporters that Tabor had been their primary concern. Author Murray Kempton described the feelings directly: 'There slept in Michael Tabor a power like Malcolm X.' Both the New York Police Department's intelligence communiqué and the FBI's COINTELPRO operations had expressly instructed officers to target people like Tabor for fear that they become the 'next Messiah'.

Meanwhile, police had still not managed to find the perpetrator of the bombing campaign in Manhattan. But a network of FBI informers had spread across the Village and the Lower East Side, and they were getting close to Sam Melville. According to reports in *The Washington Post*, Jane Alpert planted the next bomb: 'On September 18th 1969 Jane Alpert put on a white A-line dress, kid gloves and a touch of make-up and tucked a bomb into the oversized handbag she had stolen from a department store. She rode the bus to the Federal Building in New York's Foley Square and took the elevator to the 40th floor where the Department of the Army had its offices.' Packed in her satchel was a Westclox alarm clock, a blasting cap and fifteen sticks of dynamite neatly packed together. Journalist Lynn Darling describes a woman methodically carrying out her plan: 'A few minutes later, she left, leaving the bomb in a room full of electrical equipment. She didn't see the bomb go off, never saw the blinding light, never heard the nerve-cracking explosion that impelled the splinters of glass, the shards of metal. She was not a witness to the violent aftermath of her handiwork.'

Over two intensive days of bombing in November 1969, Alpert, Melville and their conspirators attacked four separate buildings: the Standard Oil offices in the RCA Building, Chase Manhattan Bank headquarters, the General Motors Building and the New York City Criminal Court Building, where the Panther 21 trial was being held. But an NYPD special squad was following their every move by now. Two undercover FBI agents, pretending to be homeless bums, were sleeping on the pavement outside their home, and a silver sedan car was permanently parked in their street. Rather than go on the run or stay holed up in her apartment, Alpert hid in full view. Every day, she packed her notebook and walked to the court proceedings. Alpert sat in the press gallery next to New York's major news journalists, her press pass signifying that she was an accredited journalist representing *Rat Subterranean News*. She would take notes, diligently record the key shifts in testimony, and periodically exchange supportive smiles with Afeni Shakur and Joan Bird, both of whom she had interviewed.

On 21 February 1970 another bomb exploded, but this time it was directly connected to the Panther trial. A group of white militants crept up to Judge Murtagh's family home at 529 West 217th Street, in Manhattan's Inwood neighbourhood, and, hiding behind the front hedgerow, spray-painted slogans on the pavement – 'Free the Panther 21' and the anti-war slogan 'The Viet Cong Have Won'. Murtagh's son John was only nine years old at the time, and recently described the scenes on a Fox News show: 'At about four thirty in the morning, I was sound asleep in bed, our entire family was sound asleep. Two bombs were detonated in the front of the house . . . They placed an explosive device under the gas tank of the family car near the back door in the garage. The first thing I remember is waking up, no doubt from the sound, my mother coming into the room, pulling me out of bed. I remember standing in the kitchen with my mother and my family. We could see flames [through] the window.' It was the finale to an ill-fated bombing spree that had begun earlier, at one-thirty a.m., in Lower Manhattan when a gasoline bomb was thrown at a police patrol car parked in front of the Charles Street police station in Greenwich Village and another was dropped or thrown on the pavement about seventy-five feet away.

John Murtagh has borne an understandable lifetime grudge against the men he accuses of fire-bombing his family home. He has specifically named Bill Ayers of the militant underground group the Weather Underground, whose name was inspired by the lyrics of Bob Dylan's 'Subterranean Homesick Blues'.

According to John Murtagh, 'they attacked two military recruiting installations in Brooklyn, they attacked a police institution in Lower Manhattan, and then they attacked my family home with us sleeping in our beds, with three separate bombs'. This was not entirely accurate. In fact, the context for Murtagh appearing on the Fox show was that the network was trying to connect Bill Ayers, by then an educationalist in Chicago, with Barack Obama. Some of the bombings he alluded to were either the work of Sam Melville or the Columbia University cell of the Weather Underground. Ayers had been involved in planting bombs in Chicago in 1969, but the fire bombs at the Murtaghs' family home were the work of the New York cell of the Weather Underground, led by Ted Gold, a student who had come to prominence during the Gym Crow demonstrations. The attack on the Murtagh family home was an act that was neither sanctioned nor supported by the Black Panthers. Two windowpanes were shattered, an overhanging eave was scorched, and the paint on the side of the car was charred. It was an attack that was debatably more theatrical than dangerous, but it heaped even more public opprobrium on the Panthers at the time. Ted Gold and three other members of the Weather Underground were killed in March 1970 when their bomb factory exploded in the basement of a Greenwich Village townhouse at 18 West 11th Street. They were preparing to bomb a military dance at Fort Dix, across the Hudson in New Jersey.

By this time the FBI knew of Sam Melville and that he was living under the false name of David McCurdy. They knew about Jane Alpert, too, and had already questioned the office staff at *Rat*. Typical of the times, the FBI also had a well-placed informant in Melville's circle. George Demmerle had been an FBI undercover informant since 1966 and was being paid $250 for every report he filed on known radicals. Melville first met him at Woodstock, where Demmerle was manning a table on behalf on another of 1969's bewildering array of fringe groups, the Crazies. Although Melville was warned to be careful of Demmerle, he rashly allowed him into his inner circle and then took him into his confidence about a new bombing target he had identified.

Melville's next mission was his last. He had noticed a group of National Guard vehicles parked near the 68th Regiment Armory at 25th and Lexington. After watching them over several days, Melville realised that the trucks were moved indoors at night. He planned to place a bomb in one of the trucks and allow the army to drive it into their own complex. Melville took Demmerle with him as a lookout, and the information was swiftly passed to the FBI. When Melville arrived at the Armory, he was overcome by FBI agents and police officers, and arrested. Melville pleaded guilty and was sent to the notorious Attica State Prison where he remained until his dramatic death. The passion he had always had for black militancy, developed over years of visiting Harlem, did not weaken. He continued to fight for better conditions in the prison until he was shot during the riots – one of the leaders and one of the few white victims who died alongside black prison rebels.

As the Panther 21 trial rumbled on it became clear that the defendants had a propaganda coup in their midst, a story that might influence a jury or tip the emotional balance of the trial in their favour. His name was Lee Berry, a twenty-four-year-old Panther who was undergoing treatment for epilepsy at the Manhattan Veterans' Hospital on the day of his indictment. He had been a soldier in Vietnam and while on active service there had suffered several fits. He informed the police department that he was in hospital but was available to be questioned there. The offer was denied, and Berry was taken by force from the hospital to the Manhattan House of Detention, where he was detained under $100,000 bail conditions. He was held for seven months, with two other prisoners, in a cell built for one. Although his attorneys complained of neglect, the claims were refuted by the Commissioner of Corrections office. His condition worsened. In July 1969 Berry's counsel returned to court with a further claim that he had been beaten by a guard, suffered an epileptic seizure, and in the struggle was assaulted with a blackjack, which lacerated his eye. The seizure was being treated as a physical attack on an officer. Berry was then placed in solitary confinement and, according to a report in *The New York Times*, 'his diet throughout that period of treatment was bread and tea. Somewhere, in the confusion of these disputes, his regular medication was withdrawn.' The report further claimed that 'it was November before Judge Murtagh ordered Berry to Bellevue Hospital for observation'. On his arrival in hospital he collapsed and was rushed to emergency care where he was operated on for appendicitis. In the confusion, the hospital removed a normal healthy appendix, and he contracted pneumonia. Berry's callous treatment had an emotional resonance that appealed beyond radicals to ordinary people. Berry's wife, who was not prominent in the Panthers, was recruited to attend rallies. She was at the Bernsteins' fundraiser the night that Tom Wolfe tore it to bits in his 'Radical Chic' essay.

When the verdict finally came, on 13 May 1971, it was a mortal blow to the NYPD. After deliberating for only three hours, the jury acquitted the defendants on all counts. When it was exposed in court that the charges had stemmed from the plotting and provocations of three long-term undercover police operations, the Panthers were cleared. Eugene Roberts had never testified in open court before. He was kept on the stand for six weeks. His shaky and self-incriminating testimony was devastating for law enforcement and the whole culture of secret surveillance. Now, the press had a story and they were unforgiving in their condemnation of the botched surveillance operation. Tony Ortega described his fellow jurors in *Village Voice*: 'Two teachers, a political science student, a Housing Authority maintenance man, a woman from the New York State Insurance Department, a retired longshoreman, an opera composer no less, two book editors, a TV-film editor, a welfare administrator, and a Post Office employee – stalwart gorgeous people all, with the New York . . . sparkle.' The jury had seen through the bombast and posturing of the Black Panthers and the deceit and collusion of the police. It is incontrovertible that they made the right decision to free the Panther 21, but their celebrating outside with the Panthers was misjudged.

The jury threw a lunch party and invited the Panthers to join them. Several did, but the star of the Panther 21 was noticeably absent. Michael Tabor had fled the country and was in political exile in Algiers. He would never return.

The Garbage Offensive: young Hispanic kids pose in front of a line of garbage in the summer of 1969. The media flocked to East Harlem to report on a local ghetto protest led by the Hispanic activist group the Young Lords.

NOVEMBER

The Boogaloo Revolution

They were an unlikely couple, who had only met that spring. He was Miguel Melendez, a New York-born Puerto Rican whose formal education had been held back by undiagnosed dyslexia, and she was an Irish-American college tutor called Patricia Sweeney, who worked for the Admissions Department of Old Westbury College, in Nassau County, New York. Work had taken them to the Midwest and they drove together in Sweeney's black VW Beetle through blizzards, reaching the Windy City twenty-four hours later. When they set off, both imagined it was on routine college business, but a chance meeting in Chicago ignited another chapter in the ever-changing story of modern Harlem. Sweeney was a Chicago native and had been tasked by the college to diversify its student intake by bringing promising talent from ghetto communities to the traditional and leafy college in Westbury, which at the time was being subsumed into the State University of New York. The college had identified Melendez – then a prominent member of the East Harlem Student Organization – as someone who could help to recruit more students from the Puerto Rican community.

He was happy to take on the role, in part to make extra money and also with the hope that he could take some time off to scour Chicago for boogaloo.

Melendez was on a voyage of discovery. He had attended St Athanasius High School in the Bronx. There he had befriended Ronnie Puente, son of the famous bandleader Tito Puente. It was the beginning of a remarkable life story that straddled the tramlines of music and social action. Passionate about understanding his roots, Melendez burrowed away in libraries, studying the history of Puerto Rican nationalism and the island's complicated relationship with America. Although at the time his knowledge was primitive – and largely emotional – he had become a convert to the cause of Puerto Rican independence. For the previous four years, he worked as a budding music promoter in Harlem, learning the ropes of the concert scene from his uncle Albie Diaz. Uncle and nephew shared a passion for the music of Cal Tjader, the percussion and vibes master who by 1969 was a veteran of the Latin jazz scene and known throughout East Harlem as one of the purveyors of the Cuban dance craze the mambo. When Tjader's seminal album *Soul Sauce* – which combined urban soul, jazz and Latin – hit the streets, kids queued for hours round the block at Casa Latina and at B&G Records on Southern Boulevard to buy a copy. The title track was a single that owed much to Willie Bobo's primitive shout-out rapping and persistent R&B beat – a hybrid that spoke to Harlem's many immigrant communities.

Although Melendez was too young to visit the Palladium on 53rd and Broadway, the one-time citadel of Latin dance music, he had met many of the greats: the Afro-Cuban jazz legend Machito; the Puerto Rican bandleader Tito Rodríguez; the Harlem-born Tito Puente, who pioneered mambo and cha-cha-cha; and two South Bronx brothers who shaped the future of salsa, Charlie and Eddie Palmieri. Just as soul music was passing through a period of fundamental change, so was its near neighbour, Afro-Caribbean dance music.

Melendez became a regular at the Latino dance clubs that spread out from the bars of East Harlem: the Park Plaza on 110th Street, the Taft Hotel on Seventh Avenue, and Brooklyn's 3-in-1

Club. His uncle ran his own nightclub – Cameos – and it was there that Melendez first heard the beats that exploded into the cult of boogaloo. 'Learning the trade was one thing, but above all I listened hungrily to the stories musicians told,' he wrote in his autobiography *We Took the Streets*. 'Hearing of their lives, the hardships they endured in the quest for success. It was like going to college. It's those stories, their legacy, that made up for the financial losses we often took, no matter how jam-packed and amazing a show had been.' Boogaloo was a new intense sound, which borrowed so much from soul music and the African-American experience that it unsettled older immigrants. One enduring urban myth claims that when the old Palladium dancehall downtown was being demolished, Hispanic construction workers painted the word 'boogaloo' on the wrecking ball, signalling the destruction of one way of life and the emergence of another.

By 1965 Melendez was a neighbourhood promoter who ran shows at Colgate Gardens, the base of an influential Bronx DJ called Symphony Sid. Fanatics branded Sid the 'jazz traitor' when he had forsaken his bebop roots to become a convert to the cause of Latin music. It was a time when subcultures were clashing and cross-fertilising – jazz into funk, soul into psychedelia, and, most spectacularly of all, the thing they called boogaloo. In the East Harlem of the mid sixties, the Cameo Club and Colgate Gardens were visited by a music revolution as the sound of boogaloo swept through every American ghetto and captured the hearts of young teenagers, many of whom were born in America but whose families had migrated to New York from the Caribbean.

It is commonly believed, even by those saturated in music, that boogaloo had its origins in Chicago, where a string of records from the local soul scene sprang up. At first, it seemed as if it was little more than yet another dance craze, a here-today-and-gone-tomorrow fad, but boogaloo had a presence and resilience that lasted well beyond the end of the sixties, fuelling feelings of self-confidence and teenage rebellion on its way. The music was primitive dance, a syncopated funk beat, with noisy party exhortations and a driving brass sound: the engine of sixties soul stripped back to the crankshaft. An early example was the evergreen

'R&B Time' (1965), an infectious single fronted by Chicago's most famous R&B disc jockey E. Rodney Jones. It was a mess of cultures, opening with a faux Chinese refrain before exploding into a relentless sax-led soul instrumental and Jones's voice toasting over the beat, demanding action and urging the dancers to reach new heights of energy. Jones was in a unique position to promote his own single and those who surrounded it on the Chicago soul scene. He was one of the so-called 'Good Guys', the regular DJs on radio station WVON – the Voice of the Negro. It was the first twenty-four-hour radio station aimed at the black community in Chicago. He reached out on the crucial drivetime slot between three and seven p.m., talking to 'everyone who was anyone' and bringing what his colleague, station director Richard Pegue, described as a '1,450 percent personality, bigger than life itself'.

Yet boogaloo's origins lay in confusion and controversy. Two unknown soul singers called Tom and Jerrio took a master tape of a rough-house dance record to ABC Records. Tom was a Chicago singer called Robert Tharpe, who had jettisoned his real name for the more romantic Tommy Darke. Jerrio was his friend, Jerry Murray. For a while both were connected to the Midwest soul group the Ideals, but they found greater celebrity as a duo performing comedy and cover versions to mainstream ghetto audiences. Then, in an audacious, or possibly crazy, move, they managed to gain access to an unreleased obscure Motown song called 'Do The See Saw' by the Contours and began touting the song as their own. Using the Detroit backing track and shouting nightclub dance instructions over the top, Tom and Jerrio issued a 'new' version of the song on what was a privately pressed label called Jerry-O. The track, now called 'Boogaloo', was subsequently bought up by ABC-Paramount who, unaware of the copyright theft, promoted it heavily until it charted. The scam was not long in being rumbled. Berry Gordy sued the two singers and claimed all the royalties. While lawyers argued over the originality and relative merits of the two songs, the term 'boogaloo' took off, and within a matter of weeks a string of new dance records hit the shops. But what no one had actually noticed was that the original lyrics of the Contours' Detroit-produced original from 1963 held a clue to what was really going on. Its lyrics referred to 'the salsa stars across the tracks' – probably the first recorded evidence of something that was instinctively happening in East Harlem: the cross-fertilisation of up-tempo urban soul music with Latin dance forms. It may also be one of the earliest uses of the word 'salsa', a common Hispanic word, but not one that was widely used about music until the early seventies.

Chicago had a thriving club scene where funk and boogaloo mutated. A family dance group called the Cash Brothers, which featured the irrepressible Alvin Cash, signed for the Mar-V-Lus and One-derful! indie labels in an attempt to find fame in the highly competitive funk market. Over a period of six years he fronted up an impressive number of dance records including 'Twine Time', 'Alvin's Bag' and 'Do The Ali Shuffle', but prominent among them was 'Alvin's Boogaloo' (1966). This was a boogaloo classic that had all the madcap ingredients of a new underground phenomenon: a stuttering funk beat, a call-and-response party atmosphere, and a sheer good-time attitude that could light up the dullest room.

Chicago may have been crucial at the birth, but when boogaloo really took off it was in Harlem, where it became a byword for dancing, partying and simply having a wild night out. Between 1965 and 1969 hundreds of records bearing the name were released, some on soul labels and others on fledgling Hispanic labels. Unperturbed by legal defeat, Jerrio moved to Detroit and garrulously founded his own record label called Boo-Ga-Loo Records, persisting with more funk party tunes – 'Papa Chew Do The Boogaloo' (1966), 'Karate Boogaloo' (1967), 'Funky Boogaloo' (1968) and 'Popcorn Boogaloo' (1968). Across the spectrum of independent soul came many followers: J.J. Jackson's 'Boogaloo Baby' (1966), Don Gardner's 'My Baby Likes To Boogaloo' (1966), The Flamingos' 'Boogaloo Party' (1966) and 'Brooklyn Boogaloo' (1966), and the Fantastic Johnny C's 'Boogaloo Down Broadway' (1968). Many more contemporary songs without the boogaloo tag used the whistle-stop party atmosphere, among them two major Chicago releases that sold well in Harlem and in Europe – 'Do The 45' by the Sharpees, a St Louis soul group who recorded on One-derful!, and 'Move With The Groove' by a Chicago boogaloo group Bull and the Matadors, led by frantic singer James 'Bull' Parks.

Boogaloo crossed over from soul and flourished in Hispanic-speaking communities. Big bands were still the staple of Latino dances, and Hispanic-owned record labels were in their infancy. So, at first, boogaloo found its way into the playlist of every major band, with very few becoming available as records. Among them were Latin percussionist and bandleader Johnny Zamot, who released 'Johnny's Boogaloo', 'Boogaloo Frog' and 'Boogaloo Baby', all in 1967; the Dominican bandleader Bobby Quesada, who released 'Bataola Boogaloo' on one of the fledgling new labels, the famous Fania Records in 1968; Johnny Colon, founder of the East Harlem Music School, who issued 'Boogaloo Blues' (1967); Willie Rosario, the conga player and boogaloo DJ at the Hispanic-language radio station WADO, who released 'Watusi Boogaloo' on ATCO; and Afro-Cuban jazz drummer Pedro Gutierrez aka Pete Terrace, who released 'Do The Boogaloo'.

Although boogaloo is now seen as a moment of fusion, in which Latin, funk and soul met and merged, it might also be described as a coming of age. For those teenagers whose origins were in Cuba, the Dominican Republic and Puerto Rico, it was their rock 'n' roll, their punk or, more accurately, their northern soul. Many boogaloo and Latin soul records were 'private pressings', small quantities of records made for friends and family, and a raw bubbling excitement was audible on what were often underfunded recordings. These obscure records, virtually invisible to outsiders – and often parents – were played at underground nightclubs and dancehalls like the Corso and Club Tropicana, which were situated on the edges of New York's intimidating Projects and seen as no-go areas for mainstream teenagers and a foreign country to the white middle classes.

Boogaloo was unashamedly feelgood music. Nothing about it talked of politics or social change, but the generation who grew up with the music – young Hispanics born in America – were challenging the compromises that their parents had made. The multi-instrumentalist Johnny Colon told *Vice* magazine: 'Boogaloo is the quintessential American experience. It's youths trying to make it, it's immigrant influence, it's musical development.' As a teenage star, whose 1967 hit 'Boogaloo Blues' became an anthem of the scene, Colon claimed that the music made kids feel as if they were no longer second-class citizens. As urban riots in the sixties distracted the media from a fuller understanding of ghetto life, the boogaloo generation began to demand more from America than their parents ever did. It was in its own coded way a music of defiance, and when teenage voices rose up in East Harlem no one shouted louder than the Young Lords.

When Mickey Melendez and his tutor arrived in Chicago, they set up a series of meetings to give advice to mainly Hispanic high school kids and distribute college literature. They also held interviews for students who had already shown an interest in Old Westbury College. One of their pre-planned meetings took them to the offices of the Latin American Defence Organization where Melendez was introduced to a young man who had a street reputation and connections in Chicago's Hispanic neighbourhoods – Lincoln Park, West Town and Humboldt Park. His name was Jose 'Cha-Cha' Jiménez, a gang leader from Lincoln Park and one of a tough generation of young Hispanics who faced off with rival gangs like the Egyptian Cobras, the quasi-political Blackstone Rangers and the Almighty Vice Lord Nation, who boasted 30,000 members. In the summer of 1968 Jiménez was arrested for possession of heroin and spent some time in a correctional facility. When he returned to the streets it was as an educated and passionate young man who proceeded to transform his gang into the Young Lords, the Puerto Rican activist group and Hispanic equivalent of the Black Panthers.

Neither Jiménez nor Melendez knew each other, and their conversation rambled in many different directions until Jiménez brought another young man into the conversation. His name was David Perez, a teenage activist who was running a campaign to have his high school named after Roberto Clemente, the Puerto Rican-born star of the Pittsburgh Pirates baseball team. Perez was interested in attending Old Westbury, and in the course of their conversations it became clear that he shared Melendez's passion for Puerto Rican independence. As the day lengthened into night, a plan was hatched to return to New York and establish a branch of the Young Lords in America's most famous barrio – Spanish Harlem.

Spanish Harlem had been mythologised in song since 1960 when Jerry Leiber and Phil Spector co-wrote an unusual ghetto ballad. 'Spanish Harlem' was originally sung by the Harlem singer Ben E. King, who had just left the soulful doo-wop group the Drifters. On release, the song was hugely popular but regarded as nothing much more than a romantic soul ballad which talked of love and roses. What was exceptional was the setting. The song tells the story of a rose that grows in the gutters of the ghetto and offers hope to the talent that might feel trapped in slum conditions. But in the song, the rose's 'black soul' and 'fiery lack of control' blooms at night; the song is lifted from chocolate-box sentimentality to a vision of hope. With the right voice, it had all the potential to transcend romance and become a song of community, pride and even resistance. By changing the colour scheme and describing the neighbourhood as 'black 'n' Spanish Harlem', Aretha Franklin – much like she had done with Otis Redding's 'Respect' – reclaimed the song. In 1971 it outsold the original, dominated the R&B and pop charts, and sold in every major international territory. Aretha's gospel voice soaring above Ben E. King's subtle metropolitan soul brought a layer of urgency to a song that had travelled from the fringes of sentimentality to the aching heart of civil rights. Despite the song's popularity, the term Spanish Harlem faded away, to be replaced more frequently by East Harlem, or the more Hispanic term El Barrio. However, a large part of the transformation of community identity in East Harlem is not down to the song or to Aretha Franklin, but to the New York Chapter of the Young Lords.

The New York Young Lords were founded on 26 July 1969. With Mickey Melendez and the Chicago student David Perez already in their ranks, membership surged over what was a hot and sticky summer. An early recruit to the cause was a member of the original Last Poets, Felipe Luciano, who like Jiménez in Chicago had recently been released from prison after a gang-related stabbing. He had been involved in a brutal encounter with a rival gang in

Bushwick, and although not the killer, he was implicated in the murder. Other early recruits were Pablo Guzmán, who became a news reporter at WCBS, and Denise Oliver, an African-American woman who, if she had lived in Central Harlem, might have gravitated to the Black Panthers. Oliver had been brought up in El Barrio along with members of the soul group the Voices of East Harlem, and while working as a community activist became more connected to her own neighbourhood. Oliver rose to the executive ranks of the Young Lords. The organisation's legal support was provided by an aspiring lawyer Geraldo Rivera, who in later life became a famous talk-show host.

Unlike many of the radical groups that had emerged in the sixties such as Students for a Democratic Society, Student Non Violent Coordinating Committee, the Black Panthers, Detroit's Steering Committee, the Memphis Invaders and the Weather Underground, the Young Lords did not rush to judge what their community needed. They simply asked them. In the summer of 1969, still only a few weeks old, East Harlem's Young Lords organised a survey of barrio residents and asked them to identify the most pressing issues they faced day-to-day. They supplemented the poll with door-to-door enquiries and, although they themselves had identified discrimination, poverty, poor housing and police brutality as the most urgent concerns, the community answered with one recurring word – *la basura*: the garbage that rotted in the streets of East Harlem. Garbage was a scourge that had intensified over many months, since a sanitation workers' strike in 1968, and it had come to symbolise the stigma of the ghetto and the failures of city government. It was not what the Young Lords had anticipated, but they listened and *la basura* became their cause. Within days of the survey, the Young Lords put a plan into action and mounted what they called the Garbage Offensive – the name was a reference to the Viet Cong's guerrilla campaign, the Tet Offensive. The subject was dominating the nightly news as the war swung inexorably out of America's control.

According to the radical pamphlet 'Palante: A Brief History of the Young Lords', the Garbage Offensive started on a Sunday. 'Piles of rotting trash had been left to decay in the Puerto Rican community, even though the Sanitation Department mover was just up the block. For weeks, the people patiently swept up the streets and bagged the trash themselves, waiting for the city to do its job. The community tried every avenue and gave the city every chance to fulfil its most basic functions. But the city bureaucracy didn't respond. Young and old, hospital orderlies, students, and store owners began dragging the trash that had been left rotting in the summer sun into the middle of the street, building barricades four feet high. And to make sure traffic on Third Avenue wasn't going to move, they set the trash on fire. When the city finally came, it was the NYPD and the Fire Department, not the Sanitation Department.'

The sight of burning mounds of garbage grabbed media attention. A contemporary report in *The New York Times* described the scene: 'people began throwing garbage and wrecked furniture into the middle of the streets. Traffic was stopped frequently; midtown businessmen avoiding the clog of the East River Drive found themselves stalled inside stifling cars in an area whose residents looked upon their discomfiture with little sympathy. The police and sanitation workers would clear one intersection and find that two blocks away – east or west, downtown or up – another one was blocked with the kind of debris that in middle-class sections of the city is not allowed to languish on the sidewalks. The Mayor's office got the message and a 24-hour pickup of garbage was begun. For a while El Barrio, that part of Harlem where the first Puerto Rican migrants settled, was cleaner than anyone remembered. With this "garbage riot", the Young Lords first made their presence felt in New York.'

The Garbage Offensive was remarkable in many ways. It had emerged organically from the community itself, it was popular across the generations, and it was photogenic. News photographers from all the main networks and newspapers flocked to East Harlem to capture images of ghetto youth sweeping the streets along Third Avenue or the fires lighting up the ghetto night. Melendez recalled in his autobiography: 'The garbage formed a five-foot-high wall across the six lanes of Third Avenue, causing an unexpected traffic jam . . . it was a theatrical scene, flames went up spectacularly as people started to scream with joy. In my mind the people – timid mothers, grandmothers, everyone – were showing the world their support for the Young Lords.' In those days, Luciano claimed, 'most Puerto Ricans were not willing to confront' and participating in the garbage offensive 'emboldened them'. Melendez agrees: 'We'd developed a colonial mentality; docile, subdued and clutched with a profound self-doubt that destroyed our confidence.'

As the summer faded into autumn, the Young Lords had learned a powerful lesson: including the community was the key to winning support. They had also instinctively grasped that 'spectacle' was their friend. Having briefly set themselves up in a vacant storefront on 111th Street, the Young Lords began a search for a longer-term community base that could act as their headquarters. In November they identified an under-used church in East Harlem, the First Spanish Methodist of East Harlem, which at the time was under the control of a Cuban émigré faction opposed to Cuban independence, and headed by the Reverend Dr Humberto Carrazana, a fiercely anti-Castro pastor. The church was barely open by day and always locked at night; it appeared to the Young Lords to be unresponsive to the community's needs. Its busiest day was Sunday when it threw open its doors to the affluent suburban Cuban exiles who returned to the barrio to pray.

A group of Young Lords turned up at a poorly attended Sunday mass. As the service began, one by one the Young Lords rose in the pews, asking the congregation what they thought the East Harlem community needed to improve the lives of local residents. Suspecting they were about to come under siege, the pastor alerted the police, and unwittingly triggered a full-scale stand-off. The Young Lords left the building but vowed they'd be back. In November they thought they had found a compromise when they applied to the church for permission to run a breakfast club project, similar to that run by the Black Panthers. Their request was ignored. On reapplication it was flatly turned down, and so they took the decision to occupy the church.

In December, in an aggressive assault, the Young Lords forced entry. They communicated with the outside world through windows, and children were handed in by local mothers who were demonstrating the need for day care. Local volunteers also accessed the building to provide a nursery. Free breakfast and clothing programmes, educational workshops and community dinners were established. The eleven-day occupation attracted celebrity visitors and food donations from business leaders. 'East Harlem was a colorful but deprived community, where people from many Latino nationalities and races shared apartment walls,' Melendez recounted. 'It was a mosaic of trades, from blue-collar workers to merchants. Above all, it was a neglected community. Many people there resided in dilapidated tenements, and in their day-to-day life had to cope with every conceivable scarcity. In summary, it was the kind of place for any institution to gain God's benediction by working overtime to help the needy.'

Although the occupation had broken the law, it was widely supported across East Harlem, and it shamed Mayor Lindsay's administration into turning their attention to Latino poverty. Two more initiatives took the Young Lords onto the front pages of the newspapers: first, a door-to-door campaign to eradicate lead poisoning in tenements; second, a hospital occupation. Many slum landlords used the cheapest lead-based paints on pipes and in hallways, and children were frequently poisoned after eating flaking paint. The campaign eventually became a mainstream cause when the *American Journal of Public Health* linked the Young Lords' activism to the foundation of the Bureau of Lead Poisoning in New York. The next 'spectacular' was in the following year, in July 1970, when 150 Young Lords occupied the ailing Lincoln Hospital in the South Bronx. The hospital was on its knees, underfunded and falling apart. According to Young Lord Pablo Guzmán, 'there was a joke in the neighbourhood that if you got stabbed on this side of the street, crawl over to the other side so the ambulance wouldn't take you to Lincoln'. There were rats in the emergency room and children who were under the hospital's care had contracted lead poisoning while being treated there. The occupation seems largely to have been supported by hospital staff, and there remain questions about hospital management's possible collusion with the Young Lords to draw attention to their plight. *The New York Times* wrote: 'Twelve hours later, after negotiations with hospital officials, they filed out of the nine-story structure in the face of a line of helmeted policemen . . . Two members of the Young Lords, Pablo Guzmán, the minister of information, and Louis Alvarez Perez, his bodyguard, were arrested as they left the building. They were charged with possession of dangerous weapons, a pair of chukka sticks, two pieces of wood about eight inches long held together with an elastic thong. The charges were later dismissed in night court.'

By the autumn of 1969, the jailed Black Panthers had another tranche of money from fundraising efforts, and Michael Tabor became the next person to be released on bail. His imposing personality and public-speaking skills made him an asset on the outside. He had written extensively on drugs in the ghetto and the failures of the New York health services to provide adequate care to addicts and frequently joined the Young Lords in sit-ins, occupations and hospital protests. A joint meeting of Black Panthers and Young Lords demanded better drug detoxification programmes and drug clinics, and there was a spate of hospital occupations, some of which were successful. One of the leaders of the occupation was Vicente 'Panama' Alba, a Young Lord who had been a heroin addict since he was fourteen years old. In an interview in *The Abolitionist* magazine he claimed that 'fifteen percent of the population was addicted . . . The concentration of addiction was on teenagers and people in their early twenties and thirties. Addiction at that time was primarily to heroin. This was an epidemic that the Black Panther Michael "Cetewayo" Tabor, one of the New York 21, wrote [about in] a pamphlet called "Capitalism Plus Dope Equals Genocide", which we used widely. In New York heroin devastated most of Harlem and the South Bronx. Young people utilized heroin very publicly, sniffing heroin at dancehalls or in school bathrooms, which led to shooting up intravenously.'

The musician Joe Bataan grew up with many of the young men and women who became Panthers or members of the Young Lords, although he himself was either in prison or too distracted by his career as East Harlem's boogaloo commander to join their fight. No one captured the spirit of boogaloo and its culture quite like the much heralded King of Latin Soul. Even in his prime, Bataan looked back on 1969 as 'a field of dreams' when the fusion of Latin, soul music and urban R&B threw up a new world of opportunity. He grew up as a gang leader in East Harlem, and in an essay called 'The Song of Joe B.', the Last Poet and Young Lord leader Felipe Luciano described the background they grew up in: 'There was a time in El Barrio when the only thing that mattered was whether you lived on Dragon Turf or Viceroy Turf. Legends persist about the shootouts between the two gangs, the all-night orgies, the humiliating defeats, the fist fights between individual warriors that lasted for hours. The Torres Brothers and George Robles of the Viceroys and Georgie Bass and Joe Bataan of the Dragons: *Ellos fueron los malos*. They were the bad ones.'

For someone now synonymous with Latin music, Bataan was an anomaly. Unlike most of his immediate gang members, he was not Puerto Rican, nor even Spanish-speaking. He was the son of an African-American father and a Filipino mother and spoke a hip version of Spanglish, which was not only a hybrid of the two languages, but peppered with words and expressions from jail talk and the musical underground. He grew up on 116th Street and attended Patrick Henry Junior High, a school infamous for producing gang members and pupils who were barely literate. His basic education was interrupted by a series of small-scale arrests, and when Bataan was inevitably incarcerated he was sent to Coxsackie Correctional Facility up in Greene County, New York. Bataan and Luciano first met in 1965, inside what was known as the 'Spain Wing' of a prison rife with interracial violence. But there was a glimmer of light in the darkness, in the form of an enlightened educational policy. Bataan was allocated a music tutor called Mark Francis, who taught him rudimentary skills and instilled in him a passion for performing. Bataan embraced Latin music, and Luciano spoken-word jazz. Somehow prison had become a boot camp for creative reinvention.

As a young teenager, Bataan had hung out in the record shops that dotted the streets of Harlem and the Bronx. He was a regular at Bobby Robinson's where he hunted down doo-wop, then soul and funk, and was a familiar face at the old Casa Alegre in the

Bronx. Casa Alegre was opened in 1955 by street entrepreneur Al Santiago and had become a seminal record shop which in time gave birth to Alegre Records, the indie label that was home to charanga stars such as Eddie Palmieri, Tito Puente and Johnny Pacheco. It was Alegre's major rival, Tico Records, that first hit on the Latin concept of the 'All-Stars' – a forerunner of supergroups – where well-known musicians from across a range of bands were brought together to accentuate scale and recognition. The Tico All-Stars broke into mainstream jazz circles with their *Descargas* albums, recorded live at the Village Gate on Bleecker Street, and were duly followed by the Alegre All-Stars, then by the momentous Fania All-Stars who were residents at the Cheetah club on 53rd Street, and finally the world-renowned Buena Vista Social Club.

By 1966 Bataan's talents had been noticed by Jerry Masucci, an Italian-American former cop and divorce lawyer who was then a producer with Fania Records – a record company that was a cultural beacon or a parasitic leech, depending on whose version of Latin music history you believe. Often compared with Detroit's Motown Corporation, Fania began as a tiny hand-to-mouth operation. It was founded in 1964 by Masucci and the Dominican bandleader Johnny Pacheco. Masucci had worked as a tourism executive for the Cuban government and while based in Havana fell in love with the music of the streets and the bordellos. The pair sold their first Latin records from the trunk of Masucci's car. Fania had its ear to the ground and was quick to connect to the youngest and most exciting talent. They launched the career of a group of Brooklyn teenagers led by a seventeen-year-old trombonist named Willie Colón whose first three records were 'Willie Baby' (1967), 'The Hustler' (1968) and his 1969 barrio hit 'Che Che Colé'. All three were raw street records, reflective of teenage life in East Harlem, and Colón's prominence on the barrio sound systems was matched by Bataan's arrival in the local market. Despite being unsophisticated about music, Bataan was streetwise and burning with ideas. He managed to convince Fania to release his debut record 'Ordinary Guy' (1967). Despite Bataan's thin and frequently off-tune voice, it had a thrilling authenticity and spoke to a generation who yearned for music that connected directly to them.

'Ordinary Joe' was followed by an infectious boogaloo version of a song called 'Gypsy Woman', entirely different in both tone and lyrics from Curtis Mayfield and the Impressions' 1961 hit. But Bataan – or more likely Fania – reckoned that enough people would confuse the two and so they could boost sales. Bataan regularly delivered; all four of his first five albums – *Subway Joe* (1968), *Riot* (1968), *Poor Boy* (1969) and *Mr New York And The East Side Kids* (1971) – were unambiguously about El Barrio, carrying imagery of the ghetto or everyday street life in New York. Bataan would go on to become a prominent figure with the great disco label Salsoul, the name derived from a cross-pollination of salsa and soul.

Puerto Ricans had been the first Hispanic group to move to New York in any substantial number. From the seventies onwards, the Puerto Rican population reached its height, numbering up to eighty per cent of the overall Hispanic community and nearly twelve per cent of the total New York population. That was in marked contrast to the city's tiny Syrian Jewish community, who were only 75,000 strong and concentrated in a tiny affluent enclave of Brooklyn. It was from this tiny and traditional sect – rather than the waves of Hispanic immigrants – that Salsoul came. Salsoul was owned by the Cayre brothers, three Syrian Jews who, according to *Forbes* magazine, 'got rich in the '70s producing Latin music on the Salsoul label and then got much richer distributing videocassettes via Walmart'. The Cayres had built their first business on the back of the cruise-ship industry running a duty-free store on board a Miami cruise liner. But the niche they spotted was seismic. Music was changing at almost every level: production techniques, the home consumer market and, most significantly of all, mobility – the demand for music on the move. In New York two electronic consumer companies sprang up. One was Crazy Eddie's, run by a souk-smart salesman called Eddie Antar, whose catchphrase for cheap prices was the self-parodying one-liner – 'he must be insane'. The other belonged to the Jamal brothers, who owned a rival chain Nobody Beats the Wiz. All were Syrian Jews. They arrived on the New York audio scene well-resourced, aspirational, and redefined how people listened to music. Their trump card was easy access to an import supply chain that brought cheap electronics from China, fiercely undercutting the domestic market. By stacking high and selling cheap, they pushed sales of home-entertainment systems, cassette recorders, 8-track cartridges and boombox radios. Stores like Crazy Eddie's were both an opportunity and a threat. They deflated sales of vinyl records and reduced their inventory of discs until the floor space needed for electronics eventually forced vinyl to disappear from sale altogether. For a time, the only New York subculture that seemed to care about vinyl at all was the underground club scene. In New York that meant the first generation of hip-hop DJs in Harlem and the South Bronx, who chased it down for funk beats.

Salsoul Records was aimed squarely at the club market. The company was hardwired into the loft parties, underground clubs and urban ghetto communities where soul, Latin and their various fusions were still a forceful presence. Bataan's releases for Salsoul were among his finest, including a boogaloo cover version of Gil Scott-Heron's ghetto morality tale 'The Bottle' ('La Botella') and the visionary 'Rap-O-Clapo-O', one of the very first rap/hip-hop records to emerge from Harlem. With time Salsoul became the very pinnacle of underground dance. Its release sheets were heaven to the initiated, featuring Loleatta Holloway, the Chicago gospel singer whose voice gave status to tracks like 'Hit And Run' (1977) and 'Love Sensation' (1980), which in turn built the scaffolding of what eventually became Chicago house music. There was Double Exposure's club classic 'Ten Per Cent' (1976), arguably one of the greatest soul dance records of the decade, and Eddie Holman's 'This Will Be A Night To Remember' (1977). Holman had won the Apollo's amateur night crown at the age of ten and enrolled at the Victoria School for Music in Harlem before moving to Philadelphia where he joined the next great movement in urban-specific soul – the Philly sound. Significantly, Salsoul had also identified a new character in the narrative of soul – the DJ and studio mixer. Over time they hired Tom Moulton, Vince Montana Jr and Walter Gibbons. It was Gibbons, a New York DJ, who remixed 'Ten Per Cent' to perfection, and whose studio creativity became a key part of Salsoul's rich success. In what is a small but not insignificant observation about the Cayre brothers and the Syrian Jewish values they expounded, Gibbons was given the job of remixing at Salsoul because of his punctuality. In a world of flaky and easily distracted DJs, Gibbons could be trusted to turn up on time.

Joe Bataan's story took him on a journey through all the dance genres of his day but he remained loyal to El Barrio and was a regular sight on the streets and in the community parks around 116th Street as his success ebbed and flowed. His 1980 single 'Sadie (She Smokes)' had one more contribution to make. It opened with the now obligatory '*uno, dos, tres*', the Latin percussion giving way to primitive street rap, and the story of a Harlem dance queen called Sadie unfolds. As the song takes off it becomes obvious that a precious new talent is helping to shore up Bataan's thin voice – the exceptional Jocelyn Brown. She would go on to record yet another club classic, the exemplary 'Somebody Else's Guy' (1984). Perhaps more than any other single record, the story of Sadie the dance queen from Harlem became the urban template of a new era of R&B – an amalgam of disco, rap and soaring vocals that was for a time known as New Jack Swing, and then evolved into contemporary R&B giving licence to D'Angelo, Erykah Badu, Mary J. Blige and Beyoncé.

By 1980 Bataan's musical career had stalled. From then until 2000, he worked at Coxsackie Correctional Facility as a counsellor, with special responsibilities for Latino youth. In an interview in the *Bogotá Post*, he once claimed that 'domestic problems, lifestyle and disputes with the music industry caused my hiatus from music. I also began working with troubled youths in detention as a counsellor for twenty-five years. This life experience helped me to grow in life and continue to further my influence in another area of work. I returned to a place where I was incarcerated, which was probably not a coincidence. I like to believe I gave back knowledge to those that were troubled early on.'

The Young Lords disintegrated in the early seventies, marred by political in-fighting and personal jealousy after some senior members were recruited into the mainstream media, who very late in the day had recognised that they had no one who could reliably and sensitively report on the Puerto Rican community. Another factor led to their demise, too. Like the Black Panthers and almost every other politically radical organisation of the times, the Young Lords had been infiltrated by the FBI and were a COINTELPRO target. A network of paid informers and undercover agents spied on, undermined and disrupted their activities. FBI infiltration led to schisms within the group, but the biggest tension of all was a disagreement that was never fully resolved at the time: whether their focus should be on domestic poverty or the campaign for Puerto Rican independence. What is not in doubt is that the Young Lords' brief but brilliant period in the radical limelight catalysed feelings of pride and identity among Puerto Ricans that had lain dormant for years.

A Christian youth speaks out at an anti-drugs protest at the front entrance of Teen City, a local café at 116th and Lenox, at the height of the teenage deaths that swept Harlem. The demonstration was a block away from the offices of Fat Jack Taylor's Rojac Records.

DECEMBER

King Heroin

Winter began to bite. On a freezing cold Saturday evening in December 1969, twelve-year-old Walter Vandermeer left his squalid three-room apartment at 305 West 117th Street and headed for a row of tenements near Seventh Avenue. This was Harlem at its bleakest. It was there, in the communal bathroom of a Harlem tenement, that Vandermeer died of a heroin overdose, the youngest recorded drugs death in America at the time. It was a death that shook America to the core, triggered new laws on drug abuse, and shone a torch on the dark characters who traded heroin on the nation's ghetto streets. It had an impact on soul music, too, but that was always secondary to the public's reaction to the young boy's demise.

He was four feet eleven inches, dressed in a Snoopy sweatshirt, and weighed only eighty pounds; he had been surviving on cupcakes, Coca-Cola and an occasional fish and chips for months. Pathologists initially assumed that he had overdosed on his first encounter with drugs. It was wishful thinking. The story was much more disturbing. Walter was streetwise beyond his years; he started sniffing glue aged six and had been using heroin since the age of ten. Every day he bought and sold $2 bags on the corners of 116th Street, and was precociously informed about the street trade in heroin. The media saw his death as symptomatic of a wider crisis at the heart of America's inner cities and because it happened at the end of the year it invited the nation's press to reflect on 1969 as a troubled one. Galloping inflation, political show trials and drug deaths loomed large, but the event that had cast the darkest shadow of shame was the arrest of Lieutenant William Calley Jr, who was responsible for the murder of 109 Vietnamese civilians in what had become known as the My Lai massacre. America seemed burdened with self-doubt, and the death of such a young child did not help public confidence.

Like so much of Harlem's story, it had happened before in a very different era. Novelist Ann Petry anticipated the tragedy of squandered life in one of the Harlem Renaissance's finest novels *The Street* (1946), in which she follows a deprived single mother Lutie Johnson as she struggles to raise a child on a corner brutalised by successive generations of poverty. Much of the book's action unfolds at the intersection where Vandermeer died. Petry's novel was in many respects a prequel to the young boy's troubled life. She describes 116th Street, blighted by unforgiving weather, and in all its forensic detail, not knowing what it would become: 'There was always a crowd in front of the Junto Bar and Grill on 116th Street. For in the Winter the street was cold. The wind blew the snow into great drifts that stayed along the curb for weeks, gradually blackening with soot until it was no longer recognisable as snow, but appeared to be some dark eruption from the street itself. As one cold day followed swiftly on the heels of another, the surface of the frozen piles became encrusted with bags of garbage, old shoes, newspapers, corset lacings. The frozen debris and the icy wind made the place desolate in winter and the people found a certain measure of escape from it by standing in front of the Junto, where the light streaming from the windows and the music from the juke-box, created an oasis of warmth.' In the forties, the Junto Bar dominated a block that by 1969 was occupied by Fat Jack Taylor's Rojac Records, alongside a cavernous basement which, in the years to come, would be the pioneering home of hip-hop – Harlem World. At four p.m. each day the sidewalk outside became an open-air market where heroin was sold flagrantly. The kingpin dealers of the day had worked out their golden hour: it was the time when NYPD police shifts changed over. For an hour, the streets were virtually denuded of any police presence and the marketplace could flourish with impunity.

Vandermeer's death provoked many different responses: some emotional, some ideological and some driven by the urgent demand to 'do something'. One direct response was a draconian era of drug legislation in the State of New York driven by Governor Nelson Rockefeller. Another was a series of presidential discussions that led to the ultimately doomed War on Drugs. Yet another was a cultural response within soul music.

Sam Dees's *The Show Must Go On* (1975) was a masterclass in lyrical writing which featured a troubled child woven through the songs, and Curtis Mayfield's painfully ironic *No Place On Earth Like America Today* (1975) came with a cover image of the perfect nuclear family juxtaposed with a breadline of the black unemployed in Depression America. Gil Scott-Heron and Brian Jackson's *Winter In America* (1974), with its freezing cold ghetto backdrop, could easily have been influenced by Petry's novel. Petry's observational writing was every bit as trenchant and descriptive as the poetic and socially strident soul music that was on the cusp of becoming commercially viable.

From late 1969 onwards, the shoots of this new tonality had begun to flourish, and songs flooded onto the market that set their stories of tough-luck love or social strife in urban ghettos usually in Harlem, Chicago or Detroit. When the Supremes released 'Love Child' (1968) – arguably Motown's first unreservedly modern message song – it broke through a perception barrier, defying the theory that mainstream audiences were not ready for pop music about teenage pregnancy. Many more came in its wake. Booker T. and the M.G.'s' follow-up to their unmistakable anthem 'Time Is Tight' was another organ-led funk instrumental called 'Slum Baby', and across town in Memphis the revitalised Elvis Presley was refashioning his image in the aftermath of a series of lame

Hollywood films by reconnecting with the city's unique cross-fertilisation of rock, country and R&B. In the early weeks of 1969 Presley was in the American Sound Studios in North Memphis recording a Mac Davis song originally entitled 'The Vicious Circle', but which sold internationally as 'In The Ghetto'. By the end of the year, synchronous with Vandermeer's death but driven by Presley's historic return to live shows in Las Vegas, the song, a story of a young life lived out in the ghettos of Chicago, became a global pop hit. The gospel-infused voices of Elvis's preferred backing singers, the Sweet Inspirations, gave the record a huge sales lift in the very ghettos the song described. The trickle became a flood. Donny Hathaway's 'Little Ghetto Boy' (1972) was a classic of its kind in which Hathaway's hauntingly beautiful voice narrates the life of a boy surviving in pool-rooms as his father robs grocery stores. The beauty of the vocals is in stark contrast to the bleak and pessimistic message of the cruelty of the world and how things are not going to change.

Hathaway's song was a major influence on Sam Dees, the soul genius from Birmingham, Alabama, who had done sterling production work for Birmingham's local indies Clintone and Moonsong. He had even released a few unacknowledged songs of his own, including the stunning 'Lonely For You Baby' on SSS International (1968). Dees arrived at Atlantic Records after a wasted year at Chess Records, and took an apartment in Harlem, determined to break New York. Hathaway's impact – either directly or indirectly – was tangible on Dees's debut album *The Show Must Go On*, a contender as one of the greatest soul albums ever. A gifted writer and an outstandingly good singer, Dees proved himself to be the sensitive master of ghetto-child soul stories. Three tracks from the album return to the theme: the opening track, 'Child Of The Streets', is the haunting family tragedy of an abandoned child whose father is a pusher-man and whose mother is a prostitute; 'What's Gonna Be' is a plea for sociopolitical change in the ghetto; and 'Troubled Child' tells the story of homelessness and abandonment in the most deprived social conditions.

It is entirely plausible that Dees was directly influenced by the attention given to Walter Vandermeer's death in the press.

Although his name was unmistakably Dutch in origin, Vandermeer's premature teenage swagger had been learned on the streets of Harlem, in the only world he ever knew. His father was an illegal immigrant from the former Dutch colony of Surinam and had jumped ship in New York's harbour district before finding a job working as an assistant in a midtown pharmacy. It was there that the authorities caught up with him. He was deported when Walter was only five months old, accused of violating immigration laws, thus leaving his wife as a single mother who across time took three more husbands. By 1969, her large chaotic family were all living in a tiny Harlem apartment, with the infant Walter sleeping as one of six to a bed. At the time of her son's death, Vandermeer's mother lived with Walter's stepfather, a Liberian immigrant called Sunday Togbah. It was a home of sorts, but the young boy found greater emotional comfort on the streets among the runaways, junkies, teenage gangsters and fly guys of Lenox Avenue. This was a life, according to *The New York Times*, 'of frightening emptiness and real dangers'. He had been suspended from Public School 76 on West 121st Street as a nine-year-old, accused of aggressive and disruptive behaviour. He was a perpetual truant, and on the rare occasions he did attend, he had to be restrained from punching teachers and attacking classmates. By now, the system was fast running out of options. In a final act of desperation, he was referred to Manhattan's Floyd Patterson House, a residential treatment centre for emotionally disturbed children, which was named after the heavyweight boxer who in his retirement years was a counsellor for the New York State Office of Children and Family Services. In his own troubled youth, Patterson had been consigned to a reform school in North Carolina. Only his success in the ring, and a genial and ingratiating personality, saved him from a life in prison.

But Walter refused to settle and had to be sedated with Thorazene. There were brief and hopeful signs of rehabilitation, and for a short while Vandermeer bonded with a child care counsellor, John Schoonbeck. On learning they both had names of Dutch ancestry, Walter described him as a 'soul brother'. Poignantly, when the young counsellor mentioned taking a holiday in Africa Walter pleaded to go with him. In Schoonbeck's absence, the boy joined a Harlem street gang, Bonnie and the Seven Clydes, who specialised in low-level car crime and street robberies. But progress was too little, too late. Vandermeer became so entrenched in Harlem street life and drug culture that he had no real way out. He had been injured in street incidents on three separate occasions: once being hit by a brick in a fight, another time in a car accident as he sprinted across a busy intersection to avoid a rival gang; and a third time when he fell from a metal fire escape. When his obituary was published in *The New York Times*, it described his daily struggle to exist: 'Walter would be out late at night hawking newspapers in bars or begging for coins at the corner of Eighth Avenue. In the daytime, when most children were in school, he would station himself near a radiator in a grocery store for warmth until chased or borrow a couch to catch up on the sleep he had missed.' A photograph on the front page of the newspaper showed Walter at a summer block party, dressed in a white vest and staring cockily at the camera, old before his time, as a brood of youngsters stood behind him like a dissident funk group.

For some Harlem commentators, his short life invited comparisons with the Harlem doo-wop star Frankie Lymon, who had died, aged twenty-five, of a heroin overdose in early 1968. Lymon had been the ultimate teen sensation in the mid fifties when anxiety about postwar youth culture was at its hysterical height. His song 'I'm Not A Juvenile Delinquent' was a cute but ultimately self-incriminating song which answered back to worried sociologists and overbearing parents. Despite his angelic face and jaunty protestations, however, Lymon was a problem teenager. At fifteen, he was already abusing drugs. 'I looked twice my age,' he told *Ebony*. 'I was thin as a shadow and I didn't give a damn. My only concern was in getting relief. You know, an addict is the most pathetic creature on earth. He knows that every time he sticks a needle in his arm, he's gambling with death and, yet, he's got to have it. It's like playing Russian Roulette with a spike.' As doo-wop was swamped by sixties soul, his career quickly faded. Then his mother died. According to the *Smithsonian* magazine, on 27 February 1968, 'he was booked for a recording session to mark the start of a comeback. Instead, he was found dead that morning on his grandmother's bathroom floor.'

Walter Vandermeer was the youngest of 1,031 people who died in 1969 from drug abuse. That was only part of the picture. A simultaneous FBI report, focusing mainly on Chicago's South Side, estimated that 720 people had died as the result of murder or manslaughter in crimes related to narcotics. It was an early and unheeded warning to communities like Harlem that the neighbourhood was careering towards a full-scale drugs epidemic. Heroin was already killing more young people than any other cause, including heart disease, cancer, homicides and youth suicides. In the next decade, drugs would wreak even greater havoc on the social cohesion of Harlem, destroying many more lives and changing the architectural character of the neighbourhood as whole buildings, and in some places entire blocks, gave way to drug factories, shooting galleries and no-go areas.

On the night Vandermeer's body was discovered, surrounded by syringes and drug paraphernalia, Dr Michael Baden, the city's medical examiner, returned home. Baden lived with his wife, the eminent psychiatrist Dr Judianne Densen-Gerber. Unusually for a highly professional doctor, he brought his job home, and witnessing Vandermeer had emotionally drained him. He laid Walter's stained white T-shirt on their bed. The sight of the child's garment, childlike in the extreme and with an image of Charlie Brown's pet beagle Snoopy emblazoned on the front, reduced them both to tears. On the back of the dead boy's shirt was the line: 'Watch out for me. I want to bite somebody to relieve my inner tensions.' Confronted with such conflicting images of childhood, the couple, already accustomed to difficult case loads, made a personal pact that something had to be done. Densen-Gerber became one of an army of well-heeled Manhattanites who made ghetto poverty and drug abuse their focus. She founded the controversial drug treatment community Odyssey House, and spent much of her life moving from society balls to ghetto demonstrations to fund improved drug rehabilitation. Walter Vandermeer's death was the spark that ignited Densen-Gerber's formidable career. In the years that followed, in a feature in the *New York Magazine*, Mayor Ed

Koch, the man most associated with the hard work of reversing New York's drug- and crime-ridden reputation, described her as 'one of those seminal forces, an original go-getter'. She was an unmistakable figure with a bouffant hairdo and rhinestone-studded glasses, who smoked elegant Cuban cigars, and through a mixture of chutzpah and sheer coincidence came to befriend Governor Nelson A. Rockefeller while picketing his home.

Until the end of 1969 Rockefeller, the Republican state governor for New York, had backed drug rehabilitation, job training and housing. He saw drugs as a social problem and not a criminal issue. But the weight of public reaction to Vandermeer's death, and the death of a fifteen-year-old girl on the same corner a few months later, toughened the political mood. Rockefeller promised new and stricter legislation. In January 1973 he had all but done a complete U-turn when he announced in a press conference his call for mandatory prison sentences of fifteen years to life for drug dealers and addicts, even those caught with small amounts of marijuana, cocaine or heroin. 'I have one goal and one objective, and that is to stop the pushing of drugs and to protect the innocent victim,' he said. The figures seemed to back him up. Federal statistics showed as many as 559,000 drug users nationwide and state police saw a thirty-one per cent increase in drug arrests from 1971 to 1972. *TIME* wrote sceptically that 'the Rockefeller Drug Laws . . . led almost immediately to an increase in drug convictions, but no measurable decrease in overall crime. Meanwhile, critics argued that they criminalized what was primarily a public health problem, incarcerated nonviolent felons who were better off in treatment, caused a jump in recidivism rates, and prevented judges from using discretion in sentencing.' Those were among the kinder words written about a drugs policy that lacked any sense of nuance, empathy or even sustainability as the already overcrowded and riotous prison population swelled.

It was many years before any kind of remorse touched the consciences of Harlem's top dealers. They had been flamboyant super flies swaggering through Harlem nightlife but now tolerance of their lifestyle was fading. Once a major Harlem dealer, Leroy 'Nicky' Barnes eventually admitted some kind of culpability:

'Heroin wreaked a lot of havoc and a lot of pain in the black community. I shouldn't have done it. Maybe I was aware, but I just didn't give a fuck. I wanted to make money, and that's what I did. Looking back, I wouldn't have made those decisions, but it's a hell of a lot different and much easier to sanitize yourself after the fact.' His local rival Frankie Lucas also admitted culpability in old age: 'I have remorse. I never sold nothing to a kid in the street, but I found out that my people had. I didn't want to sell to kids. I didn't want to make them junkies. I didn't want to be a part of it. I justify it by saying during my time, I couldn't get a job on Wall Street, not even washing toilets. I went to school three days and the teacher wasn't there two of them. I had to make a living. I didn't want to be just a damn bum in the street. So that's what I did.'

Excuses piled up like garbage as Vandermeer's death percolated through New York society. Up in Harlem, a local playwright called Al Fann was well advanced with an episodic youth-theatre play on addiction, pitching the idea among adults and older teenagers. Aghast at the fate of Vandermeer, he adapted his play to accommodate vignettes that were closely modelled on Walter's death. Fann cast a group of eight Harlem teenagers in the play, renamed it *King Heroin*, and began the arduous job of attracting local residents to the show. The term 'King Heroin' spread as virulently as the drug itself. In its original usage, the term simply meant the biggest and the best. It was already a well-worn commercial term. Southerners referred to the cotton production economy as 'King Cotton'. Budweiser was sold as the 'King of Beers', and one of the best-selling cereals of the day was Quaker Oats' King Vitaman.

Fann cast himself as the play's central character, a complex but likable police officer called Lieutenant Hendricks, who worked the streets around 117th Street and was on speaking terms with the hookers, pushers and runner boys who did errands for the drug lords. As part of the immersive rehearsals for the performances, Fann sent his young cast onto the streets to observe the street people as they went about their daily routines. They discussed what the theatre company called 'Harlem's silent statues' – junkies who stood or slumped in the same position for hours, virtually unnoticed by passers-by. It was an observation that the young Nile Rodgers had made while watching his junkie father and his friends descend into a stupor. 'They often slept standing up,' he wrote in *Nile Rodgers: Le Freak*, his painfully honest autobiography, 'and this group narcolepsy could strike in the middle of some dynamic conversation . . . Eventually our living room would be filled with black-and-white hipsters suspended in time and space, while I ran through the petrified forest of their legs.' Al Fann impressed on his teenage cast that their first acting task was to capture the existential loneliness of the junkies and the false and painted cheeriness of the hookers. 'The community had learned to ignore the junkies on the street,' he told *Ebony*. 'Citizens walked by and cops drove by. Nobody even looked at them, it was amazing.' It was this feeling of pathetic listlessness and social isolation that *King Heroin* aimed to capture.

The play opened at the St Philips Community Theater in the neo-gothic Episcopal Church on 134th Street, where it was well received and attracted interest from bigger theatres downtown. In an unusual marketing strategy, the show even provided a small fleet of cars to drive mostly white audience members from Midtown Manhattan up to Harlem. The uptown pilgrimages of the Jazz Age were long gone and the odysseys that so many had made across the years had stuttered to a close. Fann was led to believe that the play had made a critical breakthrough when the New York State Narcotics Commission offered to fund a film based on it. But as they negotiated the deal the Commission withdrew its grant offer, accusing the play of 'lacking a solution at the end that would send audiences away with hope'. Ironically, the play was not alone in not finding a hopeful solution. The Narcotics Commission, the prison system, social workers, community activists, the police and the entire educational system of America had also failed. Heroin was winning.

The term 'King Heroin' soon entered the bulging dictionary of soul music when James Brown recorded a semi-rap funk single by the same name. Brown had first stumbled on the term by sheer chance when an ex-convict called Manny Rosen – who had served time with Walter Vandermeer's brother at Rikers Island – recited a rap poem to him. Rosen was a counter clerk at the Stage Deli on Seventh Avenue, and Brown was performing there. The poem was a clever piece of street doggerel which narrated the story of heroin from the perspective of the drug. Almost certainly Rosen had appropriated the name from prison narratives, or even from the Harlem play. Like many of Brown's recent releases, it was a clever amalgam of street smartness and self-regard, acquired in a deli from a title stolen from the theatre. Brown had by now reached a pivotal moment in his career. He was still tied to the Cincinnati label King Records but had built up his own subsidiaries – among them People Records and the Brownstone label – and was on the verge of signing a five-year deal with the US conglomerate Polygram. It was a deal that would give him greater global reach and all but secure his wealth. Brown's marketability was immense: equally robust on record and on the live stage, he had a style that seemed to be hardwired to the ghetto but was sufficiently flamboyant to reach out to broader audiences. He was the self-proclaimed 'hardest working man in showbiz', and a press release from the early seventies broke down that pronouncement into raw data. 'James Brown will perform 335 days this coming year, losing as much as seven pounds each performance. In an average month he will give away 5,000 autographed photographs and 1,000 pairs of James Brown cuff links. He will wear 120 freshly laundered shirts and more than eighty pairs of shoes. He will change his performing costume 150 times and will work over eighty hours on stage, singing, dancing and playing at least 60 songs, on one of more than eight instruments.'

He was a phenomenon, but for the first time in his professional life his political associations had driven a wedge into the black community. He was now loved and loathed in equal measure. Always the consummate businessman, he now owned radio stations, publishing companies and a management agency and, in the words of the hip-hop stars he came to influence, was enthralled by 'cash money' and being 'paid in full'. But Brown's self-enrichment came at a price and some of his business decisions had taken him too close to the candle. By 1969 he was regarded as a man too easily seduced by the powerful. He had attended White

House dinners with President Johnson and, in what many saw as an act of ghetto betrayal, endorsed President Nixon's 1968 presidential campaign and assisted his drive to reduce public funding and develop private enterprise in the inner cities. The nationwide success of 'King Heroin' also won Brown a questionable honour as an anti-drugs advocate and further commendation from the then Californian governor Ronald Reagan. More pertinently for the evolution of soul music, Brown had taken the underground prison-rap style to a wider commercial audience, preceding the birth of rap and hip-hop by at least a decade. What he was less keen to promote were his connections with law enforcement. By 1969 he was assisting the FBI in Georgia, warning them of any incursion by black militants or members of the Black Panther Party. Although his support for the FBI stopped short of being a paid informer, he later admitted that he was against what he described as the 'outside agitation jive' and saw it as his moral duty to inform the authorities. By 1969 it was not easy to determine the provenance of James Brown's morality. He turned down an invitation to perform at the Harlem Cultural Festival, baulking at the fact that the festival was free, and unimpressed by the idea that he should devote his services to the community. He was free to do so – but equally Harlem was free to judge him accordingly.

King Heroin was traumatising New York in 1969. There were 1,031 narcotics deaths that year, up from 654 a year earlier. At the time city officials estimated there were over 100,000 drug addicts in New York and 'that it would be impossible to pinpoint the actual number of dope users'. Dr Earl Jung, head of the city's drug abuse programme within the high school system, estimated that 'a large percentage' of the 100,000 addicts cited were of school age. Vandermeer's death was the tip of the iceberg. In the previous year more than 200 persons aged nineteen years or younger had died in New York City from narcotics-related causes: teenage life was cheap.

The 'plague' of heroin addiction had become a *cause célèbre* for the Reverend Wyatt Tee Walker, senior pastor of the Canaan Baptist Church of Christ located near the notorious corner of 116th and Lenox. He launched a series of high-profile demonstrations that brought 300 members of his congregation to premises where it was believed heroin was being distributed. Their righteous anger was concentrated on Teen City, a popular soul food hangout. A fifteen-year-old girl had recently died in the apartment of the owner, Edward Hamm. He was arrested and charged with homicide for failing to summon help after she had overdosed. The Reverend Walker conducted an open-air service using the trunk of a white Mustang as his pulpit and claimed with conviction, 'I am convinced God is concerned about the perdition.' Concern was not restricted to Christianity, either. Muhammad's Mosque No. 7, on the same corner, had been the spiritual home of Malcolm X prior to his assassination. It had been rebuilt after being destroyed by fire and now sat in the epicentre of the heroin marketplace. Muslims regularly protested on the corner and frequently targeted the premises of Fat Jack Taylor's Rojac Records directly opposite. Community campaigns attracted momentary attention but often faded fast at the point of a gun. In June 1969 community leader Charles Kenyatta, who had been waging a campaign against dope pushers, was critically wounded while sitting in a car outside 2050 Valentine Avenue in the Bronx, a victim of retaliation.

Rolling Stone, then in its infancy, but already extending its journalism from rock music and counterculture to social affairs, published a lengthy investigation into Walter Vandermeer's death. Alfred, a young Harlem teenager, told the magazine: 'I started smoking grass at 13, but I got tired of it after about two months. I moved on to sniffing heroin and later I started shooting. When I was 13 I went to junior high school in the Bronx; that's where I had my first shot. I skin-popped it in the back of the auditorium because teachers don't hardly look there during the change of periods. I started liking it so I stole from my brother. Then I got money from my father. I'd tell him I was going to a dance or something just to get money so I could get high. Then I started catching a "jones", what's known as a habit. I was always getting cold, feeling sick, I couldn't eat nothing and I kept throwing up. When I got to 16 my mother told me either I go to Phoenix House or else to the Rockefeller program. So I chose Phoenix House because people said the Rockefeller program was like jail. My mother took me there one time for a test to prove whether or not I was an addict.'

The early days of *Rolling Stone* shone a light on counterculture that explained the contradictory power of drugs to enhance creativity and yet destroy communities. The unlocked imagination was already one of the major defences of LSD, but heroin took on different and more challenging questions. Lou Reed's song 'Heroin', released by the Velvet Underground in 1967 and produced by Andy Warhol, *enfant terrible* of the New York art scene, carried all the weight of a pioneering single. It was too honest, too brutal and not condemnatory enough for a consumer market already fearful of the drug, and so was either banned or discouraged by radio stations. After he left the Velvet Underground, Lou Reed's 'Perfect Day' (1972), a song that cleverly and poetically reflected the singer's heroin abuse, was different again. It had enough ambiguity to sneak through the net of concern, and the agony of dependency was buried beneath images of perfection – the zoo, films and drinking sangria – which helped to disguise the darkness of heroin in the eyes of radio and television. Hints, layered images and hidden implications became the only way that mainstream pop and rock could cope with heroin, and lyrics were often disputed for decades into the future. The Rolling Stones' 'Brown Sugar' (1971), recorded at that great R&B haven Muscle Shoals Sound Studio in Alabama, is still to this day a song rich in interpretation. Although credited to the band, it was written mostly by Mick Jagger at a time when he was dating the sixties soul singer Marsha Hunt, and so it has variously been deciphered as a song about interracial sex, cunnilingus and powdered brown heroin. Jagger has since admitted he would never write such a raw song now.

The term 'Jones', like 'King Heroin', soon reverberated around street talk and soul music. The Temptations and producer Norman Whitfield were at the top of their form with their 1969 album *Puzzle People* and the track 'Don't Let The Joneses Get You Down' captures the group in the midst of their psychedelic soul period. Another of Fat Jack Taylor's acts, the Detroit duo Chico and Buddy, recorded a song called 'A Thing Called The Jones' (1968) on Tay-Ster, which tells the now familiar story of the junkie who steals from his mother to fund his habit. Follow-ups came thick and fast, some by well-known artists like Hank Ballard's 'I'm A Junkie For My Baby's Love' (1971), but many more were raw street funk singles on highly localised labels that escaped the quality control of major labels. They included the Universal Messengers' 'Why You Want To Be A Junkie?' (Turbo Records, 1973), 'The Joneses' by the Cleveland ghetto funk band S.O.U.L. (Musicor, 1974), Charles Pryor and Power of Love's 'What They Doing (Funky Junkie)' (1974), Walter 'Butterball' Davis and the Exciters' 'Nobody Cares For A Junkie' (1974), Deep Heat's 'She's A Junkie (Who's The Blame)' (1975), Earth's Delight's 'Junkie Hustle' (1975) and funk supergroup War's 'Junkie To My Music' (1978). By the early seventies the Joneses was street slang for heroin withdrawal symptoms. One of Baltimore's best disco funk bands took the name the Joneses and released a debut record 'Mary Mary (Don't It Make You Feel Bad)' (1974), a barely disguised song about marijuana, and their most famous follow-up was another encoded drug song 'Sugar Pie Guy' (1974).

But as rock and soul sought to disguise the tracks of heroin a very different honesty was emerging in soul music. A generation of artists, mostly from the independent soul scene, were beginning to tackle the ghetto and all its social problems, releasing records that were trenchant in their descriptions of heroin and the havoc it was causing in the inner cities.

The brilliant Sam Dees was the major pioneer. In 1973 he recorded the brutally descriptive 'Signed Miss Heroin' (1973), a deceptive love letter which casts the drug as an all-pervasive ghetto bitch capable of destroying morals and emotions as the stomach cramps dig deeper into the soul. This is an anti-love song in its rawest form, matched only by the towering 'Home Is Where The Hatred Is' (1971), a ghetto odyssey by Gil Scott-Heron and Brian Jackson, sung to self-lacerating perfection by Esther Phillips, whose journey to free herself from addiction was not yet complete. Within a few short years of each other, James Brown's 'King Heroin', Sam Dees's 'Signed Miss Heroin', Esther Phillips's 'Home Is Where The Hatred Is' and the Dramatics' neo-biblical 'The Devil Is Dope' (1973) were in the record stores.

The Dramatics had lost two of their founding members after the tragedy of the Algiers Motel incident in Detroit in 1967, when a rogue unit of cops killed three black teenagers during a curfew at the height of the city's troubles and savagely beat Larry Reed and Roderick Davis. The next generation of the group – led by Ron Banks – signed for Stax/Volt in Memphis but continued to record in their native Detroit. In 1973 they produced an underground concept album, *A Dramatic Experience*. The cover depicted a horned devil – symbolic of heroin or the pusher man. Either way, it is an image designed to scare rather than to seduce.

Michael Tabor, who was out on bail and back on the streets of Harlem, had a profound and personal understanding of the heroin epidemic. He had been born and bred in the jungle of apartment blocks on 134th Street, worryingly close to the 32nd Precinct Station House, where he was well known to the local police as a teenager. Tabor had grown up when doo-wop singers sang beneath the streetlamps and watermelon men tramped the pavements, desperate to sell their load before the rind discoloured. Tabor excelled in sports. He was one of the neighbourhood's outstanding basketball stars and a familiar figure in Rucker Park, the warren of wire-fenced public courts which was once described as 'the Wall Street of Basketball'. Rucker was an uptown institution. It was named after the basketball pioneer Holcombe Rucker, who worked for the city's Parks Department and whose legacy was the annual summer tournament held at the courts. The Rucker courts were located on 155th Street, near Harlem River Drive, across the East River from the South Bronx, and so perfectly placed, like a metal mesh no-man's land where the ghettos met, where soul music blared from car radios, and where gangs congregated to watch or to play. This was the Apollo Theater of basketball, where the precociously gifted ghetto stars met to show off their skills. Every summer, as the sun-burnt days stretched on until midnight, rival teams from across the Five Boroughs would converge. From doo-wop to hip-hop, it was places like Rucker where the soul battles were at their fiercest, where groups were formed, rivalries intensified and talent scouts hovered, looking for a bite.

Tabor progressed to the Roman Catholic Rice High School on West 124th Street, recruited by the school more for his hoop skills than his catechism. His schoolfriend Jesse Fowler remembered their teenage years: 'playing on the roof tops of 137th Street, stealing into the firehouse near Seventh Avenue when the firemen were out just to slide down the brass pole a few times'. Tabor was good, very good, but he paled in comparison to Ferdinand Lewis Alcindor (who took the Muslim name Kareem Abdul-Jabbar in 1971), the Catholic league's champion; or East Meadow's Julius Erving (Dr J); or Earl 'The Pearl' Monroe, a Rucker star who visited annually from Philadelphia's high school league. Together, that generation of inner-city players changed basketball, bringing a flamboyant street style to the game. Among Harlem's many great players, the crown went to the mercurial Earl 'The Goat' Manigault, the boy with the strange name who invented basketball's now ubiquitous 'slam dunk' and brought the personality of basketball screeching into a new era. With a swaggering bravado, his gravity-defying aeroplane spins and trademark celebratory grip round the rims of the basket, 'The Goat' reigned supreme. Manigault got his nickname from mispronunciations of his surname but, in a gesture of self-promotion the equal of any rapper, he often claimed it was an acronym for the Greatest Of All Time.

Although he was only six foot one, Manigault had extraordinary leverage and an uncanny ability to hang in the air. When the crowds had dispersed, he would practise into the small hours, picking up a quarter coin from the backboard and replacing it with another coin, to test his balance and finesse. Abdul-Jabbar called Manigault 'the best basketball player in the history of New York City', telling the street basketball magazine *Slam* that 'he was so agile, so quick . . . Basketball was his total means of expression.' Manigault stood out in a subculture bursting with ego and extroversion, and was destined to become a successful sportsman, before he took to heroin. In 1969, at the very point that college scholarships were being offered and he had accepted an offer from Laurinburg Institute in North Carolina, he was hit with a three-year jail sentence for drugs possession. Manigault spent the next sixteen months in Green Haven Prison in Stormville, NY, his college scholarship cancelled. On his return to Rucker, he bewitched them again, but the word was out, and college coaches now treated him with caution. Manigault served another jail term from 1977 to 1979 for a failed robbery and ended up working as a painter/gardener for the recreation department, living out much of his adult life close to destitution. In an article published in *The New York Times* entitled 'A Fallen King Revisits His Realm', Manigault told the reporter: 'For every Michael Jordan, there's an Earl Manigault. We all can't make it. Somebody has to fall. I was the one.'

Tabor had admired Manigault from a distance and watched with dismay as heroin tore him down. His own basketball ambitions faced a different kind of challenge, and it was not entirely due to his heroin addiction. His mother Grace died when her son was still a raw impressionable teenager. The night she died, Tabor put on his Rice High School basketball uniform, the only thing he owned that had truly made her proud, sat on her bed and cried inconsolably for two days. Everything he had achieved was down to his mother's ambitions. Grace had worked tirelessly to deflect her son from the flashy superficial attractions of the ghetto, encouraging him to learn and to find work. She had encouraged his basketball aspirations, reasoning that they held the key to unlocking a college degree, and ensured his successful entry into Frederick Douglass Junior High School – by some distance the most educationally renowned school in Harlem. The great African-American poet Countee Cullen, one of the catalysts of the Harlem Renaissance, had taught English and creative writing there; and James Baldwin, one of Harlem's most treasured writers, had edited the school magazine. Tabor was aware of both of them, and the intellectual and literary role that his school played in the chemistry of black pride. But basketball held a greater sway and so he returned nightly to the courts where heroin was rife.

On the cusp of leaving Harlem for a college place, he went off the rails and took to hanging around the courts and street corners, trying to ward off depression and becoming consumed by drugs. Although he was already a self-taught scholar of black history who had shown interest in music and literature at school, his mother's death led him to despair. Then, things suddenly turned around. He gravitated towards a crowd on the corner of 125th Street and Seventh Avenue to hear the Black Panther leader Bobby Seale enrapture a boisterous crowd. Among the crowd, unknown to Tabor at the time, were Alice Faye Williams, Joan Bird and a precocious fifteen-year-old, Eddie 'Jamal' Joseph. Within a matter of weeks, they were in the same briefing room, training to become the nucleus of the Harlem Black Panthers. Tabor had not only seen the light, he had seen something even brighter: a solution to the scourge of heroin that had gripped him and ruined the life of Earl Manigault. He used his knowledge of the local drug trade to his advantage and became the Panthers' expert on heroin. One night, when asked by the group how he had kicked the habit, Tabor responded with a short lucid lecture on the role that heroin was playing in the community. By all accounts he was a compelling speaker, capable of impersonating the sonorous gospel style of Martin Luther King and the deep bass singing style of Temptations singer Melvin Franklin. He looked around the room and asked a simple question: if America spends billions on trying to eradicate heroin – through the prison system, heavy-handed policing and the education system – why is it that the only organisation that has had any success in rehabilitating damaged heroin users and hardened drug criminals is the mosque? As he made his point, Tabor gestured westward to Muhammad's Mosque No. 7 on 127th Street, then the home of the Nation of Islam. His pointing finger invited his audience to consider this rarely acknowledged truth. Despite all the money spent trying to change the behaviour of recidivist criminals, the only effective antidote was the Nation of Islam. Tabor then made the obvious leap: if the Muslims can do it in the name of religion then the Black Panthers could do it in the name of the ideology of Black Power. He himself was proof of its powers of redemption.

While in prison, in 1969, Tabor wrote the trenchant and well-argued essay 'Capitalism Plus Dope Equals Genocide'. It begins with his own story and graphically describes what he considers to be 'the scourge of the Black colonies of Babylon', 'the Plague': heroin addiction. At the core of his argument – much inspired by his own experiences – was a classic Marxist analysis of the problem.

He concluded that: 'As long as our young Black brothers and sisters are chasing the bag, as long as they are trying to cop a fix, the rule of our oppressors is secure and our hopes for freedom are dead.' He targeted every layer of drug culture: the rival teenage gangs, the beleaguered and indentured pushers, the flamboyant hustlers, the street corner deals, the rogue cops and corrupt officials, the bars and nightclubs, and then the organised criminal gangs and legitimate businesses through which drug money is laundered. He left no area of Harlem life untouched – with the notable exception of basketball – and, although at times his writing is framed in the jargon of late sixties political theory, it is an astonishing, unflinching work. Nor was it meant only to be read.

When out on bail Tabor put a crude version of his thinking into practice. He became the leader of the Black Panthers' street squad (known as TCB, for Taking Care of Business), a unit of armed militants who targeted the drug gangsters and the factories where they batched up heroin into deals. Using his African *nom de guerre*, Cetewayo, he, along with Jamal Joseph and two other Panthers, raided the drug dens at gunpoint, destroyed the drugs and returned the money to Panthers HQ in Harlem. In his autobiography *Panther Baby*, Joseph described a raid on a drug factory run by William 'Goldfinger' Terrell. 'Drug dealers would take over apartments, using some for sales and many others for dope dens, called shooting galleries. A junkie could buy a bag of dope and then go across the hall to shoot drugs in one of the rooms furnished with broken-down couches or discarded mattresses. Before the drugs were sold in the dens they were prepared in other apartments known as factories.' He described how one of the Panthers would rub black pepper in their eyes to make them look desperate and addicted, then knock pathetically on the door looking for junk. When the door slowly opened, a rifle butt would be jammed in its hinges and the Panthers would kick their way in. With paramilitary precision, the unit would destroy the heroin, confiscate the scales and remove the cash in carrier bags. What they never did was involve the police. It was clearly a dangerous, possibly suicidal, mission but it was one that the Panthers believed was essential if the community was to be transformed. 'Put faces on those junkies, lives in those desperate, watery eyes,' Joseph wrote. 'Black men who in another place and time could have been soldiers, could have been warriors, scholars, architects, doctors, lawyers. Black women who could be, should be, teachers, doctors, lawyers. Teenagers who should be dancing, dating, sporting, with eyes that are red with studying late as opposed to eyes that are dying from chasing heroin.'

At the Panther 21 trial, Tabor attracted attention far from Harlem when he made the inspired decision to defend himself. In a city fixated with the legal profession, he cut a bold presence. His big bass voice and street-smart intellect kept him in the news as the trial twisted and turned. He was ruthless in his condemnation of the undercover officers who had infiltrated the Panthers and frequently reminded the court that they had either proposed or, in some cases, actually perpetrated the crimes that he was being tried for. His personality had all the divisive and theatrical energy of 1969 – confident to the point of belligerence and impudent in the face of authority. He refused to defer to the court but, just to remind people that he was on top of his brief, he once went out of his way to congratulate Judge Murtagh for his progressive attitudes to street prostitution. Halfway through the trial, a further turn of events changed Tabor's life. After another successful round of fundraising, the Panthers' defence committee had raised enough money to post bond for another prisoner. This time it was Michael Tabor who drew the successful lot and so he returned to the streets of Harlem to lead an initiative to open drug detoxification clinics in the New York ghettos. But a fratricidal war between factions of the Black Panther Party had taken hold and Tabor was forced into taking sides. In what was, in effect, a prequel to the infamous hip-hop wars of the 1990s, where East and West Coast were pitted against each other, the original Oakland Panthers found themselves in bitter dispute with their northern comrades. Bobby Seale, Huey Newton and the prisoner-turned-firebrand intellectual Eldridge Cleaver could no longer be in the same room without resorting to violence. Tabor inevitably sided with the Harlem branch, which was still reeling from the mass arrests and nearly three years of infiltration and disruption. They aligned with a faction that had gathered around Eldridge Cleaver, his wife Kathleen, and the international wing of the organisation, based in Algeria. In a moment of intense factionalism, which was undermining the movement, Tabor broke his bail conditions and sought political exile in Algeria, along with his wife Connie Matthews. There he became a prominent member of the International Branch of the Black Panther Party.

Tabor's decision to abscond further intensified the factionalism. Even towards the end of her life, Afeni Shakur spoke bitterly of her hurt and contempt for Tabor's disappearance. She claims that while in jail awaiting trial, the Harlem Panthers had struck an agreement that none of them would jump bail and that they would stay united, to fight their case in court. She never spoke to him again. Tabor was convinced, wrongly as it turned out, that he was about to be sentenced to life in prison. He had no confidence that the system would free him and his fears were legitimate. Ironically, having escaped to Algeria and then been exiled to Zambia, Tabor was acquitted in his absence and all the charges against him were dropped. It was widely presumed that he would return to Harlem to continue his drug rehabilitation work and take up a leading political role. He consistently refused to do so. Tabor spent the remainder of his life in exile, living over thirty years in Africa and finally settling in Lusaka, Zambia, where he died in 2010. By then he was a nationally known radio DJ, professional journalist and passionate advocate of African popular music. Many before him had flirted with the idea of Back-to-Africa but Tabor delivered on the dream. His exile was America's loss. Tabor was a serious talent and had the intellectual energy to be a formidable critical voice in Harlem, the place he still called home.

For Walter Vandermeer there was one final humiliation. His funeral coincided with a city-wide gravediggers' strike in January 1970 and his burial was delayed. Seventeen hundred gravediggers took industrial action and went on strike in forty-four cemeteries across New York. The young boy's hearse – paid for by charity and public donations – waited to be called forward into the cemetery. And then the snow started. It was gentle at first, barely covering the ground. It had none of the ferocity of Detroit in 1967, when snow strangled the Motor City, silenced the noise of industry and fell like a premonition of worse to come. Nor did it fall like the freakish and conspiratorial snowstorm of March 1968 in Memphis, which changed Martin Luther King's travel plans, forcing him to return to the city in April, where he was assassinated. Nor was it the Harlem snow that Ann Petry had described in her novel *The Street*, snow 'blackened by soot until it was no longer recognisable as snow'. This was a different kind of snow and it floated down on Walter Vandermeer's ivory-coloured casket – soft, quiet and deathly grey.

Donny Hathaway: the future of soul.

EPILOGUE

The Future of Soul

The hotel manager of the Essex House Hotel on Central Park frantically called the Midtown North Precinct of the NYPD on 54th Street. A man had either fallen or jumped from one of the hotel's windows. It was yet another fatal mystery in the remarkable story of sixties soul.

Donny Hathaway's career had stalled, and he had all but disappeared into his own world. Long periods of hospitalisation and a strict regime of prescription drugs had stabilised his mental health, and those closest to him thought he was well enough to record again, but on Saturday, 13 January 1979, his crumpled body was discovered thirteen storeys beneath his locked room. No suicide note was found.

He had just returned from a dinner with his friend and collaborator Roberta Flack and his manager David Franklin. Earlier that day he had been producing a session with Eric Mercury and another ex-recruit from the ranks of Black Power, the New Jersey soul singer James Mtume. During the session, Mtume claimed that Hathaway was behaving irrationally, had refused to take his medication, and was paranoid that his music was being stolen by a suction machine in the studio which he claimed was being controlled by an evil white man. It was a sad and delusional last day in the life of one of soul music's greatest talents.

Hathaway left Flack in the hotel lobby. Their parting words were lovingly mundane. Hathaway had asked her to keep him a piece of the ginger cake she had served earlier that night at her apartment. Soon after midnight, her phone rang and she heard the news that her friend was dead. Like Marvin Gaye and Tammi Terrell a decade before, Roberta Flack and Donny Hathaway had been cast as lovers – although they were only ever close friends – and their romantic duets – 'You've Got A Friend' (1971), 'Where Is The Love?' (1972), 'The Closer I Get To You' (1977) – set a new benchmark for great soul love songs. The guitarist George Benson, who worked closely with Hathaway in their Harlem days, said after his death that 'he was a natural talent . . . I learned a lot by sitting by him. He started singing and he'd hit everything. I'd think, I wish I had a voice like that . . . He was not a loud singer and that's what made his voice so beautiful.' Benson's point is crucial. What marked Hathaway out as a pioneer were his acts of defiance. He refused to sing like a whisky-soaked R&B singer and turned away from the vocal showiness of the great gospel singers, despite having been a childhood gospel prodigy. Hathaway insisted that soul music could be as subtle and as layered as any other form of art, and he preferred gentle insinuation to raw power. He once dismissed James Brown as a comedy character acting out 'crude vaudeville' for the easily pleased.

During one of his last sessions with Flack, Hathaway recorded the peerless 'Back Together Again' (1979), a song that to this day remains an intriguing mystery of intense voices: the voices that were plaguing his troubled mind, the soothing voice of Flack, his ever-present friend, and the spiritual choirs floating over them. Modern electronica and the studio voices echo and respond to each other like auditory hallucinations. Deep in the mix – as if the past is determined to stay relevant – you can hear the call-and-response of old-style gospel, soft and low-key, beneath the relentlessness rhythms of club music. The music of the church was now as likely to be heard on a hedonistic dance floor as in church itself.

In 1969 Hathaway's 'The Ghetto' had opened up new possibilities for black American music. Symphonic, socially relevant and surging with creativity, it pointed to so many new futures, and although he himself never lived to see the story fully unfold, soul music took Hathaway's guidance and evolved into a hundred different sounds.

The decade inevitably ended, but sixties soul defied an early death. The infectious Motown catalogue, boogaloo party sounds, throbbing sex machinery of urban funk and noble pleas for greater racial tolerance have played a part in popular music ever since. It has been a story of evolution and revolution cheered on by a vanguard of artists and dance music collectors who have refused to let the music die. But, if a death is required, then we can be very precise about the day that sixties soul died. It was 15 May 1969, when Governor Ronald Reagan ordered the California Highway Patrol and the police to charge a group of students in a public park, on the edges of the University of California, Berkeley, triggering seventeen days of rioting.

It was a horrendous time in the history of American law and order. Paramilitary officers, their badges obscured to avoid being identified as National Guardsmen, attacked the crowd with fixed bayonets. One hundred and fifty-eight students were injured; some sustained gunshot wounds and head wounds. The incident was pre-planned and became known in countercultural circles as 'Bloody Thursday'. The People's Park had long been a bone of contention between students, local residents and the University of California. Like the land grab that had enraged Harlem in 1968 and triggered the Gym Crow riots, the University of California planned to develop the area as part of the expansion of the Berkeley campus. The park was the traditional meeting place for students to study, make friends and fall in love, but as sixties radicalism hardened, the park became a gathering place for demonstrations and occupations. The presence of radical bohemian students provoked the conservative Governor Reagan into a characteristic rage. He described the campus as 'a haven for Communist sympathizers, protesters, and sex deviants' although never elucidated on what deviance had taken place. The spark that ignited the trouble was a relatively low-key student rally about the Arab–Israeli conflict. Reagan seized his opportunity and instructed the National Guard to move in.

Just as the rioting reached its peak, something strange, possibly prophetic, happened. A tour bus carrying Motown musicians from a concert at the Winterland Ballroom in San Francisco became caught up in the rioting. As the bus tried to navigate Dwight Way, on the fringes of the park, it was encircled by fleeing students. The violence escalated and became ugly. Inside the bus were the Four Tops: lead singer Levi Stubbs, his Asian-American schoolfriend Abdul 'Duke' Fakir, tenor singer Lawrence Payton and Renaldo 'Obie' Benson. By chance, Benson had a window seat. He stared out in disbelief as young students, much younger than he was, were battered to the ground, stamped on and beaten with rifle butts. Governor Reagan was adamant that his troops had acted with restraint and told journalists: 'Once the dogs of war have been unleashed, you must expect things will happen, and that people, being human, will make mistakes on both sides.'

Benson's witnessing of the 'dogs of war' unleashing their violence had a lasting impact. He was a gifted singer, but not a songwriter, nor a musician. After he returned home to Detroit the bloody scenes continued to play on his mind and he recounted the story to his friend, songwriter Al Cleveland, who at the time was sharing his apartment. Together, they fashioned a song that became one of soul music's greatest compositions, Marvin Gaye's epic 'What's Going On'. Across the summer of 1969, as Donny Hathaway's 'The Ghetto' dominated inner-city airwaves, Benson and Cleveland touted the song around Detroit. The Four Tops collectively turned it down, resistant to anything that smacked of politics, so Benson offered the song to another Motown group, the Originals, but there was no take-up. During a Motown tour of the UK in 1970, Benson arranged to meet the protest singer Joan Baez, believing she would appreciate the song's sentiments. She listened graciously but again no deal was struck. It was only when the Four Tops returned to Detroit that Benson finally offered the song to Marvin Gaye.

'What's Going On' broke through the dam of caution that had been built up by Motown's senior management. Among the flurry of songs that soon followed were Edwin Starr's agitprop song 'War' (1970); Marvin Gaye's 'Abraham, Martin, and John' (1970); the Temptations' funk sermon 'Ball Of Confusion (That's What The World Is Today' (1970); and Marvin Gaye's state-of-the-nation concept album also named *What's Going On* (1971).

Much has been made of Marvin Gaye's greatest album. Its roots were firmly planted in the historic themes of the late sixties. Detroit had been caught up in a deadly insurrection, and his brother Frankie, a radio operator in Vietnam, had returned home to recount his experiences in combat. The two brothers exchanged a series of letters between Detroit and Vietnam over the course of three years, and Frankie's first-hand accounts of war found their way into the lyrics of the album. 'I saw all the things I never wanted to see,' Frankie told Marvin on his return. 'I was in places I never wanted to be . . . You couldn't stand up: you had to crawl through the mud over things that moved when you touched them. It rained so much that everything on the ground rotted and smelled like week-old garbage, from the heat, rain and humidity . . . Once you see people dying, cut up, or being tortured, day after day of that you get desensitized, then paranoid . . . Still you want to believe there's a reason.'

Fighting depression, facing a ruined marriage and trying to control a raging cocaine habit, Gaye recorded an album that dwelt on the scarred surfaces of the inner city: police brutality, lack of welfare for children, the trauma of veterans returning from Vietnam, and the dark failures of society that were engulfing Detroit. But much like Donny Hathaway's 'Thank You Master For My Soul' (1970), with its strangely prophetic line about the walls of his room not being the walls of his grave, society was viewed through the prism of the singer's own personal insecurities and the troubled anxieties he felt about the role of God and formal religion. Both Gaye and Hathaway struggled to reconcile their religious upbringings with the social landscape around them, to the point of questioning the very existence of God. It was a crisis for many soul singers of that generation, and one that infected Hathaway more than most.

Sixties soul had successfully secularised the sound of gospel but now tougher questions were being asked. 'What's' Going On' had itself been transformed from its original concept. Benson told the writer Dorian Lynskey that Gaye 'added some things that were more ghetto, more natural, which made it seem [more] like a story than a song . . . We measured him for the suit and he tailored the hell out of it.' No group across the entire catalogue of sixties soul could match the infectious style of the Four Tops. In twelve triumphant months from 1965 to 1966, they had released 'I Can't Help Myself (Sugar Pie, Honey Bunch), 'It's The Same Old Song', 'Something About You', 'Shake Me, Wake Me (When It's Over)' and 'Reach Out I'll Be There' – classic Motown songs that came to define what sixties soul was all about: an irresistible beat, instantly memorable lyrics, and those towering gospel voices unleashed on teenage love. Benson's gift to Marvin Gaye broke profoundly with the era they had grown up in. As the society around them fractured, singing about teenage love seemed anachronistic and irresponsible, and, whatever its past, the future of soul would never be the same again. Harlem had seen to that.

Harlem's story was one of restless innovation. The fusion with jazz, the hardening of street funk, the rise of the DJ, and the orchestral arrangements that led to disco and the seeds of hip-hop pointed to a more diverse, and dislocating, future for black music. These changes bubbled beneath the surface of the final chart returns of 1969. Motown still dominated the top singles of 1969. Along with Aretha Franklin, the Detroit label occupied all of the top five places on the *Billboard* charts. But beneath the top slots a wave of new sounds was emerging: some influenced by counterculture, others by a more racially polarised country. Significant among their number were Sly and the Family's Stone's 'Everyday People', The Impressions' 'Choice Of Colors' and the 5th Dimension's 'Aquarius – Let The Sunshine In'. And an entirely unknown group from Washington DC called the Winstons – all college friends of Donny Hathaway – occupied the number nineteen slot with a cleverly political dance record called 'Color Him Father'. What no one knew then, nor could have predicted, was that the B-side – an R&B instrumental simply called 'Amen, Brother' – would become the DNA of a radical new form of soul music. One isolated fatback drumbeat, originally played by the drummer Gregory Coleman, was lifted from the song and over time become the most sampled breakbeat of hip-hop and modern R&B. The 'Amen Break', as it is now known, became a nagging and underlying presence in the music of NWA, 2 Live Crew, Salt-N-Pepa and Mantronix, then, as it surfaced from the hip-hop underground, it found its sampled way into songs by Oasis, the Prodigy, David Bowie and Björk.

The first shoots of hip-hop were clearly visible in Harlem in 1969. Although the nearby South Bronx Projects were famously home to pioneering turntable wizards like DJ Kool Herc and Grandmaster Flash, it was the record shops on 125th Street that became the locus of hip-hop's distribution. Bobby Robinson's Records, the makeshift base of the Enjoy label, had first launched with King Curtis's 'Soul Twist' in 1962 and become home to R&B veterans Titus Turner and J.D. Bryant, but they diversified with funk to become one of the first fully fledged hip-hop labels, releasing old-school slabs by the Funky 4+1 and Grandmaster Flash. Robinson's rival, Paul Winley Records, a shop with origins as far back as fifties doo-wop, was by now in deep legal trouble for bootlegging George Benson's music, and had turned to pressing rap records (mostly by the owner's daughter Tanya 'Sweet Tee' Winley). Beyond the shops were the venues that became hip-hop landmarks: the voluminous Audubon Ballroom, the site of Malcolm X's assassination, was an old-school venue for the first generation of rappers and the theatrical home to Grandmaster Flash and his radical musical montage 'Adventures On The Wheels Of Steel' (1981). Most stridently of all, there was Harlem World, a hip-hop haven set up by the Allen twins and Fat Jack Taylor in the subterranean floors of a disused Woolworth store. It sat, buried beneath Rojac Records, on the street corner where Harlem's heroin market was at its most brazen – where Walter Vandermeer had died. Harlem World became a gangsta institution. Initially straddling soul and funk, it soon became the home base for hip-hop artists such as the Cold Crush Brothers, Grandmaster Caz, Lovebug Starski and the schizoid Dr Jeckyll & Mr Hyde (first known as Harlem World Crew).

In July 1977, taking advantage of the city-wide electricity blackout, the hardcore rappers from Harlem World stocked up on electronics by robbing stores. Many of them recorded early rap tracks with Taylor, on his reactivated Rojac and Tay-Ster labels – the imprints that had once promoted Big Maybelle, the International 'G.T.O.s', Clarence Reid and Lillie Bryant. Taylor hired the Allen twins and a young woman called Deborah Jones to manage Harlem World, and it proved to be yet another coincidence among many. Jones was the teenage niece of Harlem's famous nightlife superstars, Joe and Sylvia Robinson, who had recently opened independent studios across the river in Englewood, New Jersey.

In 1969 the Robinsons owned a suite of labels including Turbo, Stang, All Platinum and, latterly, Sugar Hill Records, which was named after the aspirational Harlem neighbourhood bordering 155th Street. Sometime in 1979 the couple returned home to Harlem at the invitation of their niece to attend a party at Harlem World. It was an eye-opener. Despite their decades at the forefront of Harlem R&B, they had never seen the neighbourhood teenagers engaged in a full-on rap battle. The couple returned to New Jersey determined to put hip-hop on vinyl and quickly arranged a session for a group of young rappers who they called the Sugarhill Gang. It was there that they produced the now historic 'Rapper's Delight', an infectious, wisecracking and surreal journey into the inventive mind of the self-aggrandising street kid. Political correctness was thrown bodily out the room as the rappers boasted about their sexual prowess, lied about their conspicuous wealth, and sneered at anyone they deemed inferior (including the ultimate action hero Superman, who was decried as a fairy flying through the air in pantyhose). 'Rapper's Delight' brazenly stole chunks of Chic's 'Good Times', which one of the Sugarhill Gang had bought in a Harlem record store. Nile Rodgers – his life as a Black Panther now ten years behind him – sued for copyright theft, but a deal was struck and 'Rapper's Delight' kick-started a global pop phenomenon.

Rap music is often described as a radical break in the journey of black music but in many key respects it is simply a continuation. In 1969 the Robinsons were already a Harlem super-couple, with tentacles reaching out from music into fashion and underground nightclubs. Unknowingly they had already released a record that had the underlying DNA of hip-hop. Frankie (Love Man) Crocker's 'Ton Of Dynamite' (1969) had all the genetic threads – the funk backing track was a recycled recording by the Robinsons' studio band Willie and the Mighty Magnificents called 'Funky (8) Corners'. Crocker was a self-aggrandising 'Love Man' who was known throughout New York as one of Harlem's top radio DJs, and 'funky corners' were a street funk trope dating back to the earliest days of boogaloo.

It was inevitable that Harlem's troubled children would be at the forefront of hip-hop. Tupac Shakur had been conceived while his mother Afeni was released on bail during the Panther 21 trial. Although his life took him first to California and ended with his murder outside the MGM Grand in Las Vegas, his mother was his greatest influence and Harlem his spiritual home. Then, in November 1969, in the week that the Young Lords led their headline-grabbing Garbage Offensive, another baby was born in Harlem Hospital. His name was Sean Combs and he would grow up to assume a bewildering array of names, most memorably Puff Daddy, and become the grandmaster of the hip-hop empire Uptown Records. Before he was two years old, Sean Combs lost his father. Melvin Combs was an associate and street general of the gangster Frank Lucas. He was assassinated in his car in Central Park West, another victim of Harlem's heroin trade.

Each death resonated. Walter Vandermeer's had nudged the conscience of America but Harlem had to endure many more years of drug infestation before the neighbourhood would see improvements, and when they came, it was as much to do with demographic change and real-estate prices as drugs policy. The income of black and Puerto Rican families gradually rose. As more joined the ranks of white-collar employment, the trend of suburbanisation, first to Englewood and Teaneck, spread more widely. Between 1970 and 1995 the percentage of the black population living in the suburbs doubled from 16.1 per cent to 31.9 per cent, and the percentage of suburbia that was black nearly doubled from 4.8 per cent to 8.1 per cent. New incomers moved to Harlem, as they had done for centuries, but this time many of them were not poor immigrants but young professionals from elsewhere, attracted to the area by its access to public transport and proximity to Midtown Manhattan. The gentrification that would ultimately transform Harlem was already visible in the late seventies, bringing new wealth to its brownstones and gradually pushing poverty outwards. It was a transformation that brought with it many obvious benefits but, unintentionally, may also have stifled the area's reputation for creativity. Some say it has suffocated Harlem's soul.

Of the characters who shaped the story of Harlem in 1969, their deaths spoke volumes about the times in which they lived. King Curtis, the most prodigious saxophonist in the history of soul music, was murdered in a street brawl. Big Maybelle, the queen of R&B and a regular on the Apollo stage, finally gave up on Harlem and died in her mother's home in Cleveland. Sam Melville, who terrorised Manhattan with his bombing campaign, died as a militant, fighting alongside former Black Panthers and Harlem street criminals in the Attica riots.

Then, most tragically of all, there was the young man who had given a subtle voice to the ghetto. Many had put Donny Hathaway's fathomless outbursts and incoherent mumbling down to genius and dismissed his irrational behaviour as the by-product of his stardom. But with time even that fallacy faded. The soul singer Eric Mercury found Hathaway deeply scary and intimidating. Roberta Flack, who had known Hathaway since college, was less troubled by his unpredictability and worried more about his periods of seclusion and deepening self-doubt. She found it bewildering that someone with such vocal skills could think they were a worthless singer, that a man with such talent could jettison his own work, deeming it unworthy. Flack has since talked of the intensity of their years together. 'Donny and I cut "You've Got A Friend" in twenty minutes, which isn't hard to understand,' she told *Edge* magazine. 'I am a musician, not just a singer, so you don't have to teach me something. I have the presence of mind and the ambition and the appreciation for my craft to sit down and practice. So I practiced, came to New York, and Donny and I did "You've Got A Friend", which went to the top of the charts. So they said, "Let's do an album." Okay, so the next thing we did was "Where Is The

Love". Donny and I finished that first album in three days! I should say that I did whatever Donny asked me to do as a duet partner. In terms of putting it together, sketching it out, bringing all the pieces together so that everybody understood what was happening – that was Donny, that was the kind of mind he had. Three days.'

Jerry Wexler, an astute observer of Atlantic's testing roster of artists, said that Hathaway was 'a tortured soul . . . a perfectionist. Sometimes he would obsess about a beat or a rhythm to the point of distraction. He could stick on one notion that nobody else could understand. And things would just stop while he tried to explain the problems and very often it was inexplicable to mere mortals.'

Increasingly Hathaway came to avoid the eyes of 'mere mortals'. He always wore an oversized cap – known at the time as a 'Big Apple' – indoors and out, onstage and off, and he often became paranoid if anyone – a waiter, photographer or well-meaning colleague – suggested he take it off. According to the UK soul journalist Charles Waring, 'Donny Hathaway was a musical supernova, he burned with a fierce, incandescent brilliance for a few short years, and then he was gone.' His death, presumed to be suicide, robbed soul music of one of its most innovative artists and denied the ghettos of North America one of their greatest ever poets. It was the tragic end of a career that King Curtis had confidently predicted would change the direction of black music. He was right.

BIBLIOGRAPHY

Primary Sources

Amsterdam News, Special Collections, Columbia University Library, New York, NY.

Black Panther Party Harlem Branch files, Schomburg Center for Research in Black Culture, Manuscripts, Archives and Rare Books Division, The New York Public Library, New York, NY.

Jean Blackwell Hutson Research and Reference Division, Schomburg Center for Research in Black Culture, The New York Public Library, New York, NY.

Blues and Soul magazine, 1968–1975, author's own collection.

The COINTELPRO Papers, The FBI Education Center, Pennsylvania Avenue, NW Washington, DC.

Harlem Community News, Special Collection, Schomburg Center for Research in Black Culture, The New York Public Library, New York, NY.

Home Select Committee on Assassination (HSCA) 1976–1979), Library of Congress, Washington, DC.

Michigan Chronicle, 1962–1972, Detroit Public Library, Detroit, MI.

NAACP Collection, cataloguing the activities of the Detroit branch of the National Association for the Advancement of

Colored Peoples and its related activities, 1909–1979, Walter Reuther Library, Wayne State University, Detroit, MI.
Newsweek, vols 68–88, 1967–1969.
New York Post, 1965–1975, The New York Public Library, New York, NY.
The New York Times, 1965–1975, Columbia University Library, New York, NY.
The Papers and Correspondence of the Reverend Martin Luther King Jr, The Martin Luther King, Jr. Center for Nonviolent Social Change, Atlanta, GA.
Wax Poetics, 2007–2010, author's own collection.

Secondary Sources

Alpert, Jane, *Growing Up Underground*, New York: William Morrow, 1981.
Beckham, Barry, *Double Dunk: The Story of Earl 'The Goat' Manigault*, Silver Spring: Beckham Books, 1980.
Blackstock, Nelson, *COINTELPRO: The FBI's Secret War on Political Freedom*, New York: Pathfinder Press, 1988.
Bowman, Rob, *Soulsville USA: The Story of Stax Records*, New York: Schirmer Books, 1997.
Boyd, Herb (ed.), *The Harlem Reader*, New York: Three Rivers Press, 2003.
Branch, Taylor, *At Canaan's Edge: America in the King Years 1965–8*, New York: Simon & Schuster, 2006.
Carlin, Richard, *Morris Levy: Godfather of the Music Industry*, Jackson: University of Mississippi Press, 2016.
Carpenter, Bill, *Uncloudy Days: The Gospel Encyclopaedia*, San Francisco: Backbeat Books, 2005.
Carr, Ian, *Miles Davis: The Ultimate Biography*, London: Harper Collins, 1999.
Chambers, Jason, *Madison Avenue and the Color Line: African Americans in the Advertising Industry*, Philadelphia: University of Pennsylvania Press, 2008.
Davis, Deborah, *Party of the Century: The Fabulous Story of*

Truman Capote and His Black and White Ball, New York: Wiley, 2006.
DiEugenio, James & Pease, Lisa, *The Assassinations*, Port Townsend: Feral Press, 2003.
Donner, Frank J., *The Age of Surveillance*, New York: Alfred A. Knopf, 1980.
English, T. J., *The Savage City*, New York: Harper Collins, 2011.
Freeman, Scott, *Otis: The Otis Redding Story*, New York: St. Martin's Press, 2001.
Gentry, Curt, *J. Edgar Hoover: The Man and His Secrets*, New York: W.W. Norton & Co., 1991.
George, Nelson, *Where Did Our Love Go?*, London: Omnibus Press, 1985.
George, Nelson, *The Death of Rhythm and Blues*, London: Penguin, 1988.
Gordy, Berry, *To Be Loved*, New York: Warner Books, 1994.
Gordon, Robert, *Respect Yourself: Stax Records and the Soul Explosion*, New York: Bloomsbury, 2013.
Hamilton, Marybeth, *In Search of the Blues*, London: Jonathan Cape, 2007.
Hauser, Thomas, *Muhammad Ali: His Life and Times*, London: Robson Books, 1991.
Hegarty, Neil, *Frost: That Was The Life That Was*, London: W.H. Allen, 2015.
Howard, Josiah, *Blaxploitation Cinema*, Surrey: Fab Press, 2008.
James, Tommy (with Martin Fitzpatrick), *Me, the Mob and the Music: One Helluva Ride with Tommy James and the Shondells*, New York: Simon & Schuster, 2010.
Joseph, Jamal, *Panther Baby: A Life of Rebellion and Reinvention*, Chapel Hill: Algonquin, 2012.
Kahn, Ashley, *The House That Trane Built: The Story of Impulse Records*, New York: Norton, 2006.
Kempton, Murray, *The Briar Patch: The Trial of the Panther 21*, New York: Da Capo, 1997.
Kot, Greg, *I'll Take You There: Mavis Staples and the March Up Freedom's Highways*, New York: Scribner, 2014.

Kotz, Mick, *Judgement Days: The Laws That Changed America*, Boston: Mariner Books, 2006.

Lucas, Frank, *Original Gangster*, New York: St. Martin's Press, 2010.

Mayfield, Todd, *Travelling Soul, The Life of Curtis Mayfield*, Chicago: Chicago Review Press, 2017.

Marable, Manning, *Malcolm X: A Life of Reinvention*, London: Allen Lane, 2011.

McRae, Donald, *A Man's World: The Double Life of Emile Griffith*, London: Simon & Schuster, 2015.

Melendez, Miguel, *We Took to the Streets: Fighting for Latino Rights with the Young Lords*, New Brunswick: Rutgers University Press, 2007.

Moore, Robin, *The French Connection*, Guildford, CT: Lyons Press, 1969.

Newsday, The Staff and Editors of, *The Heroin Trail*, London: Souvenir Press, 1974.

O'Reilly, Kenneth, *The FBI's Secret File on Black America, 1960–1972*, New York: Free Press, 1991.

Pepper, William F., *An Act of State: The Execution of Martin Luther King*, New York: Verso, 2003.

Pickering, Leslie James, *Mad Bomber Melville*, Portland: Arissa Media Group, 2007.

Posner, Gerald, *Motown: Music, Money, Sex and Power*, New York: Random House, 2005.

Ribowsky, Mark, *Dreams to Remember: Otis Redding, Stax Records and the Transformation of Southern Soul*, New York: Liveright, 2015.

Ritz, David, *Divided Soul: The Life of Marvin Gaye*, New York: McGraw-Hill, 1985.

Salvatore, Nick, *C.L. Franklin, The Black Church and the Transformation of America*, New York: Little Brown & Co., 2005.

Singleton, Raynoma Gordy, *Berry, Me and Motown*, Chicago: Contemporary Books, 1990.

Smith, Suzanne E., *Dancing in the Street: Motown and the Politics of Detroit*, Cambridge, MA: Harvard University Press, 1999.

Sugrue, Thomas, *The Origins of the Urban Crisis: Race and Inequality in Postwar Detroit*, Princeton: Princeton University Press, 2005.

Thompson, Heather Ann, *Blood in the Water: The Attica Prison Uprising and Its Legacy*, New York: Vintage Books, 2017.

Vincent, Rickey, *Party Music: The Inside Story of the Black Panthers' Band and How Black Power Transformed Music*, Chicago: Lawrence Hill Books, 2013.

Wanzer-Serrano, Darrel, *The New York Young Lords and the Struggle for Liberation*, Philadelphia: Temple University Press, 2015.

Ward, Brian, *Just My Soul Responding*, London: UCL Press, 1998.

Warner, Jay, *Just Walking in the Rain*, Los Angeles: Renaissance Books, 2001.

Wexler, Jerry, *Rhythm and the Blues: A Life in American Music*, London: Jonathan Cape, 1993.

INDEX

Notes: Where artists have been known by more than one name, the entry is under the most used name with cross-references to the other names. Where names have no particular emphasis (for example LL Cool J) the entry is under the first name or letter.